THE OUTLAW AND THE HITMAN

Also by Caesar Campbell

Enforcer
Wrecking Crew

THE OUTLAW
AND THE HITMAN

INSIDE THE CRAZY WORLD OF AUSTRALIA'S MOST LEGENDARY BRAWLER, BIKER & ENFORCER

CAESAR CAMPBELL
with Donna Campbell

MACMILLAN
Pan Macmillan Australia

First published 2016 in Macmillan by Pan Macmillan Australia Pty Ltd
1 Market Street, Sydney, New South Wales, Australia, 2000

Cataloguing-in-Publication entry is available
from the National Library of Australia
http://catalogue.nla.gov.au

Other Authors/Contributors:
Campbell, Donna

Typeset in 12.5/16 pt Sabon by Midland Typesetters, Australia
Printed by McPherson's Printing Group

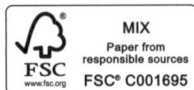

MIX
Paper from
responsible sources
FSC
www.fsc.org   FSC® C001695

The paper in this book is FSC® certified. FSC® promotes environmentally responsible, socially beneficial and economically viable management of the world's forests.

I'd like to dedicate this book to my father and mother. Dad was the toughest bloke I ever knew, but he always had a soft heart for his family. Mum was the gentlest and kindest lady, the perfect match for Dad. She had to toe the line when Dad died at just 46, and again when two of my brothers died in 1984, then another in 1987. She showed mental toughness that would put most men to shame. Mum and Dad have 93 children, grandchildren and great-grandchildren, 70 per cent of whom are male. We all miss you and love you Mum and Dad. You'll never be forgotten and we know you're together in heaven.

CONTENTS

'I had been blessed since my teenage years with the ability to knock someone out with one punch from either hand. I'd whack them and it was lights out. I'd roll through the place and knock everyone out, tie 'em up and wait for them to come around. I'd do the finger-snapping first. It was quick and clean, but it didn't always work. It's amazing how hard it can be to separate people from other people's money.'

– Caesar C

PROLOGUE

Up in the cold country where I live now, there's a heap of bikers who are retired from different outlaw clubs. We have a bit of a yak when we run into each other down the street and sometimes we get together for a ride into the mountains or a drink and a session of bullshit at the pub. There's plenty to talk about. As old-school bikers, these blokes have lived lives of hard-hammering fun, sex and violence. But you've got to leave room for a bit of mystery too.

In 2014, one of the blokes, Irish, pulls up a chair next to me and puts his bourbon down on the table beside my orange juice. He's a thick-set guy with shoulder-length red hair and a lot of grey coming through his bushy old beard. He wants to talk about Kings Cross back in the days when we both practically lived up there, back in the days when it was dirty and glowing. Before the council had ripped up the footpaths for even the first attempt at cleaning the joint up by installing a fancy pavement, back when you knew who owned the cops and any attempt to enforce early closing hours or any other wowser law became just another way for everyone to make a quid.

Irish and I are talking about the Cross and the hard men of the era when he remembers a story that went around at the time, but has now largely been forgotten. 'What about the Widowmaker, Caesar?' he says. 'Did you ever hear about him? Was he real?'

'From what I heard, he was,' I say. 'He was like the Grim Bloody Reaper. Once he tapped you, you stayed tapped. But he wasn't like the other show ponies up there. Whoever he was, he was smart enough to stay unknown.' I look over to another one of our little gang across the table. 'Hey, Chance,' I say, 'Irish here wants to know if the Widowmaker was real.'

'Oh shit, yeah,' Chance says. 'I heard from a reliable source that he took out 20 blokes in one night.'

'What'd he do with 'em?' Irish asks.

'Took them out shark fishing,' I say.

'Yeah, bloody oath,' Chance says. 'People are the best bait.'

'But he can't have fed them all to the sharks,' Irish says. 'What'd he do with the bodies that were left over?'

'What do you think he did? He tied 'em to a motor and dropped 'em overboard. Hey Caesar, remember that Nascar motor you dropped into your Falcon – fuck that could go.'

Every time we change the subject, Irish keeps wanting to come back to the Widowmaker. He's fascinated by the myth of this phantom killer who never got caught, and that crims were terrified of even though none of them knew who he was. Irish tells a few yarns that he'd heard about the hitman, some of which might even be true. Chance is sitting there looking at me, trying hard not to crack up.

So we keep bullshitting with a few Widowmaker stories of our own, making the hitman's feats ever more unbelievable to the point where he could have been a Batman villain. Irish eventually catches up with us.

'Youse two are having me on.'

'We wondered when you'd wake up to it.'

'But the Widowmaker did exist, didn't he?'

'Yeah,' I say, 'he did.'

'You knew him?'

'I'm not saying I knew him. Chance probably knew him better than what I did.'

'I don't know about that,' says Chance.

'So what happened to him?' Irish asks.

'As far as I know, he got away with it all, never got busted and is now living a quiet life in retirement.'

I can't bring myself to tell him that the Widowmaker has retired here, to the Snowy Mountains, and is in the room with us.

Ninety-seven per cent of the story I'm about to tell is fact. The other three per cent has been fudged. You can figure out why. But the Widowmaker was real and he lives to this day. He's got death riding on his shoulder at the time of writing. I know what it feels like. I've had death riding there a few times myself. So often, in fact, me and death have become good mates. So often that you lose your fear of him. Lose your fear of everything.

*

It is 21 December 2014. I am down visiting family in Sydney and I happen to be with my nephew, cutting through the car park of the Auburn RSL club on our way to pick up a takeaway feed. Three blokes approach us. Middle Eastern appearance, about 30 years old. They look like bikers, but they aren't wearing patches, so it's hard to tell.

Before I know it, the lead bloke, a similar size to me, has a gun in his hand and he's pointing it at me. 'Get down on your knees and beg for your life and I won't put one in ya.'

'Go punch it up your arse.'

You see, I'm like one of those gunslingers in the old westerns who wants to retire but can't because he has to keep facing up to all the young guns who want to make a name for themselves by taking on the fastest gun in the west. Well, I've got news for you boys. I'll be 70 by the time this book comes out and beating me only proves that you're a weak cunt who takes on old men. It happens so often, Donna hates taking me out. They'll recognise me from the books or some biker magazine. 'You're Caesar Campbell. I could beat the shit out of you.' 'If you can't, there's something wrong with you.' It just amazes me. When I was in my 20s – in the 1960s and '70s – if I'd had a go at a bloke in his 40s I would have been seen as weak. I was still pretty good in the 1990s, but I'd lost 40 per cent of the power in my right side from having been hit by two 12-gauge shotgun blasts at Milperra. And I had the knuckle shot out of my right little finger so it's hard to make a fist. Getting harder every year.

And these drongos see me shuffling across the car park with a badly swollen ankle. And they want to take my colours. They want to take my honour. But those are two things a Campbell will never give away.

'I'm fucking serious,' the lead bloke says. 'Beg for your life or it's over.'

'I fucked your mother the other night and I'll fuck you up the arse next.'

He's about 5 metres away and edging closer, getting shitty, his jaw clenching.

'Be a fucking a man,' I say. 'You've got no balls, you gutless prick. Your mother gave the worst head job I've ever had. Don't stand there like a woozy fucking sheila. Come and put that barrel on me chest. If you're gunna pull the trigger, kill me like a man. Show your mates how you put Caesar Campbell down like a dog. Come and do it. Put it right here on me heart.'

He's not too bright, because I can practically see the steam coming out his ears as he marches up to me, holding the gun sideways with all that gangsta style he's been practising in the mirror since he was a 15-year-old hood in a tracksuit.

He puts the barrel against my forehead. A lot of people might see their life flash before their eyes in such a situation. I see opportunity. There's an old trick of swinging the barrel of a gun away with a backhand kind of motion and I got it about 75 per cent done, but like I said, I'm not the Caesar Campbell I used to be. The gun fires and I feel a godawful burning in my right hip. I pull the gun off him and knock him to the ground, pistol-whipping him, as they say in the old west.

I look up to see my nephew has rushed forward to take care of the other two blokes. I know he is ripped, with muscles on his muscles, but six packs don't count for much when bullets start flying. Even though he leads a straight life and this is all new to him, they haven't scared him one little bit. He is pounding shit out of the other two and showing just how staunch he is. His courage allows me time to steady and aim. One in the lead guy's right knee. One in his left.

I empty the shells from the remaining chambers into my hand.

My nephew helps me over to his car. It's a you-beaut rocket like the kids drive these days and I bleed all over it. Blood and leather don't mix. He gets me back to a family member's house. Donna is there. 'The Woman', as everyone knows her. She grabs the first-aid kit in our car. She has some special tools in it, because she's used to pulling bullets out of me. Even now that I'm in my late 60s she knows she can't leave home without it. Anyway, the bleeding's not too bad and she has a bit of a probe around with me lying up on a table pulling faces with the pain. Holding it in. She figures out that the bullet has hit the top of my hip bone and gone downwards, coming to rest at the top of my thigh, where she can feel the lump under the skin. She gets out the trusty buck knife and razor blade. She cuts it out, stitches it up and gives me a tetanus shot. It's amazing what she keeps in that kit of hers.

My nephew is standing there with this shocked look on his face. He's read the books, he's heard the stories from my mouth, but this is the first time he's lived it. And he's on a bit of a high. Pumped. Remember, he's a straight who has just punched on with three armed bikers and beat the shit out of them. He wants to talk about it and relive the glory, but his wife's giving him shit. 'You freaking idiot. What about your kids? What about me? What if you'd been killed?'

I can kind of see where she's coming from. 'You wanna stay the way you are,' I say. 'You've got a good life. Living the outlaw life isn't easy. It's probably the most dangerous thing you can do.'

'You're lucky,' The Woman says, handing me the slug. And I can see she's right. It's a Teflon-coated nine mil, so it had just burrowed a hole straight through. If it had been a hollow point, it would have shattered my hip.

I have a quiet Christmas, recuperating. In early January, some of the old bikers – Chance, PJ, Scotty and Grizzly – come around to see how I'm going. I'm not too bad. We chat for an hour or two before The Woman comes in and tells them I need a bit more rest. While

I nod off for a couple of hours, they go into the lounge room and she makes them a feed. When I wake up, I hobble out of the bedroom into my recliner, and as all outlaw bikers do, we spend the rest of the night bullshitting to each other.

Little do I know that later that month, on Australia Day, I'll be in a coma, in a chopper flying to Canberra Hospital. My wounds have gone bad. I've got renal failure, septic shock, my lungs have collapsed. Donna and my son Daniel are told I'm not going to make it. It looks like those wannabes in Auburn might have got me after all. But I've been in this situation before. I'd been left for dead on a hospital gurney after the Milperra ambush. Parked out in a corridor, I'd had the sheet pulled up over my head until a nurse coming on duty noticed me twitching. I'm pretty hard to kill.

And after nine days in a coma in Canberra, I start to come good again. I can see Donna in the distance and I'm moving my hand around, but I can't see it. She seems to be 100 yards away. I keep trying to reach her. Next thing I know, this thing's taken off my face and there she is. There are my sons and my brothers, Bull and Snake, and Bear and Cub and my sisters and Mum. My poor mum has come to Canberra even though she has cancer.

I drift away again to another place. I see more brothers – Shadow, Wack and Chop, who died at Milperra or soon after. I see my dad and my grandfather, and they're wearing Bandido colours, which is pretty funny since granddad was a cop. I see Snoddy and all these other Bandits, like Hombre, who've died over the years and who are now up there in the Ride Forever chapter, where the tanks are always full and the roads are long and windy and you've always got the sun on your back. Joining them doesn't seem like such a bad idea.

There are so many old-time bikers who have left us over the past ten years. They're the generation that was there at the start of the outlaw scene and they're just disappearing. As I come into consciousness at Canberra Hospital over the next few weeks, I know I've got to get more of the stories down and I figure I might as well raise a few ghosts from Kings Cross while I'm at it. I've known a couple of real-life gunslingers and I can tell you that they don't always die in a hail of bullets.

The Cross in the 1960s, '70s and '80s was an extraordinary place. If you were smart enough and tough enough, you could get away with murder.

And a few other things.

CAESAR'S LAW
I

HOW TO DISARM A BLOKE HOLDING A GUN TO YOUR HEAD

It's something you've got to practise over and over. How you do it depends on what sort of gun the bloke's got and which hand he's got it in. Some people only practise with someone holding the gun in the right hand. But the first time you come up against a southpaw, it's as though you never practised at all. The gun's on the wrong side. So you've got to practise with both hands.

If the bloke is standing off you, you've got to get him to come into range so you can get at him. Always stand with your hands around belly button height. Keep them there the whole time you're talking to him so he's not suspecting anything. If you start lifting your left hand up as he's walking towards you, he's going to know something's on. If your hand's already half way up it's got less distance to travel. This again is all practice. You've got to practise your speed. You do things like catching a tennis ball on a string. Practise taking a marble out of someone's hand. Put a candle out by sweeping it with your hand, touching the wick without knocking the candle over. When you can do all that, you're ready to start practising with a gun.

So if a righthander is pointing a gun at your forehead, you lift your left hand up and, with a backhand motion, knock his arm just down from the wrist. As his arm's going away, you slide your hand up the five or six inches and grab the gun and grab his thumb, making sure you keep your thumb on his thumb with your hand over the top of the barrel or the chamber if it's a revolver. You bend the hand down and back towards him. That puts him off balance and then you whack him in the throat with your free right hand.

1

THE CROSS

Everybody sees things differently. For a lot of people, Kings Cross in 1965 was about the hookers and the illegal gambling joints. For others, it was the neon lights or the bohemian cafés and the crazy characters that hung out in them. Maybe the rock and roll – you could see the Easybeats or Billy Thorpe most weeks. For me, the Cross was about the bikes and the strippers. I always found it easy to pick up strippers. So the Cross represented an endless supply of beautiful young women. And great-looking Triumphs and Harleys.

I'd wanted to be an outlaw biker since Three Fingers from the Spot Boys gave me a ride on his Triumph when I was 13. So in my late teens, I'd go up the Cross on my Triumph Bonneville rigid and just check them all out. I'd see what sort of clubs were around and which one might suit me. But the more I thought about it, the more I figured it would be better to start my own club and fill it with my mates and my brothers.

I formed the Gladiators on my 19th birthday, in July 1965. (In my first book, *Enforcer*, I said it was 1969, but that was a mistake.) We rode into Kings Cross on our Triumphs and Beezers (BSAs) with our denim cuts and our Elvis hair and we pulled our bikes up right alongside the more established clubs parked along the strip. They were all checking out the new kids, giving us the stare, but we didn't need to prove a thing. My brother Wheels was six foot five and our mate Peaceful was six foot seven, so that made enough of an impression for those who didn't know us. The other original members of the Gladiators were my brother Bull, plus our mates Lurch, Rhino and Tank. I'd been coming up the Cross with my dad since I was eight years old. He knew a lot of people there and everybody could see I was a chip off the old block. By the time the Gladiators arrived, I'd already pounded most of the bouncers on the strip.

And my brothers and I had already found our way into blues with some of the other really tough families from around Sydney, like the English brothers from Bankstown and the Cobb brothers from St Marys. So the Gladiators were born fully mature and ready to take on the world.

The Vietnam War was just getting hotted up and soon the Cross was changed by all that American money that flooded in on R&R. We noticed it most in the form of more blokes wanting to fight us.

I rode past the navy wharf at Garden Island one day when a Yank boat came in and there were at least 1500 sheilas down there – all secretaries and office workers waiting to get picked up by big-spending Yanks. We'd see them hours later in big groups. Roaring drunk. Whenever anybody wants to prove how tough they are, they seem to go looking for an outlaw biker. You'd get 20 or 30 GIs and they'd just pick out a few bikers and it would be on. If it was too badly one-sided, the other clubs would join in to batter the Yanks.

By the late 1960s, you had all the hippies in Victoria Street in their Kombi vans parked bumper to bumper down one side of the street. These long-hairs would set up their little camps and you'd see half a dozen of them sitting round a camper stove cooking themselves up a feed of beans or something. They'd walk around the Cross selling jewellery and hand-woven handbags to the GIs and sailors and all the other blokes engaged in the war they were protesting about.

In 1968, I was flicking through a magazine called *Biker Lifestyle* when I saw a picture of a club called the Tribesmen. They were wearing leather cut-offs and I thought: *Fuck, that looks so much better than the denim vests we're wearing.* So I found a woman at Rozelle who did leatherwork. She measured up all the Gladiators and made up vests. It took her two and half times as much leather to do vests for Wheels and Peaceful as it took for her to make mine. And I was no little guy, but it goes to show what mountains they were.

Except for one member of the Hells Angels, we were the first club in Sydney to have leather cuts and most of the other clubs soon followed. We got our leatherworker to make us gauntlets and wrist guards with the big dog spikes on them. If anyone tried to grab you during a fight, they'd cut themselves to pieces, or you could use the wrist guard to give your opponent a side swipe in the face and cut 'em open that way. Most of the other clubs followed us on that one too.

The hair was getting longer. Some blokes were starting to grow beards. But my brothers stuck with the old rocker kind of haircut for a few years yet.

The 1960s and '70s were a great time to be an outlaw biker. You didn't have huge clubs with chapters all over the state and all over the country. With the possible exception of the Hells Angels, it was just single clubs with single chapters of about a dozen blokes. And just about all of them used to get up the Cross on a Friday night. A lot of the clubs don't exist anymore. Like Corporation of Sin, the Norsemen, the Saracens, Salems Witches, the Hangmen, Sons of Satan, Satans Slaves, Devil's Dozen, the Gargoyles, Ghostriders, the Pagans, Headhunters, Executioners, Vikings, Warlords, Knights, Demons, Galloping Gooses (one of the real tough small clubs), Hades Henchmen, Undertakers, Assassins, Death Riders, Zombies, the Gravediggers, Motherfuckers, Satans Council. I could keep going. You add that list to the big clubs like the Hells Angels and the Finks, plus some of the other clubs that were small then but would later become big like the Rebels, the Gipsy Jokers and the Comancheros, and you get the picture. There was a complex ecosystem of alliances and feuds and peace agreements. And it was all held together by honour. Tough blokes who kept their word and wouldn't take shit from no one.

The Cross was always regarded as neutral territory, though. It didn't matter if you were at war with another club, everybody kept themselves under control and made sure nothing happened up the Cross. Some clubs had a permanent animosity and they'd make sure they were parked opposite each other so they could stare at each other the whole night and the other clubs would just be waiting for something to erupt. In my whole time of going up the Cross, though, I never saw two clubs getting into it. Sometimes individuals would get stuck in, but the clubs showed restraint. I saw plenty of clubs get into lots of foot-ballers, marines, soldiers, and sailors, especially the Yanks. But never each other. All the outlaw clubs honoured the code. It's too bad it doesn't happen these days. I know there's clubs out there that still honour the old ways, but there's a lot that don't.

When I started outlawing, you didn't need a lot of rules to run a club. You lived by the code. You lived by honour, loyalty, courage and respect for your brothers. There was a saying that went, 'There's nothing so special as love and loyalty, except the love and loyalty an outlaw biker has for his brothers.'

Up until the early 1980s, clubs were usually made up of eight to 20 members. The whole idea was about being with a bunch of blokes you called your brothers: riding, partying and bluing. You backed your brothers up no matter what. Not because you had to, but because they were your brothers. There was just a different feeling about riding in those years. Now it's all about who's going to be the biggest club and who's got the biggest club-house. It's not about getting together with your brothers, going for a run and pulling up at some paddock on the roadside just before dark, setting up camp, building a log fire and all the blokes sitting around having a beer and telling yarns and just being together. Now they sleep in motels. The old-style run has been forgotten. Not that I'd object to a motel on a run these days at my age, but back in them days that was what it was about – being together.

You didn't care about money. If a brother didn't have the money to go on a run, everyone would whip around and make sure he had enough. If a brother's bike broke down, you helped him rebuild it. Everyone chucked in parts, chucked in money. And if a bloke left a club under good circumstances, he left with everything except his colours. He left with his bike, he left with his honour. These days it seems that if you leave a club you leave your bike behind. I'm not saying all clubs do this, but I know a few that do.

A lot of people aren't going to like what I've just said, but that's always been my way. I say what I think. I don't play politics. Never have. Never will. I'm not here to be liked.

Back in the '60s and '70s, you had some really hard men. Men who just wanted to ride their bikes and party with their brothers, but most of all protect their brothers and honour the colours they wore, no matter what club it was. I remember when I first met Haystacks and Nino Palazaro from the Gipsy Jokers. They were a force to be reckoned with. Haystacks was one of the biggest men in town and Nino was the number-one contender for the light heavyweight championship in boxing, as well as being a martial arts expert. He was definitely one of the hardest outlaw bikers going around.

At the Hells Angels, they had Guitar and Gerry, Ball Baring and Little Billy. They were hard men.

The Nomads had Metho Tom and Angelo. In the very early 1970s, Metho Tom and the Nomads were up the Cross. Tom was on a Triumph, which was unusual for him because he was a real Harley man. He was doing a whirly on the main drag when a car hit him. Well, Tom was on the wrong side of the road and – I don't think anyone will mind me saying this –when he came off he was under the car, but his brothers moved him and the bike to the right side of the road and moved the car onto the wrong side. Tom became national president and built up a strong club.

A man who ran a small club called Corporation of Sin, Les Markham, had a reputation as one of the toughest guys in the bikers scene. I didn't get to meet Les until I was jailed over Milperra in the late 1980s, but he really impressed me by being a top bloke as well as one of the strongest men I've ever laid eyes on.

And then you had my brothers from the Sydney Gladiators – I considered them to be the hardest of all.

There were hard men in just about every club. Unlike today where things seem to be settled by the gun, up to the early '80s it was always settled by the fist – or the boot, or the chain, or the bat, or the knife. An old lady can pull a trigger, but it takes a man to stand up to another man and punch on. That's the courage you need to defend your colours, whether you're facing one man or 30. You go down swinging. Not that we ever did go down in the Sydney Gladiators. We were never beaten, no matter what the odds.

CAESAR'S LAW
II

BEARD MAINTENANCE

The secret to keeping your beard in good order is keeping all the food out of it and using a good conditioner. I use Dove. I shampoo and condition it every time I shower. I trim it myself, unless I'm a bit crook and it's getting shaggy. My son Daniel does it then.

I got my first beard when I was about 25, around 1971. I've had one ever since. Donna's never seen me without one. I had a full on beard when I started seeing her, then I trimmed it so it just ran down neatly from my sideburns. Then I got sick of that and have had the goatee since the mid-1980s.

A lot of young blokes are getting them now and I don't mind that at all. I think any bloke should do what he wants when it feels right.

2

THE WILD ONES

Sydney was a small town in those days and, if you hung out in the right places, you'd often have brushes with fame. And sometimes it was just out of the blue. When I was going over to Newtown to do a bit of *muy thai* training, I used to walk or jog as part of my cardio workout past a little cul-de-sac off Illawarra Road. One day I was going past and there were the Easybeats trying to get a huge amplifier into a transit van. They were just starting to get known. Stevie Wright yelled out, 'Hey mate, can you give us a hand?' I lifted the amp into the back of the van for them and after that I'd see them around on and off. They ended up giving me tickets to one of their concerts. They got more famous over the years.

One night I was leaving the Whisky à Go Go in William Street. It must have been about 1965 or '66. I walked out onto the footpath and there was Australia's king of rock and roll, Johnny O'Keefe, with his dukes up, facing off with eight or nine yobbos. He let go a couple of beauties and decked two of them before the others jumped on top of him. I wandered in and threw a few bodies into the nearby walls, decked a few others. JO'K looked up and went: 'Big feller!'

'John, what are you doing?' I said. 'At your age, you shouldn't be picking fights with half a dozen blokes.'

'I thought there were more than that,' he said, smiling.

We wandered off up to the main drag into one of the clubs and he bought me a drink. When JO'K was around, the women flocked to him. But just as many came over to me as came over to him. I think he was a bit shocked about the pull of the outlaw biker patch. We hadn't been properly introduced to each other by this stage. Of course, I knew who he was. He'd hosted his own TV show for years by this time. But one of the girls did the formalities, saying, 'Johnny, this is Caesar Campbell.'

'Oh, I've heard of you and your brothers,' he said. 'You Campbells are famous round these parts.'

'We might be well known in the Cross, but you're an icon all over Australia,' I said.

'That's nice of you to say so, Caesar.'

'What do you like being called? Johnny, John, JO'K?'

'Just call me Johnny.'

We talked about people we knew and about boxing. Johnny knew how to throw a punch. We had a good time. Anyway, he ended up with a stripper, Brandy. I already had a date for the night, so we were walking down the main drag of the Cross and people were stopping Johnny everywhere: 'Mr O'Keefe, can I have your autograph?' The girls from 13 to 50 were all over him.

We were going down past Surf City and he was parked around the back. He had a brand new Jag. He wanted me to have a look at it. 'Come on, sit in it. Feel what the seats are like.'

So I took my cut off.

'What are you taking your vest off for?' he said.

'I can't wear it sitting in a car.'

'Why not?'

'That's just what a lot of outlaw clubs do. We don't wear our cuts in cars. We wear 'em on our bikes.'

'Well, you learn something new every day.'

I sat in the Jag, looking at the fancy wooden dash, while people flocked around him wanting to talk and get his autograph.

'Caesar,' he said, 'I'm playing at the Stadium next week. Do you want to come?'

'Yeah, I'd like to. Can I bring me brothers?'

'Bring whoever you want.'

He pulled out a ticket and wrote on the back of it: 'Admit Caesar, Gladiators MC and whoever is with him', and he signed his name.

We turned up at the Sydney Stadium and found our seats were in the fourth row. The Delltones were on too. It was a top show. We went backstage afterwards and I introduced my Gladiator brothers to Johnny. He ended up inviting us to a party somewhere between Vaucluse and Bellevue Hill, Sydney's two poshest suburbs. There was Col Joye, Brian Henderson, Lonnie Lee and a whole heap of well-known singers and entertainers. Unlike when we were out on the street when everybody wanted to talk to Johnny, at this party, everybody wanted to talk to us. They wanted to know what it was like to be a 'bikie' and whether the stories they'd heard were true.

I couldn't cope. People were cornering me everywhere, sometimes forming a circle of eight or nine around me wanting to hear the stories. I only stayed about 90 minutes.

I grabbed a chick who was pretty well known and still is today. We went back to her place and had a really good night. Apparently some of my brothers had equally good celebrity nights too. Some missed out, but that's the way it goes.

It always amazed me how JO'K used to front up for his TV show, because he always had black eyes and swollen cheeks. He was such a fiery little bloke, always bluing. Anyway, that was Johnny O'Keefe – top bloke, top singer and, to me, still king of Australian rock and roll.

The big rock and roll venue in the Cross in the 1960s was Surf City, a converted movie theatre that got demolished for the railway station in the '70s. It was a slaughterhouse. There were hundreds upon hundreds of people in there, band after band. One night, Billy Thorpe had gone outside to have a joint or something after playing a set, back in the days when he was still all neatly done up in a little suit and a skinny tie. I was watching as a bloke with a few mates behind him decided he was going to belt the big pop star. I imagined that his girlfriend must have been screaming and drooling over Thorpe and the bloke couldn't handle it.

Fuck that, I thought. I already knew Thorpie. A mate of mine, Brian Gale, lived next door to Thorpie's lead guitarist, so I used to bump into him and the Aztecs every now and then. So I wandered over to help.

Thorpie couldn't fight his way out of a wet paper bag. I thumped the blokes and he thanked me. It was pretty straightforward.

*

I WAS up at the Pink Pussycat one night when it was up under the Coca-Cola sign. The famous stripper Sandra Nelson was performing. Part of the reason she was famous was that she took off more gear than the law allowed. Strippers were meant to have those little tassels on their nipples and keep at least something on downstairs, but she'd get it all off, and if a member of the press was there or if the coppers hadn't been paid on time it would result in a raid or whatever. So Sandra had been able to cross over into the mainstream with all the publicity about her huge, untasselled tits. The afternoon papers loved her and she was always going on the telly, but this night she was doing what she did best, getting her gear off.

I was leaning up against a wall down the back enjoying the show when one of the bouncers came up to me and said he needed to take a crap. 'Will you watch the door for me, Caesar?' he said.

'Yeah, I'll watch the door.'

So I was standing there when Sandra came out. 'Are you working here now, Caesar?' she said.

'Nah,' I said, a little taken aback that she knew who I was. 'I'm just giving Boof a break. He's gone to the throne room.'

'Oh, right. How about we go out one night?' she said, all up-front.

'Yeah, that'd be good.'

So we did. I got her on my Harley and we rode down to Harry's Café de Wheels for dinner, then I took her the 45 kilometres up to Palm Beach. She was flashing her tits and cars were almost running off the road. In shopping centres, blokes' jaws were hitting the footpath. She was a really nice chick. We got on well and let's just say we enjoyed a very pleasant, romantic evening.

We went out a few more times over the next couple of years and during that time she took me up to the offices of Mr Sin, Abe Saffron. She said I should meet him. Unfortunately, he wasn't there but she just went straight on into his office. I was expecting all his heavies to barge in with their pieces drawn at any minute, but nobody came. Sandra ended up getting all romantic on me again, so that was interesting.

When she eventually introduced me to Abe Saffron, he wasn't what I expected. I knew he wasn't a big bloke, but I'd heard how he had all the coppers and judges and politicians in his pocket, so I expected someone a bit forceful, tough. He was more like an accountant, a bank manager. Medium handshake. Easygoing. But he liked to be called Mr Saffron.

CAESAR'S LAW III

WHAT TO DO IF CONFRONTED BY A BUNCH OF BLOKES THAT WANT TO BASH YOU

The best thing to do for an ordinary bloke, if there's two opponents, is hit the closest one as hard as you can straight in the nose. You want to break it, and in doing that both his eyes will start to swell. For about thirty seconds that bloke's eyes will be watering and he'll be seeing black and red. That gives you the chance to go the other bloke.

There's always the good old kick in the nuts for him. Or you can hit him in the throat. That's my favourite thing. You've got to be really careful though. If you don't know what you're doing, you can end up killing someone. You've got to know how hard to hit them. And you want to do it just a bit to the side of the Adam's apple. Not full-on. If you want to take them out, well, hit them direct there and they're gone. But if you just want to incapacitate them you hit them on either side and about a third as hard as you can hit, depending on how hard you can hit. You've got to practise these things. It's why those blokes that throw one punch end up killing people. You shouldn't be out there throwing punches if you don't know how and where to hit someone. I've never killed anyone with a single punch – not accidentally.

3

ROUND-RINGING

Since leaving school around 1960, I'd just knocked about doing what I could for a quid. For about 16 months, I worked in a piggery out at Mulgoa on the outer western fringe of Sydney, castrating the boars and doing whatever needed doing. I made money on the side by going into pubs and sussing out who the local thugs were. Every pub in them days had a pug who thought he was the best in the district, so I'd challenge them and get a bet going. I did a bit of bouncing in pubs . . . whatever I could get my hands on.

I know it sounds egotistical, but I was born with the ability to knock people out with one punch. My old man and my grandfather, Joey, could do the same. So could most of my brothers. In my first fight at school, I went *whack* and knocked the kid out. From the age of seven, Dad used to take me to Hannebery's gym in Newcastle, where Dave Sands – 'the best fighter never to be world champion' – used to train.

About 1972, word got around that Abe Saffron was going to start up an underground fight scene. It was going to be bare-knuckled. No rules. Nothing was off limits. He wanted to do it right, so he planned to bring out top fighters from all over the world and face them off against some locals. I wasn't that interested at first. I knew what I could do and didn't think I needed to prove anything to anyone.

But the infamous Mr Big of Sydney, Lenny McPherson, got in my ear about it. 'Come on, you and your brothers reckon you're pretty tough. Why don't you prove what you can do?'

McPherson was no mate of mine. I think he was keen to see me involved because I'd thumped a few of his blokes over the years and he wanted to see me get thumped back.

I let him goad me into going down and trying out. They had auditions down at the Finger Wharf at Woolloomooloo. It was still a functioning wharf back then, but it was hardly used at all. It just had this huge empty warehouse space. I decked a few blokes and I was in. I was going to be Mr Sin's main representative against the fancy overseas fighters.

The first bloke they brought out was a six foot four African–American who used the name Ray Evans. He'd apparently been a navy Seal instructor.

I arrived in my car and was allowed to drive onto the Finger Wharf by the wharfies who were manning the gate and were effectively security for the fight. Lenny McPherson was in sweet with them, so he'd teed all that up. Everyone else had to park outside and walk up the long, thin wharf with the huge old wooden warehouse running right up the middle of it. I was alone, wearing my black satiny *kyite* training pants and bare feet. I saw all these people, blokes in suits and women in nice clothes, and I thought, *Shit, what have I got myself into?* I was always taught not to do things in front of witnesses.

I didn't have a second, but one of the knockabouts up the Cross, Little Lenny Baker, seemed to take on the role. All I had in my sports bag was a bottle of Coke for after the fight. I didn't think it would go long enough to justify having a water bottle or anything like that. Little Lenny said to me, 'If you want to make the money, bet on yourself on the side. Do you think you can take this bloke?'

'Yeah.'

'Well, ask for your appearance money up front, give it to me and I'll get it all on you.' So we did that. I was a rank outsider, so there was potentially a lot of money to be made. And I trusted Little Lenny. Everybody did.

All the punters formed a circle behind a big chalk ring drawn on the rough old wharf timbers. I could see my opponent, Evans, at the far end of the circle. He was stretching his leg out and all this sort of stuff, so I grabbed my leg and put it up alongside my ear. He probably didn't expect to see a big hairy biker do that. I was doing a lot of *kyite* – a Korean martial art – at the time and could do the full front splits. I could jump off a chair and hit the floor in the full splits.

Evans looked at me and pointed to the ground, telling me I was going down.

Big Lenny McPherson yelled at me, 'You're gunna get killed, Campbell.'

There were no bells or refs. The fight began with a nod of the head from Evans and me.

He came straight at me and let fly with a kick to the hip and I thought, *The next one's probably going to go to the head.*

The way I was taught to fight from the age of seven with boxing, then wrestling, judo, *muy thai* and *kyite* was to just go on autopilot. There was a famous boxer who used to say that before he went in the ring he could see the fight in his head. He could see the other bloke throwing punches and how he would counter. That's how I saw mine. I could see what was going to happen in this fight as soon as I saw Evans and the way he moved. The way he warmed up. I was zoned in.

He went to kick me in the head and I was ready. I put my arm up and moved to the side, so his foot glanced off my arm. He spun around and sprayed out another kick with the foot. I bent down and fended it with my other arm, rising as I pushed his foot away and making him lose his balance.

That seemed to rile him, because he made the mistake of spitting at me. With him doing that, and with Big Lenny still there at ringside with his voice above all the others, telling me I was going to get killed, I went into another zone of blackness. I waited for Evans to come in towards me and I drove my foot hard into his left knee. I felt it bend, satisfyingly, as his leg snapped. He slumped to the floor. There was a whole lot of yelling from the crowd, but I can't say that I really heard it. I got in behind him, wrapped my arms around his neck and sent him on a long holiday. One-way ticket.

I didn't feel a thing. It was just a fight. He got what he deserved.

His blokes came over and bent down to look at him. One of them threw himself over the fighter in a kind of embrace. There was just silence in this cavernous space. I turned my back and walked out through the crowd in the eerie quiet. There were a lot of fine-looking folks wide-eyed, open-mouthed, staring at me, staring at the black body on the floor.

Big Lenny made his way towards me. 'You were lucky,' he said.

I got Little Lenny to go to my bag and open the glass bottle of Coke for me.

The body was left for Abe Saffron and his associates to clean up. I wouldn't have a clue what they did with it, but as I was to learn, they were pretty good at dealing with that sort of thing. There were never repercussions. My only injury was a dirty great splinter in my foot from the wharf timbers, so I decided that if I fought there again I'd better wear runners.

The fights started coming along every few weeks. They were often at the Finger Wharf, but they'd also be in garages and factories on bare concrete. Some were in disused office buildings and I'd find myself fighting on polished timber or parquetry.

Abe had the coppers on side so that, wherever the fight was, the local sergeant would make sure his boys weren't around. When it was at the Finger Wharf, the sergeant at Darlo would send the troops up to Paddington. No copper ever came near one of my fights.

I'd never know the person I was up against until the last minute, but they were almost always guys with big reputations from overseas. It was only the ones who pissed me off who ended up on those long vacations.

More people started coming to watch, not that they allowed a lot in, but certainly more money started to go through the books and that was what it was all about for Abe and his mates. There was no entry fee, but it was only the known big punters who got invited and, if there was a blow-in who was there because they knew someone who knew someone, they'd have to flash a big wad of cash to prove that they were serious before they'd be let in. I heard about some enormous bets: $100,000, $200,000, which was enough to buy a flash house in the Eastern Suburbs back then.

Because a lot of my fights were ending so badly for my opponents, it got to the point where there were two sorts of betting: whether I would win and whether the other bloke would walk out alive.

I certainly never bet on that one. That wouldn't be right. I never set out to deliberately send someone away, it just happened sometimes. They'd poke me in the eye or say something that'd set me off and I'd just lose it. I'd have the crowd going, 'Kill him! Kill him! Kill him!' That's what a lot of them came to see.

A Miss World finalist used to be there all the time with some girlfriends. They were the worst. They loved the blood. I'd sometimes see them during the fight before mine and they'd be there with their fists clenched and the veins popping out of their necks. These good sorts going, 'Kill him. Kill him.'

For all the victories I started pegging up, the big money blokes like Lenny McPherson never got behind me. Aussies have got this thing where they think if the bloke's from overseas he's got to be better. That was good for me, because it meant that Little Lenny and then later my brother Shadow kept getting good odds and we cleaned up. The prize money in the beginning was thirteen grand, but we made more from the bookies.

The only big fish who bet on me all the time were Frank Packer and his son, Kerry. Those two thought that Aussies really could be as good as anyone from overseas.

The highest paid escort in Sydney at the time was a sheila called Roberta Roberts. She was about 20 years old, studying at university, and if you wanted to spend the night with her you were up for thousands of dollars. Big Lenny and George Freeman both had a thing for her, but she used to hang around George more. To piss them both off, I'd just whistle her over and get her to plait my hair before a fight. She'd be caressing my scalp and I'd be looking at Lenny and George and they'd be staring switchblades back at me.

But for all that, I'd be concentrating on my opponent across the circle. I could tell just by the way they walked whether they had a bit of style about them. A lot of them used to spend five or ten minutes warming up and, in that time, I was picking out what martial art they practised, what type of fighting they did. The way they jabbed, the way they kicked. I always warmed up before I came in. I wasn't giving *nothing* away.

Little Lenny would be hovering around. He was an old boxer in his day, a welterweight prelim fighter, not good enough to shoot for the title, but good enough to be on the card. And he loved being amongst it all. Telling me who was in the crowd. 'Col Joye's here,' he'd say. 'Brian Henderson's over the back there.'

One time I saw this sheila in her 50s come in with a chauffeur carrying a satin pillow for her friggin' Maltese terrier to sit on.

'Who the fuck's that?' I said to Little Lenny.

'I think that's Lady Fairfax. You know, owns the *Herald* and everything.'

'You gotta be jokin'.'

'Fair dinkum.'

I heard that she had a bet, but I don't know who she backed.

CAESAR'S LAW
IV

THE PERFECT PUNCH

If you watch a good boxer, you'll see them line up their opponent with a left jab or two then swing the right hook. When he's throwing it, he's moving his hip with it so the weight of his body is behind the punch. You need that to get the full force.

Your thumb is tucked in and your wrist has got to be straight, otherwise you're going to break it. That's why they tape boxers wrists up – to keep them straight.

When you're throwing your punch, your power is coming from your entire body. You're generating force from the stomach muscles and hips, through the shoulder and down through your arm.

It's a beautiful feeling when you get it right, which I always did.

4

THE HITMAN

Another regular spectator at my fights was a guy by the name of Johnny Regal, or JR. Everyone up the Cross knew who Johnny Regal was – Australia's number one hitman. He had a short fuse and a quick gun hand.

So Little Lenny would always announce him to me when he saw him in the crowd among the other colourful characters. After my 13th fight, I was up at Sweethearts, the café in the Cross that was yet to be made famous by the Cold Chisel song, when this Johnny Regal came up to my table and asked if he could sit down.

I nodded and took a sip from my shake.

He said he was impressed by the way I fought, the way I kept winning.

For my part, I'd thought of him as a bit of a Hollywood gangster. He dressed like a spiv, always with a long leather coat in either brown or black. His hair was slicked back in the old teddy-boy style. His trousers were flared and his shoes were pointy.

And I'd also seen that Johnny Regal didn't mind letting his coat flap open to flash the twin 9 mm Berettas that he always wore in a double shoulder holster made from black leather. Anybody who was anyone up the Cross knew who Johnny Regal was and when he walked down the street they stepped out of the way. And I'm talking about everyone – including Mr Big (Lenny McPherson) and Mr Las Vegas (George Freeman). The only ones who didn't step out of his way were the citizens – the ones who came to the Cross to stare at the girls, to peek into the strip clubs and, some of them, to fight.

JR was a quick-tempered little bloke. I suppose he wasn't that little, but to me he was. He was about five foot ten and about twelve and a half stone. He was always getting into fights with people from the burbs. He was a tough rooster, but the thing was, he couldn't fight his way out of the proverbial paper bag. He always had black eyes and busted noses. He'd fight anyone. He never backed down and he never pulled his guns on the tourists from the burbs. I always thought, *Geez, that bloke's got some balls but, fuck, he can't fight.*

I think we clicked because I liked the cut of JR's jib. The fact he never pulled his guns on the yobbo tourists told me that he operated by a code. That he was in control. Because it was a different story for those who lived in our world.

One night, before I'd met JR, I was up at the legendary all-night rock venue, the Manzil Room, where JR always sat in the same booth as if it was his own private throne room, no matter who was sitting there when he arrived. It was loud and dark as usual when another well-known standover man decided he was going to show off to his new girl. I watched from a nearby table as this bloke said a few things that JR didn't like and JR just reached into his leather coat, pulled out a Beretta and shot him in the knee. The bouncer grabbed the standover man and threw him out into Springfield Avenue. The standover man clearly hadn't read the rule about not getting shot inside the Manzil Room, because JR was allowed to stay.

Anyway, the night he came up to talk to me at Sweethearts, we got on well. We kept bumping into each other up the Cross and we got to know each other. He ended up inviting me to his house at Arncliffe for dinner. I became a bit of a regular out there. His missus, Cheryl, was a top lady and a great cook. She told me I was the first person he'd ever had over for tea.

He told me how he was just a kid from Rockdale who fell in with the local gang, the Rockdale Boys and, not being much of a fighter, gravitated to guns. I don't know how he went from the Rockdale Boys to a hitman, just that he hung around the Cross in a hotted up FC Holden and things took over from there.

He was about eight or nine years older than me, so he'd had enough time to get good at his trade. After I'd been over there a few times, he invited me to follow him down a set of stairs into a basement. I made sure I was a step behind him as we walked down the narrow staircase. I considered myself a good judge of character and I felt like we were good friends, but I was still walking into a basement with the country's number one hitman. I instinctively made sure I had plenty of time to break his neck if I had to.

He turned on the lights at the bottom of the steps and we were standing in a huge concrete cavern that must have extended out under the entire backyard.

'It was built as a bomb shelter during the war,' he said. Cheryl later told me it was the reason he bought the house.

It was almost 20 metres long and 10 metres wide and he'd set it up as a target shooting range. It was solid cement stacked with sandbags so the bullets wouldn't ricochet. The targets were on a pulley system so you could set them at different distances without having to walk.

'Do you want to learn how to shoot?' he said.

'Sure.' I didn't tell him my old man had spent 12 months teaching me all about guns at a range under the Commonwealth Bank in the city. So I let JR give me some pointers and he put up a target. It was pretty close and I hit it.

'Do you want me to move it back a bit further?' he said.

'Put it back as far as you can. How far do you have it?'

'I have it right down the far end.' After a few goes to get my eye in, I was getting eight out of ten in the bullseye.

'And you said you'd never shot a gun before?' he said.

'I never said that. I said I didn't like using guns. I prefer to use me fists.'

He was getting nine out of ten in the bullseye and he was quite obviously a very good shot.

After we finished, we had an interesting conversation where he started telling me a little bit about what he did.

✳

AROUND THIS time, JR told me that there was someone he was keen to introduce me to. So one day we went into an office above the Pink Pussycat. It was Abe Saffron's Kings Cross office. We walked in and JR introduced me to 'Mr Sin'. I'd been introduced to Abe a few years earlier, but I didn't let on to JR about that. Abe could see what the go was and he went along with it.

I'd already gathered that Abe was JR's main employer and it soon became clear that JR was interested in having me do some jobs with him. I told him that wasn't my go. (Over the next five or six years I did help him out here and there. What those jobs were, however, will stay between Abe, JR and me. Let's just say it was interesting work and something I'd done before, but only for my club.)

JR started to twig that I already knew Mr Sin when I started calling him 'Abe'. JR sulked for about ten minutes, then wanted to know why I hadn't told him that I knew Abe. 'You made me look like an idiot.'

'You're the one that wanted to introduce me. I never said I didn't know him.' He got over it.

I arranged to go back the next day and meet Abe again at his main office in the Lodge 44 Motel in Edgecliff. I went into the office behind the main reception desk and up a flight of stairs. Abe said there was a job I might want to do. Some Lebanese in the Eastern Suburbs wouldn't hand over $150,000 they owed him. 'I'll give you $5000 if you can get it back,' he said. That was the equivalent of the average annual salary in 1973.

'No thanks, Mr Saffron,' I said.

'How much do you want?' he asked.

'Thirty-five per cent.'

'Thirty-five! The most the top collectors get round here is five,' Abe said.

'Well, you can get one of them to go get your money for you,' I said.

I got the job.

I'd just bargained Australia's top crime boss up to my price and it felt pretty good. But I only got paid if I came back with the cash. Maybe he only agreed to 35 per cent because he never thought he'd see the money again. His other collectors had failed him on it. I just had to do better than them.

He wrote down an address and I hopped on my bike and rode over. It was a block of flats in Waverley. I knocked on the door and these three big Lebs were standing there with that look that said, 'Who are you? This better be good.' I didn't bother with formalities. Or conversation. I put my foot through the door and I just went *whack, whack, whack* and suddenly they were all lying on the floor.

I shut the door behind me and checked the flat to make sure no one else was there. I tied them all up and waited for them to regain consciousness. As soon as their eyes started opening, I started breaking fingers. I didn't have to break many before I learnt about a false bottom under one of the bedroom cupboards. I pulled out a bag and threw it at the feet of the smallest one. I untied his hands and sat him up. 'Okay, start counting.'

It took a long while, but we eventually got to $180,000. I tied the counter back up and walked out the door with the bag and all the money. I rode back to Abe and handed him his $150,000. He handed me my $52,500 cut and I got back on my bike and left.

I had found my calling.

BEST SONG EVER

'Unchained Melody' by the Righteous Brothers. I just like the lyrics and the tune. We were living in the Dandenong Ranges in Victoria when I first heard it on the radio. I was hanging around with Bad Blood, the first outlaw club in Australia, and I was going to Allen's milk bar in Sassafras. All the blokes and chicks from around would rock in there. It was just like Arnold's in *Happy Days*. You had the booths and be drinking out of glass Coke bottles and the big heavy glasses for your milkshakes. You'd spin tunes on the juke box and have a burger. They were good times.

My next favourite song is 'The Power of Love' – the Jennifer Rush version, not Celine Dion's. That whole you-are-my-lady-and-I-am-your-man thing was important to Donna and me when I was stuck in prison. The song became pretty special for us.

5

TAG-TEAMING
WITH THE
GLADIATORS

I made it a rule in the Gladiators that as my brothers turned 18 they came straight into the club. They didn't have to prospect – the biker equivalent of an apprenticeship. The other members were fine with that at first, but as Shadow, Wack, Snake and Chop came through, the other fellers started to get a bit alienated because my brothers were just straight into bluing. It was all fights and women. That was the way the club went. Other clubs stayed away from us and we developed the reputation as the meanest, most unstoppable club in town. That's how Jimmy Anderson, who ran a few clubs for Abe Saffron, came to name us the Wrecking Crew. Every time a new bouncer turned up at one of his places my brothers, often Snake, felt they had to try them out.

As the 1970s got going, the hippies changed. Instead of sitting there making their beads, you'd see 'em lying in the gutter with needles sticking out of their arms, or sitting there shivering through withdrawal waiting for some old lady to come along for them to roll.

The outlaws learnt early on that smack and bike clubs didn't mix. Some blokes in the smaller clubs got into it and started ripping off their mates' bikes to get money for a hit. The bigger clubs never tolerated it. If anyone brought it near us, they got smashed. To this day, if you go near smack in any club you get stomped and your colours are taken.

People have this idea of outlaw clubs that it's always 20 or 30 members going around picking on three or four Joe Citizens, but more often it's the other way around. What people don't understand, though, is that outlaws are different from normal people. There's this brotherhood, the code of honour that we live to.

I can remember one Friday night in the early 1970s – there were clubs everywhere. Ten or twelve Gipsy Jokers were sitting on their bikes, not annoying anyone, just yakking on, talking to a couple of strippers. A group of about 20 American soldiers – I'm not sure if they were army or marines – decided that they wanted one of the sheilas and the Jokers told 'em to fuck off. The Yanks were straight into them. All us other clubs watched with great interest as the Jokers kicked the living shit out of these soldiers. Now, I wouldn't bet me balls on it, but I'm pretty sure Ugly was one of the Jokers up there that night. And a most impressive demolition job they performed too.

At the Rock and Roll pub, right near the Finger Wharf at Woolloomooloo, there was this time we took on all these wharfies – Painters and Dockers who were visiting from Melbourne. We had this thing where if we were really outnumbered we'd get into a circle so everyone covered everyone else's back. The Painters and Dockers charged us. We put our backs to each other and they hit us and bounced off. Once we got going, we moved the circle round, rotating it, and we mowed the wharfies down like a whipper-snipper.

Another night, we were outside a club owned by the hard man Joe Meissner. Half-A-Mo was on the door. Half his suit was checks, half plain and, as his name suggested, he had half a moustache.

Anyway, the famous American wrestler Tex McKenzie was there with the wrestler Mark Lewin, 'master of the sleeper hold'. I fancied myself against Lewin, because I reckoned I had a better sleeper hold than him. I'd learnt it doing my martial arts. But it ended up being me and Tex McKenzie squared off against each other. He was a man mountain – six foot nine. I went *Boot!* with a left-foot side kick into his knee and as he came down I hit with a spinning elbow into his jaw and he was out cold.

Next thing I knew, there was this five feet eight inches, 19 stone ball of muscle coming at me at 100 miles an hour. It was Bulldog Brower, another one of the then-famous TV wrestlers. My brother Chop, who must have only been about 19 at the time, stepped out with his elbow raised and Brower's legs went out from under him. Chop would have copped a year's suspension if he'd tried that in the rugby league, but there were no refs here.

That left me and Mark Lewin. It was like an episode of *Ringside Wrestling*. But he didn't want anything more to do with me. He backed off. 'I've got no fight with you guys. You Aussies are crazy,' he said, his palms facing out towards me.

Tex McKenzie didn't turn up for the next episode of *World Championship Wrestling*. They said he'd 'had an accident in training'. But the next night, Bulldog Brower came looking for us, running round the Cross wearing a dog collar with all these spikes sticking out. He was a like a guard dog that's been riled, all aggro energy, head spinning, ears raised, spitting foam. He must have been a nutcase. He certainly acted like it on TV and he looked like it now. He had these huge arms. He'd bench press enormous weights before he'd get in the ring on TV.

This night he had another wrestler, Brute Bernard, with him. Bulldog Brower wanted another go at Chop, and Chop wanted to get stuck into him. But we grabbed hold of Chop and wouldn't let him go. There were a bunch of coppers over the road watching, so Chop would have copped a lot of grief if we'd let him loose. Brute Bernard had hold of Bulldog, holding him back too. 'That's it. That's it,' Chop was shouting. 'Hide behind your mates.'

Bulldog Brower said something back, but I couldn't understand it. It was more like a dog growling. I said to Brute Bernard, 'Why don't you pat him on the head and calm him down? Give him a bone, like a good boy.'

'Who are you?' Brute Bernard said.

'Who are you?' I said, even though I knew exactly who he was. I liked watching him wrestle.

'I'm Brute Bernard.'

'Is that supposed to mean something to me?' I said.

'And who are you?'

'I'm Caesar Campbell.'

'Ahh, so you're the big cooler up here.' I later got told that was a slang word Americans used for the top bouncers or top bluers.

Anyway, Brute Bernard got Bulldog Brower and turned him in the opposite direction and we took Chop back to the bikes, with Chop trying to get back to him the whole time like an angry terrier on a chain. The situation was no longer serious – it had become just funny.

6

BOOTS, BANDANAS AND ANIMAL DOCTORS

I'm sure Abe used to like to think he was on good terms with the outlaw bikers. If you had colours on, you just walked into Abe's clubs and got treated well, whereas some other places didn't want to know you. Most nightclubs wouldn't let my brother Snake in because he was so bad-tempered when he'd had a few and was always beating the shit out of bouncers, but he was always welcome at Abe's joints. Me and my brothers always got free drinks at the Venus Room, which was our favourite hang.

I think Abe used it as a prestige thing with his colleagues like George Freeman and Lenny McPherson to show them that he had the bikers onside. And as part of that, word got back to us one day in 1973 that he was offering $150 to every outlaw biker who would ride from the Rock and Roll Hotel in Woolloomooloo up through the Cross and back to the Rock and Roll. The only catch was that all they were allowed to wear was their boots and bandanas.

About 70 blokes took part. A lot of club members brought prospects to mind their clothes. Some of us sat on our cuts because we didn't trust prospects to mind our colours, which we considered our most treasured possession. Everyone could see what club I belonged to, though, because my colours were tattooed on my back.

So the 70 bikes set off from the pub and thundered past the navy docks at Garden Island before we hooked up the hill and round into the Cross. Blokes fell on the footpath laughing, sheilas cracked up, as the bikes came hurtling through the main drag, then we did the big righthander onto William Street before another righthander and back to the pub.

Everyone was on a huge high as we took our boots off to put our jeans back on, then our colours. Abe had given JR the cash and he was standing there with a great fat wad handing out the $150 for each bloke's participation, plus there was an extra $500 prize for the biggest erection. I'm not going to tell you who got that. Let's just say this bloke did his club proud.

*

AROUND THE same time as this, we had a whole lot of Maoris coming over from New Zealand trying to stake a claim in Sydney for clubs like the Mongrel Mob and Black Power. One night my brothers and I were out the front of the Venus Room just chewing the fat, minding our own business, when next thing we knew, all these cars were pulling up and a whole lot of humongous Maoris were pouring out and rushing towards us. We could tell from their faces that they weren't here to give us the traditional nose-rub greeting. Within seconds, we were punching on. Then we heard a gunshot.

'Bull's been shot,' Shadow called out. I looked over and saw Bull holding his gut. Somebody pulled him back into the doorway as we all instinctively formed into a circle around him. The Maoris were still coming at us and we kept punching on. The whole attack was totally out of the blue, but it wasn't hard to guess that since we were regarded as the toughest club in town they thought that if they could get over the top of us, it would put the scarers through all the other clubs. So, outnumbered, we were desperately trying to protect our brother and save the honour of our club. All of a sudden, I got pushed from behind and I saw that it was Bull, back on his feet trying to burst back into the fight. And he did, too. He got out there and was whacking on with this big Maori.

Everybody used to think you couldn't hurt a coconut by hitting him in the head, but Bull proved otherwise. We beat the shit out of them. We got the one who shot Bull, and Bull stomped him. Crushed his hands to jelly. I don't think people realised till then how tough Bull was. He was quiet. He was our sergeant and he'd mostly just sit back with his bourbon and cruise along, keeping an eye on things. He'd only come to the fore when there was serious trouble. And here he was with a .357 in his gut, acting like it was just a .22.

We took the gun and went straight in to see Abe. We gave him the gun as a thank you for his generosity with the Bandanas and Boots Run. And we needed his advice on what to do with Bull's wound. He gave us a referral to his favourite doctor, The Animal, a very well-known Eastern Suburbs doctor who also ran a fancy horse stud at Picton, a bit over an hour's ride out of Sydney.

We took Bull out there in the car and The Animal had a look at him. He had the full veterinary set-up, with an enormous X-ray machine for horses.

Bull got the horse X-ray and The Animal showed us the picture of the slug sitting in his guts. He put Bull under with a general anaesthetic and took out the .357 slug, closing the wound with a very neat little stitch job. After a week or so's rest, Bull was as good as new.

*

KNOWING THE Animal was to come in very handy over the next few years.

I was at the Rock and Roll one night about 1975 when there'd been a bit of a dispute between two blokes in the front bar. They took it outside round the back and a whole lot of their mates followed. I heard engines revving and a lot of yahooing going on for a long while before one of the barmaids, Tammy, came rushing over to me. 'They've got Kitty round there,' she said. 'She needs help.' Kitty was just a young chick who worked behind the bar. I wandered out and found that they were pushing her around and ripping at her clothes.

So I thumped a few of them and next thing I knew I had a snub-nosed .38 pointed at me from about 3 metres away. Before I could even start to do anything about it, the darn thing went off and I felt the thump in my right hip. The bloke who fired it seemed as shocked as I was, giving Kitty the time to grapple with him, which allowed me the time to get in and smash him. I took the gun off him and put one in his left knee and one in his right, just like I'd do almost 40 years later when I'd be shot in that same right hip. Only this time I also put one through the other guy's hip, right where I got it.

It turned out that the bullet had gone through me. I went to The Animal for treatment. He stitched up the hole, neat as can be, and I was good to go.

7

SLAVES TO A GOOD PARTY

Around October 1975, Satans Slaves put on a big party called the Outlaw Run at a 120- or 160-hectare property owned by a couple of their members near Oberon, in the high country west of Sydney. It was invitation only and most of the bigger clubs weren't invited, but 20 of the smaller clubs were. The Gladiators had a reputation for being a bit hard to get on with, but I was on good terms with Satans Slaves' president, Demon – a fair-sized bloke who could look after himself. The main reason we got invited, though, was that Demon hired us as security.

I had three of my brothers on the gate all the time and they checked the blokes as they came through. If they thought anyone was suss, they'd just pull 'em over and go through their gear. We confiscated guns, but we weren't so worried about knives. They were told straight up that there'd be two to three of us on the gate all the time and if anyone caused any trouble there was only one way in and one way out. We took turns going around the property on these old Triumphs the Slaves had given us. It got pretty muddy and we hacked the Triumphs around the paddocks, checking the campfires and the stage area. We had some prospects at that time and we had them doing most of the work while we enjoyed ourselves.

A few clubs there had a bit of animosity going, like the Hangmen and Hades Henchmen. Or the Executioners and the Rats. But they knew that if they started something they were going to have to take us on too.

There were a couple of hundred outlaw bikers. There were strippers, something like ten or twelve bands on the back of a semi-trailer. The bar was in a big shed, all powered by a noisy old diesel generator.

One of the most popular activities was jousting on motorbikes – where two blokes would ride at each other holding long poles with old boxing gloves tied to the ends. Whoever knocked the other one off got the money. However much it was, it wouldn't have been enough to pay for the damage to the bikes, but it was all good fun.

They also had an old Land-Rover with a tractor tyre tied to it by a length of rope. Three blokes would get on the tyre and be dragged around a paddock, which got cut up into a complete bog. Whichever bloke held on the longest stayed on it while the next two challengers got on. At the end of the weekend, whoever lasted longest got the money. It was great entertainment and a lot of laughs. We conned some of the strippers to have a go at it starkers and that was a sight to see.

That was what it was all about in the 1960s and '70s. Partying, riding your bike, and women. It was a bloody good weekend. I don't think there was a single fight. And if there was, they did it well away from the rest of the clubs.

Satans Slaves could be proud of themselves. It was one of the better runs I can remember.

Especially the strippers. One of my brothers, Wheels, fell in love with one of them. Every second stripper is named Bambi, and this one was too. They had the hots for each other something fierce. Every time she came off stage she came straight over to him. I don't know if he was with his current old lady back in 1975. If he was, I'm sorry about that, Wheels. That's the life of an outlaw.

We had such a good time that at the end of the weekend when we came to get paid, we told Satans Slaves to donate the money to their next party. Unfortunately, they got shut down in the next 12 months by a club that was not so much bigger than them, but harder. It was a shame, because they put on one hell of a do.

The only downer that weekend was the run back into Sydney. At Mount Victoria, going through fog, the Gargoyles were involved in an accident. Two of them died later in hospital. I didn't know the Gargoyles that well, but I'd met a few of them over the weekend and they seemed like a good bunch of blokes, proper outlaws – partying, riding, having a good time. We felt their loss.

8

AN URBAN LEGEND

About six months after JR had introduced me to Abe, we were up the Manzil Room when we bumped into an outlaw biker I knew called Chance. JR seemed to know him too. Chance was the sergeant-at-arms of his club, which I won't name. He was about my height, my build, but his beard was a bit longer. A lot of people used to think he was another Campbell. I'd seen him up the Cross for years, but we were just nodding acquaintances until one night when he got into a blue with about 20 Road Barons. Well, there were about a dozen patched members, the rest looked like hang-rounds. I just happened to be passing by and I saw Chance was doing pretty well against them all by himself. I didn't like the Road Barons. We'd had a few run-ins with them. But I'd always had a lot of respect for Chance's club. So I got stuck in and together we sorted them out. After that, we always had a yak and sometimes a drink together.

That night at the Manzil Room, Chance, JR and I talked for a bit over the always-loud music and during the following months the three of us started hanging out together more regularly. We were up the Manzil Room again one night, must have been about 1976, when I came back from taking a leak to see the two of them deep in conversation, with their heads close together shouting to make themselves heard over the band. When they saw me coming back, they stopped and looked at each other like they were in agreement about something.

'Caesar, I've got a question for you,' JR said. 'Have you ever heard of the Widowmaker?'

'Only as a rumour,' I said. For a few years there'd been talk about this hitman who could make his targets disappear without trace. And for those targets who didn't just evaporate, he had an ability to make their deaths look like natural causes. The underworld lived in fear of having him on their trail. But the whispers made him sound so good at what he did – almost supernatural – that I was not convinced that he actually existed.

'The Widowmaker is no rumour . . .' JR said, pausing with a smug grin on his dial. 'You're sitting here looking at him.'

'You?' I said, a little disbelieving. Sure, JR topped people for a living, but he was hardly a man of mystery.

'No, not me.' He nodded towards Chance.

I took a moment to digest this information, looking between the two of them. 'Why are you telling me?'

'Well, Chance says he's known you for a long time and we know we can trust you.'

I asked JR if he minded if Chance and I had a word by ourselves. So JR went off to the bar and I turned to Chance. 'Why do you want me to know you're the Widowmaker?

If I did what you do and no one knew who I was, I'd want to keep it that way.'

'Nah, well, there's a couple of jobs I've got coming up where I thought you might be able to help. I've been to your fights. I know you're not squeamish. I've seen what you've done to blokes in the ring. Both of us live the same life, the life of the outlaw. You're one of the few one percenters outside my club who I respect.'

'Why don't you get one of the blokes in your own club to help you?' I said.

'I don't want to involve my club in what I do. I trust you. We've known each other for a long time. My club respects yours and I know the feeling's mutual. Me and you, we're painted in a similar vein.'

'What about JR? Why don't you take him with you?'

'JR's good at what he does, but he hasn't got what I need. Some of the jobs I've got coming up . . .' He paused for a while. 'Let's just say I need someone who's not squeamish about causing a bit of pain.'

This was all very interesting, but I wasn't just going to dive into something like this. 'If you want me to help you, I want to know a few things. I'm not a dummy. One of them is this thing about how no one ever finds your bodies. If there's going to be trust between us, I want to know how you do it. You already know a few things about me from coming to me fights. It's got to be a two-way street. You could always rat me out for what I've done in the underground fighting, so I don't think it's too much to ask you how you get rid of these people you whack.'

'All right, I'll tell you a few things,' he said. 'One is, I never whack a woman. I always have to know for sure that the person I've been asked to hit really needs to be hit. I've done politicians, a couple of cops, businessmen, but you know what the main thing is that they have in common?'

'What?'

'Most of the blokes I've whacked have been paedophiles. That's why I enjoy doing what I do . . . and the money. If a bloke's a paedophile, it has to be proved to me. I don't care if it's a politician, or a cop, anyone – if they're molesting kids, they're going to be put in the ground.'

'So you bury them?'

'Nah, that's more a figure of speech.'

'Well, how do you get rid of 'em?'

'Two ways. One is I take 'em out through the Heads. The bloke I work for has got a nice little cruiser. Wrap 'em in chicken wire and barbed wire. Chain 'em to an old engine block and dump 'em over.'

'Let me guess: the barbed wire is so that when they start to bloat it cuts into the skin and lets the gases out and stops 'em floating to the surface.'

'Well, I'm not going to have to explain too much to you.'

'What's the second way?' I asked.

'You know the little pie company there down around Edgecliff?'

'Yeah, they make a lot of the pies that [a well-known pie company] sells.'

'If I whack a bloke, I take 'em down to the little factory. It's not hard to get into. They've got a very nice big industrial mincer. I'll undress the bloke, shave his hair and put all the hair and clothes in a plastic bag, then I'll get one of the big containers from the freezer and put it under a mincer. I'll lop off an arm, then a leg, head, put 'em through the mincer, then I'll chuck a bit of the other mince on top of what I've done, because there's a bit of a colour difference. Next day, the minced-up body goes into pies and gets shipped to [the pie company].'

'That's the last time I eat any of their pies,' I said.

'Well, the general public seem to enjoy the odd politician, businessmen or priest. Anyway, Ceese, it's up to you.'

I didn't give him an answer and he kept telling me about his craft. He mentioned a well-known cabaret artist. 'I couldn't make him disappear like normal, so I made him have a heart attack.'

'How'd you give him a heart attack?' I asked.

'A needle full of potassium chloride.'

'Oh yeah? How come the coroner doesn't pick it up?'

'The amount I use causes a heart attack. But for the coroner to pick it up, you've got to have the autopsy within four hours, otherwise it disappears. There is some extra potassium there but when you die the body produces some extra potassium. You work it out. The body's got to be found, which can take two, three, four hours, up to a day. Then the cops rock up. It's kept there for a while before it gets shipped to the coroner's office. There's no chance you can be found out. There's been a few heart attacks like that, not just in the entertainment industry. There was a property developer who turned out to be a very nasty man. Let's just say that, with blokes like that, before I put 'em in the ground, I want them to feel a lot of pain . . . and I know that you know how to cause pain without leaving marks.'

'Yeah, I can do that. I could teach you. It's just nerves and pressure points. They can cause excruciating pain.'

'Nah, I wouldn't have time to learn before these jobs. Besides, like I said, the three jobs I've got coming up . . .'

'Okay, what do you need me for?'

'Before I get to these blokes, there'll be a lot of security, which will have to be taken out quietly.'

'So you want a few necks snapped?'

'Something like that.'

*

56

EVEN NIGHTS when I was working, I'd do what I had to do, then go home, get my bike, put my colours on and head back to the Cross. JR, Chance and I would catch up at the Manzil Room, the Carousel Club or Sweethearts – it changed a bit over the years – and we'd talk about work. Listening to Chance and JR talk about how they went about their business and the different ways of offing people was educational. Especially with Chance.

JR was an expert at beating security systems, but in the end he was more a bullet in the back of the ear, one in the throat, one in the chest sort of guy. Then he'd have his team turn up and get rid of the bodies, similar to what you see in recent movies when a hitman makes a call and a couple of cleaners will turn up to deal with the body and tidy up the scene. There were blokes that really did that then. They might not have been as slick as what you see in the flicks – a bit rougher round the edges – but they got the job done professionally. They made it a lot easier for blokes like JR, Stan 'The Man' Smith and the bald, fedora-wearing guy they called 'The Frenchman' to ply their trade.

Chance was different. A lot of his hits had to look like accidents or at least mysterious disappearances. He knew how to do all that, but having said that, he could also be less subtle. Chance liked to play it rough when he got the opportunity.

He got three or four jobs where he had to hit gangs in the Haymarket. Everything was different in Chinatown. You always knew that if you did anything down in the Haymarket, the only way it would come back at you was if the people that you rubbed had relatives who'd come seeking revenge. The people in the Haymarket would never call the cops, no matter what, so you could afford to play it a bit loose down there, and Chance liked to show his skills. Especially after I trained him up in some moves which he combined with his own considerable talents.

We'd be sitting there yakking and it could take up to an hour and a half to hear what happened when Chance had been to Chinatown. JR always wanted full details, so sometimes it took longer. JR was a bit on the bloodthirsty side. And the Widowmaker was good at telling a story. He made it like you were hearing a movie.

One time they did a job down there together. They walked into some gambling den and popped nine blokes. *Bang! Bang! Bang!* 'We walked out, blood everywhere, and never heard a thing more about it. The Chinese, or whoever it was running the place, cleaned up their own mess. You don't have to worry about much down there. Just the comeback. We went in all balaclavaed up, so if you do it the right way, you get no problems.'

I hated getting cornered by JR when he was in the mood to hear your stories. With me, he wanted my round-ringing yarns. He'd pester me about how I felt when I did what I did to a few of my opponents. He was always saying, 'You're no different to us, you've sent people on extended holidays and been paid for it.'

'Yeah, but I don't do it for a living.'

And Chance would butt in: 'But in a way you do. You're fighting blokes for money and sometimes they end up in a very, very bad way. Other blokes are taking bets on how they're going to end up.'

'Yeah, but I don't ever intentionally go out to do that. Sometimes it happens because the blokes piss me off. Or Big Lenny stirs me up.'

'Yeah, I noticed that Big Lenny gets under your skin.'

'Yeah, he enjoys doing it.'

'Tell us about the time you fucked with that navy Seal.'

58

If JR was in the mood for a story, I'd tell him that I had to leave because I had club business to attend to. JR knew that club business always came ahead of anything else. He never questioned it. So that was my get-out-of-town card.

All outlaw bikers will have at some stage told their old lady or someone else that they had club business and would be away for a few days. Everyone knows better than to question them on it. So those words do come in handy.

*

ONE TIME, JR was out of town for a couple of days on a job, but when I hadn't seen him for about a week, I thought something was wrong. I rang his house and Cheryl answered. 'I think you better come over here, Caesar.'

So I rode over to Arncliffe and walked in the door and there was JR, lying on the lounge with a bandage on his stomach at belly button level.

'And what happened to you?' I said.

He looked at me sadly and Cheryl answered for him. 'He got just a bit too cocky, didn't he? Thought it was a soft target. Didn't do his homework.'

'Well, well. The great JR shot doing a job, eh?'

'Don't laugh,' he said. 'I know it was my fault. Mistakes can happen to the best of people.'

'Yeah, but you've been doing this for eight years now.'

'Nearly nine.'

'And all that time you've always told me it didn't matter how much security was on, that you could slip into anyone's house or hotel and you could get past all the security and pop the guy and no one would even know you'd been there till they found the body.'

'Yeah, well, that's true, but I have to cop it. I was slack. I didn't do the surveillance work I should have done.

An extra bloke happened to come in just as I finished the target and I copped one in the side, then I had to put him down and that was sloppy work. I know that.'

'How'd you get back here with a slug in your side?'

'I rang up The Animal. You're going to have fun with this. He put me on to a vet. The vet stopped the bleeding and put the stitches in and when I got home I went out to The Animal's place. He X-rayed me and got the slug out. You wanna have a look at it?'

'Oh, yeah.' So Cheryl went and got a little bottle that had a few slugs in it.

'You've been shot before?' I asked.

'Yeah, this is the third time.'

'Well, you are sloppy.'

'Nah, the other two was up the Cross when I was blindsided. Anyway, that's the one I got four days ago,' he said, pointing at a nice big bullet.

'.38?'

'Yeah, the prawn had one of those cop .38 specials. They pack a bit of a whack.'

'You're lucky it didn't get into your liver. If it had got in there, you'd have been in big trouble.'

'Yeah, you've told me that before. I suppose in the business I'm in, I should know that stuff. What was it again?'

'If you get hit in the liver, the blood's a black colour . . . Chance already knew that.'

'Yeah, you outlaw bikers . . . you know just about every fucking thing, don't ya?'

'Come on,' I said, having some fun with him, 'just because we've messed up doesn't mean we have to get crotchety. I've come over here to sit down with you. I'll even feed ya a bowl of chicken soup if your woman wants to make it up.'

'You would?'

'Yeah, I'll sit here and spoon it to you if you want.'

'Nah ... that'd be weird. But you'd really do that for me?'

'Of course I would. If you couldn't feed yourself, I'd feed ya.'

'That's what I've got a woman for.'

'I know that, but we're really good mates.'

'Caesar, you're more than a mate to me. You're like the brother I've always wanted.'

Cheryl chimed in, 'Yeah, Ceese, JR would be shattered if anything happened to you in those fights you're in. He really worries when they bring in those overseas hotshots. He does. He really worries.'

'Well, quit worrying. I've had 34 fights and nothing's happened to me yet. I've beaten everyone they've been able to throw at me from Japan, Malaysia, America, Russia.'

'I know, and that navy Seal,' JR said.

'Well, yeah, there you go.'

'Yeah, remember when you first started they didn't have the prelim fights. But when they realised how quick yours were, they added them on so the people could get their blood.'

'They love their blood, don't they?' I said. 'Have you noticed the sheilas that come to the fights? Sometimes when I rock up early and I'm watching the fights before me, I can hear the sheilas screaming, "Kill him! Kill him!" and the chant goes up, "Blood ... blood ..." It's not the blokes. It's always the women, and some of the worst are those actresses and the socialites.'

'You don't have to tell me. If I wrote a list of some of the women who attend your fights, I could sit back and wouldn't have to work again. I could blackmail 'em and make millions.'

'Come on, you're doing all right at what you're doing. Blackmailing's a dirty business.'

'Yeah, nah, I wouldn't do it,' JR said. 'I was just saying, but if people knew who went to your fights, they'd be shocked.'

'I didn't think you'd even think about doing something like that,' I said.

'I wasn't. I was just saying. Geez, you're irritating. Remember, I'm a sick man.'

'Ohhh, poor diddums, you got a little cut from a .38.'

'What if I got hit by a .357 Magnum?'

'Then you'd have something to squeal about.'

We sat there for a few hours talking like this and I watched Cheryl change the bandage. There was a bit of a hole there, all stitched up. JR was a real colourful feller. He wasn't scared of nothing. If he'd fought as well as he did his job as a hitman, he would have been the toughest bloke in Sydney. He was fearless, but he was a bit of a bitch about his wound, telling us how painful it was at every movement.

'You're a wimp,' I said.

'You know who you're talking to?'

'Yeah, a fucking crybaby ... How long till you're coming back up the Cross, Mr Sooky Pants?'

'Not for another three or four days,' Cheryl chipped in. 'The doc doesn't want him going anywhere till the stitches come out.'

'Nah, I'll be up there tomorrow night or the next,' he said.

'No you won't,' she said. 'You'll do as the doctor told you.'

'Yeah,' I said. 'You wanna listen to The Animal. If you don't, next time you need fixing, he might not do it. It's not often you can go to a top surgeon to get fixed up on the sly. You're very lucky to have him, and so are most of the other blokes doing the heavy work up the Cross.'

'Yes,' said Cheryl, 'a lot of people are lucky that he's got that love for animals.'

About three nights later, I was up the Cross with my brothers. They were eyeing off some Ghostriders when I saw Chance go into Sweethearts. 'Keep an eye on me bike,' I said, and followed him in for a yak.

'When's your next fight?' he said.

'In about a week, I think.'

'Do you know who you're fighting?'

'Nah, you know how it goes. They stopped telling me who I'd be fighting so I couldn't do any checking up on their style.'

'That's a bit weak.'

'I think they're getting sick of having me as their champ. And I think they want the fights to go longer. With me winning fight after fight, I think they're losing money.'

'Nah, they were in the beginning,' Chance said. 'I know that from talking to Baz [George Freeman's bodyguard]. They didn't want you to find out they're now backing you. They don't want you getting a big head. But they are sick and tired of seeing you win. You're like St George in the rugby league. People used to go along just hoping to see 'em lose. They had to change the rules to beat 'em.'

'Yeah, I've followed the Saints since I was a nipper,' I said.

'Hey, have you seen JR around?' Chance asked.

'Yeah, but I'll leave it to him to tell you what happened.'

'It's just that I rang his place the other night and the old lady told me he was a bit crook and you'd been over there feeding him chicken soup. I was trying to picture it in me head, you sitting there spooning him this fucking soup.'

'Nah, I didn't feed him any soup. That was just a joke on the night. Hang on! Speak of the devil. Here comes Mr Suave himself.' In came JR in a spiffy coloured shirt and with his leather coat wide open, flashing his twin-rig for all to see that he was back in business.

'Fuck me roan, if the coppers weren't so afraid of him he'd go away for five years just for carrying those Berettas.'

'You're not wrong, Caesar.'

JR was still a bit stiff and sore, but he was on the mend and keen to get back to normal. He told Chance how he got sloppy in his surveillance work and mentioned the suburb of Northbridge. 'Were you in Perth?' I said.

'Yeah.'

'Let me guess. Your sloppiness had something to do with pussy.'

'Yeah.'

'What happened to the "no girls while on the job" business?' I said.

'Caesar, if you and Chance had seen this bit of pussy, you'd have broken all ten of the commandments to get some of it. She was flaming red hot. I spent the night with her when I should have been doing surveillance. I fucked up. I admit it . . . and it was worth every ounce of lead I copped for it.'

'Just to break in, are you ever going to stop bringing those bloody Berettas up here?'

'Why would I?'

'Well, one day a copper who doesn't know how things work will see you flashing 'em about. And you'll be straight inside.'

'And I'd be out five minutes later. Fucking Abe owns every cop in Kings Cross, Darlinghurst and most of Sydney. He owns cops in Melbourne, in Queensland. Nah, I'm not worried about wearing 'em.'

'Yeah, I s'pose you've got a point. Abe does have a bit of pull with the boys in blue.'

Chance chimed in: 'C'mon, you haven't told me what happened to make you spend a week at home except it had something to do with getting sloppy with a sheila in Perth.'

JR told him how he clocked the target and was turning around to leave when the extra bloke came in the room with the .38 drawn and got him in the gut. Then he added a bit of detail he hadn't told me in front of Cheryl. 'I've gone pop, pop. One in the head, one in the chest. Down he went.'

'Fucking lucky you use those silencers all the time,' Chance said.

'Never leave home without 'em. Matter of fact, I carry an extra two.'

'Two? I can see you carrying an extra one, because one might not work. But you've already got two. Surely one of them's gunna be working.'

'I just like to be safe.'

I had to have my bit. 'Well, you weren't that safe over there, were ya?' I said. 'Does Cheryl know the reason you got shot?'

'Fuck no. Don't you go telling her.'

'I wouldn't do that.'

'It was club business,' he said, laughing.

'Don't you go "club business" with me, Mr Regal. Anyway, you can tell Chance all about your trip. I can see one of me brothers looking for me. If I've got time, I'll catch you in a bit,' I said, going out the door.

Wack was over the road. 'What's the problem?' I said.

'Aahh, there's some Hungarian or Pole wants to fight Bull. But there's a big group of 'em with him.'

'Yeah, all right.' We had a prospect with us and I told him to watch the bikes. 'We'll be back in a sec.' We went down Springfield Avenue, then into a little lane off the side where we saw Bull standing up to this bunch of blokes.

He turned and said quietly: 'Give me a couple of minutes with this bloke before youse all jump in.'

The Gladiators had a one-in-all-in rule. We didn't care if it was just one bloke having a go at one of us. If he wanted to fight a Gladiator, he was going to fight us all. You never knew if he was carrying a razor or a knife or a piece. If you waited to see who won, your brother could end up being stabbed, sliced or shot. My rule was, as soon as the first punch was swung, everyone went in and got the bloke. Then again, that went the other way too. If there were 30 blokes taking on seven of us, we took on all 30 of them.

But Bull deadset wanted the bloke to himself, so we bent the rule, just this once. Bull got stuck into this hefty Hungarian who threw a few nice punches. Bull got in under him and was thumping the shit out of him when one of his mates let one go on Bull from behind. That proved my point. If you wait, your brother can get hurt.

So the rest of us went in. We downed the main guy and the kinghitter first and then got into the rest of 'em. As usual, half of them took off. When it was over, there were eight of them on the ground and the rest of 'em were standing on the corner of Victoria Street looking up the lane at their mates. A bunch of outlaws from different clubs were standing at the other end of the lane, having come down for a stickybeak after seeing us all going around the corner.

We got back to the bikes. We'd only been gone 15 or 20 minutes. All the brothers wanted to go to the Venus Room, but I said I was going back to Sweethearts. Snake turned to me. 'You going over there with that bloody hitman mate of yours again?'

'Yeah, he's me best mate outside of the club.'

The prospect's name was Happy. He was a grumpy sort of bloke. Always looked like someone had stolen his last dollar and run off with his girl. He was about six foot, pretty hefty and a good bluer. 'Just sit here and watch the bikes, Happy. I won't be long.'

'No sweat, Caesar.'

I went back to Sweethearts. Chance and JR were still there. 'Well, that didn't take long,' JR said. 'What was it? I want everything in full.'

I told him the story and explained to JR how blokes always seemed to want to take on the outlaw bikers. 'Especially when there's sheilas around. They think they're gunna impress these sheilas, as if they're taking on the toughest blokes in the world.'

'Well, that part's probably true,' Chance said.

'Yeah, but you get sick of it after a while.'

'You and your brothers get sick of fighting?' JR said.

When I told JR about how half these Hungarians had run off and left their mates, he got all indignant about it. 'If I was with a mate, I don't care how many blokes there was, I wouldn't leave him no matter what.'

'I know you wouldn't.'

I told him how, as an outlaw, your club and your family always came first. 'But outside of that, there's room for the odd good mate . . . and you're the odd good mate. With emphasis on that word "odd".'

'Oh, you're funny.'

'You wouldn't love me if I wasn't.'

'You push your luck sometimes, Caesar.'

'Now, now. Let's not get ahead of ourselves, Mr JR. Now, what could you do to me?'

'What do ya think?'

'I'd rip your throat out before you could get one of those Berettas out. I'll tell you what, since you're not worried about flashing 'em, how about you go for one of them right now, where we're sitting, and I'll betcha I can knock you out without even throwing a punch before you get it out of the holster.'

'Don't take him up on that, JR,' Chance said. 'He's sitting too close to ya. You haven't got enough room to move. I know what he's gunna do. He's gunna grab you around the larynx and in ten or twelve seconds you're going to be out cold.'

'You can't take a joke anymore, big feller,' JR said.

'Course I can. You didn't really think I was gunna knock you out, did ya?'

'You sounded like you were going to.'

'You know my policy. I never pick on anyone I know I can beat. And I never pick on people who can't defend themselves.'

'Ha, ha,' he said, with an exaggerated laugh. 'You really are a card.'

JR and I mucked around like this all the time. It worried Chance. 'Do you really think that youse two should talk to each other that way? One day, someone's going to push it too far and something's gunna happen.'

'I've got no intentions of hurting JR. Have you got any intentions of hurting me, JR?'

'No.'

Chance said, 'I'd like to be a fly on the wall when youse two are alone.'

'You know what happens to flies on walls,' I said.

*

THROUGH ALL this time, I'd kept notching up wins in the round ring.

The earlier preliminary fights before mine used to have a referee who could stop the fight. But in my fights – always the main bout for the night – there was never a referee. The way a fight ended was that if you beat the bloke into the ground and you turned and walked away from him, it was over. But if you wanted to keep stomping on him, or break some fingers, you could do that. There really were no rules. Everything went.

I remember having a bloke in a camel clutch one time. I held him with one hand and I used the other to pluck out his left eyeball. I got on top of him and was sitting on his back with his arms pulled back over my knees. It's the same position where if you wanted to you could grab him by the chin and snap his neck, but I let go of his head and put my hands into his collar bones and leaned back hard, snapping the collar bones.

He was a mess and I remember Little Lenny asking me what he'd done to piss me off.

'Nothing. It was just the way the fight went.'

There was an ex-world heavyweight *muy thai* champion from Thailand. I've got a lot of respect for *muy thai* and I've had all my kids do it. This bloke was a really hard one to fight. He kicked fast and hard and he used his elbows brilliantly to really get me a few good ones in the ribs. I thought, *Well, I have to fix this bloke quick before he does me some damage.* So I broke his leg with a side kick and I had his arm at the same time up over my shoulder with my arm going over his. I grabbed his wrist and went down on his elbow. That snapped his arm. He went down and I turned my back and walked away.

Then I felt someone coming up behind me, so I spun around and grabbed him by the throat. It was one of the *muy thai* master's seconds. He was kind of bowing and looking respectful, so I let him go and he pointed to his boss. 'Master wish to honour you,' he said. I looked over at the master and his minions were holding him in a standing position so he could bow to me. *This is a new one*, I thought. I bowed back.

I respected him a lot. He was a hard bloke to fight and he hurt me.

Big Lenny was always there stirring me up. He'd make sure he was close to me and just before the fight, he'd be like, 'You've had it this time, Campbell, we've brought in someone who's going to murder you. You're nothing but a bum, Campbell.'

'Yeah, we'll see, Lenny.'

It seemed to me that the fights weren't fair, because I had this thing that at any time I wanted I could just go whack and knock the bloke out. But Abe wanted a bit of a go, so I'd have to draw them out a bit.

I was really into wrestling and I used to like using wrestling holds to end fights more than thumping someone. But I'd still use a punch if I wanted to. Like when I fought this big Malaysian bloke and he'd obviously done *Krav Maga*, the martial art developed by the Israeli army. We're going at it, kicking, and he poled me in the eye with his thumb and I thought, *You prick*. So he shaped up to go again and I just went *Whack! Bang!* And that was it. I turned and started walking away before he hit the ground. It seemed like an unfair advantage.

Most of my fights only lasted 90 seconds to two minutes. That's why, when I shaped up for my very last fight, against a German called Wolfgang Gertz, I stood there and let him whack me for a while. I wanted to see what I could take, because I felt like I'd never been pushed before.

I said in *Enforcer* that Wolfgang was my toughest opponent, and he was, but I did just stand there for the first few minutes letting him pound away. Shadow was yelling out, 'Bash him. He's killing ya.' And Big Lenny was there yelling, 'You're fucked now, Campbell.' I eventually put my hand up to my face and felt my lip hanging down.

I thought that I'd been pushed enough. So I gave it to him. Even then he was hard to put away and the fight lasted a full seven minutes. It was brutal but fair.

Shadow and I took Wolfgang for a drink afterwards. And we kept in touch over the years. He got into the underground fighting in America and made a squillion. He came to visit me once and wanted me to go to America with him so he could arrange some fights for me, especially in Las Vegas. But I didn't fancy leaving Australia. I had my club and the old lady and the kids by then . . . but I'm getting ahead of myself.

I'd had 44 fights for 44 wins, with 11 of those ending very badly for the other guy. Sometime soon after I retired, Abe pulled back from the fight scene as well. I think he reasoned that it was just a matter of time before some reporter started asking why this was going on and why weren't the cops doing anything about it. The fight scene continued on a much smaller scale with our local scrappers lined up against each other, but it was never the same again once the top overseas fighters stopped coming.

CAESAR'S LAW
VI

FAVOURITE MOVIE

*T*he *Adventures of Robin Hood*, with Errol Flynn, was my favourite movie. I loved the whole rob-from-the-rich-to-give-to-the-poor thing.

My favourite actor though is John Wayne.

In more recent times, I loved *Mission: Impossible – Rogue Nation*. I never liked Tom Cruise when he first started out, like in *Risky Business*. But when he got into the action movies I read an article on him that said he was one of the only blokes in Hollywood who did his own stunts, and that a lot of them were more dangerous than the ones Jackie Chan did. So I've got a lot of respect for him. And *Rogue Nation* was a top flick.

9

BROKEN PROMISES, BROKEN FINGERS

My collecting work was going well. Abe only ever called me when his other collectors had failed. This ensured I only got the most interesting jobs.

I developed a routine where I'd go out and have a look at the place for probably a week to see who was going in and who wasn't. Then I mostly just used the same method I'd used at Waverley. I'd drive out there, knock on the door and whoever answered – unless it was a sheila – got decked. Like I said, I had been blessed since my teenage years with the ability to knock someone out with one punch from either hand. I'd whack them and it was lights out. I'd roll through the place and knock everyone out, tie 'em up and wait for them to come around. I'd do the finger-snapping first. It was quick and clean, but it didn't always work. It's amazing how hard it can be to separate people from other people's money.

That's when I'd reach for my tool kit. I'd pull out a pair of needle-nose pliers and ask again where the dough was. If the answer lacked sincerity, I'd get a good grip on a fingernail with the pliers and pull it straight out. This required that their nails be long enough for the pliers to grip. If the target was the worrying kind who chewed their nails down – and Lord knows with me on their case they should have been – I'd have to go back to the tool kit to pull out a darning needle. Sometimes they'd give up just with the sight of the needle. If not, I'd get it under the nail, twisting and pushing until the nail was up enough for the pliers to get under . . . and then I'd rip it out.

If that failed. Repeat. I had ten fingers to work with, so there was plenty of opportunity to bring them round to seeing the world from my perspective.

On the very rare occasions where a real tough nut was still holding out, I'd get a syringe filled with water. I'd tell the customer that it was battery acid. 'You know what'll happen as soon as I inject this into the corner of your eye? The battery acid's gunna boil at ten times the rate it is now and it's gunna blow the eyeball out of its socket.' That always got results.

After spending all this intimate time together, you formed quite a relationship with the customer. If they pleaded that they didn't have the money, I'd know when they were lying. If they were telling the truth, I'd just go back to Abe and tell him: 'They haven't got the dough. Simple as that.' It was then up to him to decide what to do about it – whether he'd take the recovery process to a whole new level. But I had nothing to do with that side of things.

I did collects in Victoria and Queensland, but it was mainly Sydney. I was always alone. I never needed help. And I never worried about dying. I had guns stuck against my chest and against my forehead, but I'd spent hours practising how to deal with that. I was fast – and once I'd taken the gun off them – furious. And so that finger collection that I mentioned in my first book had a few additions made to it, courtesy of Mr Saffron's business associates.

If people just handed me the money without fuss, I'd leave with what they gave me, but if they tried anything or bullshitted to me and then I found the money and they had extra, like those Lebs in Waverley, I'd always keep the extra for myself.

There were times where I got more out of it than Abe did. I remember one time at Pymble I went over to collect $200,000. It must have been the early 1980s, because these guys were cocaine dealers. I've got to state up front that I never had anything to do with the drug industry directly. And Abe wasn't into it either, but in this case he'd made an introduction. These Maoris had a lot of coke and they had been looking for a buyer. I think Abe introduced them to one and he was owed a cut. But when it came time to pay up, they forgot the matchmaker.

I did my usual thing, rolling through the house, until one of them pulled a police .38 special. He put it into my chest. I moved the barrel with a backhanded side sweep. The gun went to my left and, as I pushed it over, I locked my hand onto the revolver and flicked it out of his hand. I picked the gun up off the floor and shot him in the knee.

Islanders, genetically, have got really good builds and they've got hard heads, but when they're tied up or if you've knocked them out – and they know you've knocked them out with one punch – they tend not to be so standoffish.

They told me there was a box under the floorboards. I needed a screwdriver to get at it and when I pulled it out and opened it, there was $500,000 inside.

If they'd just handed me the $200,000, that would have been it. But I went back to Abe's office and gave him the dough. He gave me my $70,000 cut and I had the other $300,000 sitting in the boot of the car.

I packed it all away in my nest egg which, with all my winnings from the round ring, was growing very nicely, thank you.

10

WASABI NIGHTS

For all the time I started spending with JR and Chance, my brothers and the Gladiators were still my main focus. And for the most part, biker life continued as ever. One night, we parked our bikes at the Manzil Room and went inside. But Shadow and Chop decided they were going to take a stroll and play some stick at a pool joint halfway down the main drag and up some stairs. On the way, Chop stopped to buy something to eat, so Shadow kept going to rack up the balls. This pool hall had a pretty well-known bouncer by the name of Black Brenda. Now, for some reason he didn't know who Shadow was and decided that he didn't like the look of him. He told Shadow to get rooted. Black Brenda was a big bloke who hit the weights pretty hard. He and Shadow started punching on. Shadow got over the top of him, so Black Brenda ran down the stairs. He saw Chop coming up with a burger in his hands. He knew Chop, so he got in behind him:

'Chop, help me, that bloke's a crazy man.' Brenda looked back up the stairs and said to Shadow, 'You're for it now, cunt, this is one of the Campbells.'

With which Chop let loose with one of his bombs and knocked Black Brenda down to the bottom of the stairs. When he landed on the footpath, other bouncers started coming over from their clubs, because they had a policy of helping each other out.

Shadow came down the stairs to see Chop standing there over Brenda, who was struggling to his feet holding his face. 'I'll be fucked,' Chop said. 'I didn't knock him out, but it looks like I broke his jaw.'

Shadow turned to Black Brenda. 'Tell me to get rooted?' and stomped on his nuts. The other bouncers were there now and shaping up to have a go when Half-A-Mo yelled out, 'I wouldn't do what youse blokes are thinking. The rest of the Wrecking Crew's just come around the corner of Springfield.'

And with that the bouncers all seemed to find more important business to attend to back at their own doors.

*

THE GLADIATORS established the Venus Room as our base in the Cross. No other bike club could come inside without our permission. If we knew them and there weren't more than three or four of them, we might let them in. You came down the long corridor and dropped down three steps into a big bar area that was lined with padded booths done out in deep red velvet. There was plenty of room for civilians to come in and you'd get the male tourists coming in for a look at the girls and the female tourists coming in for a look at us.

'Are youse the Gladiators or are you the Wrecking Crew?' they'd ask. It used to really piss me off that we were becoming better known as the Wrecking Crew than our club name.

'Well, what's on our back?'

'Gladiators.'

'Well, that's who we are.'

The Venus Room was connected to a brothel upstairs, but you had to go outside and back in next door to get up to it. That's where we ran into Shultz. He was the minder for the hookers. We got to know him pretty well and he was one of the few people my brothers considered tough enough to let into the Gladiators. He was a powerlifter who missed out by a pound from being the Australian champion. He was only five foot ten, but he had a 64-inch chest.

So he joined up and became one of us. It took two skins to make his vest too.

One night we were up at the Venus Room. Snake had wandered out to check the bikes when these eight footballer types went to come in with their girls. As usual, these blokes thought that having a go at an outlaw biker made them look tough in front of their girlfriends. It was eight on one, so that shows how tough they really were. Snake always carried a great hefty chain around his waist with a big padlock on it. He'd only bring it out when he was really outnumbered and he had some trick where he could unhook it and have it in his hands real fast. So he did that and weighed into these blokes.

Meanwhile, we were all sitting at our booth yakking on, oblivious to what was happening outside. It could be pretty loud in there. You couldn't hear any of the street noise. One of the working girls, Rachel, came running in screaming about what was going on. So the rest of us brothers sprinted down the corridor. By the time we got there, there were all these blokes lying on the footpath. One was propped up against the wall and we're looking at his jawbone poking through the skin. When Rachel saw it, she pirouetted then swan-dived, and if it hadn't been for Bull catching her, she would have landed on the footpath and probably cracked her head open like all these bloody footballers.

*

ON ANOTHER night at the Venus Room, Shadow decided it was time to get his revenge on Chop for the famous Vicks VapoRub incident. Anyone who's read *Enforcer* will know what I'm talking about – suffice to say that it involved the substitution of Vaseline with VapoRub and some very sore organs.

Now, Chop used to like a cocktail that looked like a green thickshake. Shadow had got hold of a 150 ml bottle of this stuff called *wasabi*, which is the same colour. It is Japanese and apparently super-hot. He gave me a taste of a pinprick of it and it just about blew my head off. Shadow got Max the bartender to mix up two of these cocktails, one for him and one for Chop, mixing half the bottle of wasabi into Chop's. Then he challenged Chop to a drinking race. They both skulled their drinks and about ten seconds later Chop's face went red. He started grabbing at his throat and it looked like he might pass out. He was belting himself on the chest all buckled over, the colour of a tomato.

Shadow looked pretty similar from all the laughing he was doing.

I ran over to Max. 'Get us some milk. Get us some milk.'

Big Max came over with a jug of milk and Chop started skulling it. I got him into a booth. 'Come on, mate, take slow deep breaths.' I grabbed some ice and put it on his chest. He could not talk for about two hours.

Shadow came over. 'That evens us up now for the Vicks.'

11

'I'M A GLADIATOR. I'M A CAMPBELL.'

There were three blokes running around with the name Tree. It got a bit confusing. One Tree was with the Jokers, another was with one of the smaller clubs and there was another who was an independent. Anyway, this last one, let's call him Lone Tree for clarity, was a big tough bloke, but he came to me one day with a problem. 'Caesar, I've had some blokes want me to join their club but I knocked 'em back and now they've taken it as a personal insult and have got it in for me. I was wondering if you could go and have a word to them for me.'

'What club is it?'

'Satans Riders. I'm not scared of 'em but, you know, when there's 13 or 15 of 'em it's a bit hard to take on the whole lot of 'em.' He must have seen me looking a bit confused. I'd never heard of Satans Riders. 'Yeah, they're a new club. I think they've been going five or six months.'

'Where are they from?'

'They hang out around Randwick, Charing Cross way.'

'Leave it with me. I'll have a word with 'em for ya.'

So the next Saturday night me and my brothers rocked over to Randwick. We did the round of pubs there, then went to Charing Cross. The Norsemen used to hang around Charing Cross till they were disbanded. And that's where we found these Satans Riders. We had a word to them and had to give them a bit of a touch-up to get the message through to leave Tree alone. I will give them credit – a couple of their blokes wanted to have a go. They had to cop a bit of a flogging to calm 'em down.

I could tell, though, that they were the type of blokes who'd want to get even. So when we got back to our local, the Illinois Hotel at Five Dock, I told my brothers we'd have to keep our eyes on those Satans Riders. 'There's a few blokes there that might want a bit of payback. And I think a couple of them might be from the old west.'

'Whaddya mean?' Bull said.

'Back shooters,' I said. 'Just watch your backs for the next few weeks.'

We didn't let it cramp our style, though, and over the next few weeks my brothers and I did all our normal things: picking up sheilas, getting into blues, and going on the odd run here and there. We were full-time outlaws. There were times we'd take off on a Tuesday for a long run into the country, getting back Friday with enough time to shower, change and head up the Cross for the night. Sometimes, we might take off on a Tuesday and be back Wednesday night. It depended how we felt – how the weather shaped up.

So, we'd come back from one of these mid-week runs and made our way up to the Venus Room for the Friday night. Chop went out to check on the bikes because the prospect, Happy, had just come in for a drink and Chop

82

wanted to give him a break. Someone heard yelling out there, so I wandered out to investigate. As I walked down the long corridor to the front door, I heard Chop telling someone to get fucked. I rushed onto Orwell Street, a fairly quiet little backstreet, to find some blokes had Chop bent over the mudguard of a car with a revolver to his head.

It was Satans Riders. There were eight of them. Seeing me, one of them yelled, 'We want the president of the Gladiators down here now.'

I sauntered over. 'You got him.'

'Unless you want your brother (they meant club brother) dead, you get down on your knees and say that the Gladiators are shit and Satans Riders rule.'

'Don't you do it, Caesar,' Chop called out.

'Don't worry, Chop, I'm not going to.' I turned to them. 'Go fuck yourselves.'

A burly bloke of theirs seemed to be the leader. 'You've got two choices,' he said. 'Keep your colours and die like a man or you can get down and beg and we'll let you live.'

'I'm not begging to no one, especially a prick like yourself.'

'All right then, Mr Hero,' he said. 'We're going to play a little game. You wanna show how tough you are? How about I break some fingers of yours, one at a time? If you make one sound, we put a bullet in your mate's head. If you want to stop it, all you gotta do is say, "Gladiators are shit. Satans Riders rule".'

With the gun to Chop's head, I didn't see that I had much choice. I gave him my hand. Three others came over to hold me.

'Okay, here we go, one at a time.' And the bloke on my hand pulled my right pinkie back till it made a noise I was all too familiar with. I didn't make a sound. I'd done the same thing to other people often enough, but this was the first time I'd had it done to me. I could see why it was so effective. It hurt like hell. But there was no way I was going to say their club was better than ours. That would have been like saying they were better than us Campbells.

We had this whole honour thing going. We were Gladiators. We were Campbells. Our dad brought us up to be proud of our heritage and no matter what, you never let anyone put shit on your name. When he died at 46, I drummed it into all the younger ones. We had this thing like a two-handed Claymore sword pushing us on: We were Gladiators, the best motorcycle club in Australia – we were Campbells, and Campbells never backed down.

So when this bloke broke my pinkie, I started repeating to myself: 'I'm a Gladiator. I'm a Campbell. I'm a Gladiator. I'm a Campbell.'

The bloke with the revolver was standing there. 'You think you're a tough bastard. You're not going to be so tough eating the shit off my boots.' I saw my brothers out of the corner of my eye. They'd followed me out and were slowly moving towards us. So I started edging to my left, making the Satans Riders think it was because I didn't want them to break another finger. Anyway, they broke the second finger and as they broke it I pushed even more to my left. The bloke who was doing all the talking and the bloke with the revolver were all watching me. I was getting towards the other end of the car. When they broke my third finger, I moved even further. 'I'm a Gladiator. I'm a Campbell. I'm a Gladiator. I'm a Campbell.'

The adrenaline was coming out my ears by this and the funny thing was, by the third finger, it had stopped hurting so much. I was focused on my mantra and how I was going to get at these blokes without Chop getting his head blown off.

One had me in an arm lock up my back. One big bloke was hanging onto my right leg like a stick-on koala bear. I was thinking of a hip throw, or a roll back to take them all with me. I decided on the roll back. I was basically just going to throw myself backwards, then deal with them where we lay.

I had my back to Chop, but next thing I knew I heard, *Bang! Bang!*

I threw myself back, taking my pile of blokes with me. I looked up to see that Chop had somehow got rid of the bloke on him and got hold of the gun – a snub-nose revolver. It spat out flames in the darkness. *Bang! Bang! Bang! Bang!* He'd emptied all six shots into these blokes' legs. Lucky there were only six bullets or he would have killed 'em. The rest of the brothers had weighed in and wreaked hell's fury upon Satans Riders. A couple of them got away. I heard one call out from the corner of Victoria Street, 'Youse are all maniacs.'

That was a bit rich, I thought.

'I'm gunna kill the fuckin' lotta youse,' Chopper screamed back and next thing he dropped to his knees over one of these wounded blokes in the gutter. As anyone who has read *Enforcer* will know, Chop had a thing for biting. Especially facial features. He got down over this bloke and bit off a nose. Spat it out. Crawled to the next one and bit off an ear.

The bloke who had snapped my fingers – he ended up with a broken arm, a broken jaw, broken ribs, some ventilation in his knees and a face that looked like a smashed-in tomato.

It was time to go. I got hold of Chop and lifted him off the ground with my good hand. 'C'mon Chop.'

With all the gunfire, I knew the cops would be there soon. The barman, Big Max, came out. He was someone who was in no way named ironically. He was one of the largest men on the planet. He took Chop off me, put him under one arm and carried him inside. He was so big he had to walk sideways to fit down the corridor.

'Put me down, Max,' Chop screamed. 'I'm gunna fuckin' kill ya.'

'Behave yourself,' I said. 'He can put you down when we get down to the bar.'

So Max did let him go at the bottom of the three stairs that led into the plush velvety bar. Chop shaped up to clobber Max, so I grabbed Chop with my left hand. 'He's only helping. Now, let him go and shut the door.'

So Max shut us in and turned off the light. We sat in the main lounge and Max had a look at my hand and put a bandage on it. Some of the girls were knocking on the front door wondering what was going on. Rachel and a couple of the other girls came in and looked at me. 'Caesar, you poor thing. Let me look at your hand.'

'Poor Caesar?' Chop said. 'What about poor Chop? I had a gun held to me head.'

The cops turned up and Max went up to the peephole. Our bikes were still out the front, but Max came back down and reported to us that the cops had a look around and left. Never even bothered to knock on the door.

12

BRING IT ON

There was this bloke called Terry Clark who'd come over from New Zealand and been up the Cross for about six months. He liked throwing his weight around and being a bit of a bully with some of the minor crims.

Clark wasn't much to look at, but he walked around like he owned the world. I didn't have much to do with him. I met him a couple of times, but I never shook his hand. I'd heard about him and what he was like. And even Abe had said to me, 'You don't want to get mixed up with him.' I'd found that Abe was a pretty shrewd bloke and if he said something like that, it was going to be good advice. To me, Clark was just a drug dealer with a mean side when it came to women and blokes weaker than himself, though years later he would become famous with the name Mr Asia.

I'd watched how when he was walking down the street, Clark made a point of not changing direction for anyone.

If the other person didn't move, they got shoved, and if they objected, he belted them or had one of his boys do it. So this day in about 1975 I saw him walking along when I noticed big Lenny McPherson coming the other way. Big Lenny was wearing his sports jacket and hat with an overcoat draped over his shoulders so that his arms were free, looking like the lord of all he surveyed.

And here was Clark, the two-bit bully in his flares, body shirt and necklaces, walking straight at him. Mr Asia meets Mr Big. I was sitting on my bike right next to the point on the footpath where they were going to collide. They came to within less than a metre of each other, eyes fixed dead ahead, when Big Lenny growled, 'Get out of the fucking way or I'll drive yer into the fucking ground.'

And Clark stepped aside.

I noticed that, after they passed, Lenny looked over his shoulder and kept an eye on Clark for a long while. He knew you couldn't trust the bloke.

A while after that incident, I was up the Cross watching the passing parade. JR was sitting on my bike – a privilege not many people got – and Chance was sitting on his. Little Lenny Baker came up to JR with a message and he quickly said his goodbyes and disappeared off to see Abe at the Carousel Club.

After a while I recognised JR's brown leather coat and his lairy black, pink and silver shirt coming back through the crowd, escorting Mr Sin. JR would often double up as a bodyguard for Abe. No one messed with JR up the Cross, so he was pretty effective at the job. Everyone who mattered knew that JR was always tooled up.

So when JR was just about level with us – near the Bourbon and Beefsteak – I noticed that Terry Bloody Clark was coming in the opposite direction. And he's still doing his old high-school bully thing of shoving people out of the way. As he got near Abe, he put his arm out to give him a shove on the shoulder. Well, JR went for his Beretta.

I jumped off my bike and grabbed JR. 'Leave it, mate. C'mon, cool it. You'll only get yourself locked up.'

Clark started mouthing off at JR. 'You're a fucking nobody. You're a little fish in a big bath.'

Chance weighed in, 'If you want to find out who the big fish is, keep mouthing off.'

I looked at Clark, who was looking at all of us, and I could see the cogs of his brain ticking over. He decided better of it, and shut up. And as he went to walk away, almost out of habit on my part, I turned around and went *whack* with a left hook and dropped him. We stood over his fallen body and JR still wanted to put a bullet in his head. Chance said, 'These are the times I wished I carried.'

Even though Chance had a lot of metaphorical notches on his gun, when he wasn't on the job he was unarmed. I dragged them both away. JR wanted to just go back and find Clark, to put him away there and then. It took us all night to talk him down. He got on to planning out a proper hit and how he'd go about it, but eventually he cooled off.

Clark – who was portrayed in one of those *Underbelly* shows by the actor Matthew Newton – wasn't well liked. He liked to hurt people when he could get away with it. Especially sheilas. This didn't go down too well with me or my brothers. It came to be a thing that he stayed out of our way.

I wasn't worried about any repercussions from Clark for decking him. At the time, I knew he was into drugs, but I didn't know how big he was in the scheme of things until later when the whole world knew. I had that many enemies up the Cross that making one more didn't worry me.

*

IT WAS March 1976 and Hades Henchmen held a huge party in an old factory down near the Cyclops factory at Leichhardt. They'd invited a select few clubs – the Hangmen, Salems Witches, the Ghostriders and the Phantom Lords. I was the only Gladiator in attendance. The party was rocking and everybody was getting on great. The band played hard. There were heaps of women. Then, as usual, it started. One of Hades Henchmen decided he wanted a sheila who was there with one of the Hangmen. A brawl broke out and before we knew it, all the clubs were into it. Being the only Gladiator, I was standing back enjoying the show, not having anyone else to look out for. There were fists and chairs, and a few blades. In all the madness of an all-in, one of Hades Henchmen pulled a blade on me, so I felt obliged to give him a good hiding. And when I was done, I cut off a pinkie finger and a forefinger for trying to blade me. Next thing I knew, it wasn't blokes from his own club coming to his defence, it was the Hangmen.

I had this knife in my hand but I didn't want to use that, so I was side-kicking, roundhouse kicking. Might have hit a couple with the knife handle. Most of the blokes back in the early outlaw days rode their bikes all the time, but they weren't always good fighters. If you had a club of a dozen blokes, you expected about four to be able to really handle themselves. The rest were just average, but they'd be good members if they were staunch and backed up the good fighters.

The six I had here were more the staunch type. I disposed of them and took another finger. That must have disturbed a few of the women, because they were screaming, so a couple of Salems Witches and a Ghostrider wanted to take issue with me. By the time I got to my bike – a Panhead, green with metal-flake gold – I could hear the sirens coming in the distance, so I kicked her over and headed for Ashfield.

I heard later that something like 60 sheilas got busted there. Lord knows what for – being rooted by bikers, I suppose. Anyway, it had been a good night at the beginning and it was a wild night at the end. And the interesting thing about it, looking back now, was that in all that biker chaos, to my knowledge there wasn't a single gun pulled. It was all fists, chains, iron bars and a few blades. That was it. The worst injuries were a couple of fractured skulls, some broken arms and a couple of broken legs. I know, because some of them were my doing. Not to mention the fingers in the lost property section.

Back in them days, your disputes were settled with your body and what you could pick up. I'm not saying the clubs of today shouldn't be armed up, because if one club is armed and they're going at the other clubs, the other clubs have to protect themselves and their members. That's the main thing about being in an outlaw club, you protect your club, you protect your brothers. I'm not running anyone down, I'm just saying different era, different cultures.

A couple of nights after the brawl at Leichhardt, I was up the Cross sitting with JR when Chance turned up. One of the favourite conversations between JR and Chance was identifying the blokes around the traps who were always armed. I thought it funny, considering JR was always tooled up. Chance on the other hand only ever carried guns while working.

They got onto the subject of blokes who carried for a living. They had a lot of respect for the armed forces, as did I, because when you are serving your country in war, there is always a chance you'd be in a unit of say 100 going up against an enemy of 1000. But the Aussie soldier stands his ground and fights. This got Chance onto the subject of one of his pet hates – the police. Chance had this thing about coppers. To him, coppers only joined the cop force because they weren't game to face up to someone in the street one on one. They needed the uniform to hide behind.

I was talking to Chance a couple of weeks ago, and I asked him if his opinion had changed. He went off the deep end. 'Changed? Look at them today – body armour, semi-automatic nine mils, Tasers, capsicum spray, batons, radios. You tell me any time you've seen five coppers take on five outlaw bikers. You never have. Tell me any time you've seen 20 coppers take on 20 bikers. Never happens. But take 20 coppers against two or three bikers and they're big men then. They've just got to make a radio call and they've got you outnumbered. That's when they're big men. Caesar, you remember the old days, when they'd take you to the cop shop and take you out the back with the excuse of asking you a few questions. You'd be hand-cuffed and you'd have to walk the gauntlet past ten or 15 of them with batons and they'd get you in there and keep you in for a couple of hours, then come in and say, "Sorry mate, we've made a mistake. You can go." "Yeah, I'd love to get you out on the street on your own, you prick." They're real tough men behind the guns and the uniforms and the Tasers . . .'

'Calm down, Chance,' I said. 'At your age, you'll have a heart attack.'

'That's the only way those pricks'd ever get me.'

13

THE EQUALIZERS

I was sitting in the pub at Cooma with my retired biker mates. They were getting stuck into their Wild Turkeys while I sipped on my orange juice talking about how often outlaw bikers had stepped in to help Joe Citizen who was getting bashed or robbed, but the cops would come along 20 minutes later and take all the credit. They'd never mention that outlaws had beaten the shit out of the thugs, then got on their bikes and taken off, not wanting any applause or thanks.

This brought to mind a time when I went to see an orthopaedic surgeon at Lewisham. I'd been referred to him by Tony Millar, the sports doctor, because I'd pulled a tendon in my bicep lifting too much weight, too often. So the surgeon, let's call him Ted, did some X-rays and I went back a few times. He asked me how I knew Tony Millar and I said I'd done a course under him on weight training and nutrition. Dr Ted steered the conversation towards outlaw biker clubs. He seemed very interested in how we operated and what sort of things we got up to. I didn't tell him much.

On my third consultation with Dr Ted, he told me the tendon was good to go. 'It's not too serious,' he said. 'You're just going to have to rest the arm. You won't need to come back to me again. But before you go, would you mind if I told you a story about a couple of patients of mine I've been seeing on and off for 20 years?'

'Sure,' I said.

'Their names are Barbara and Harry. He's in his early 70s and she's in her mid-60s. They're a delightful couple but have had a few problems with their hips and knees so I see a fair bit of them. They live in Canterbury and, for the past four months, the house next door has been rented out to some appalling drug addicts. Barbara and Harry tell me that about a dozen live there and the group have made their lives a misery. The hooligans go to the toilet on their lawn, they've smashed their car window. Things are getting stolen . . . I suppose what I'm saying is, um, how much would it cost me for you and some of your friends to pay these fellows a visit?'

'You don't have to pay me nothing,' I said. 'I wouldn't take money off you to help out an old couple like that. Give us your phone.' I made a couple of calls to my brothers and turned back to the doctor. 'Can you give Harry a ring and tell him we'll be around there in three hours? Tell him not to worry when he hears the bikes pull up. They can make a bit of a racket.'

So Dr Ted got on the phone to Harry right then, and a few hours later my brothers and I thundered into this nice little street full of brown brick houses near Canterbury High. It wasn't hard to pick Barbara and Harry's place. There was a pile of garbage on the bonnet of an old

EH Holden and one of the front windows was boarded up where it had been smashed. We knocked on the door and an old guy peered through the curtains off to the side.

'Dr Ted sent us,' I called out.

The door opened slowly and the old couple looked a bit sheepish, but they invited us in and we sat down for a yak. They had one of the best-looking pied Staffordshire bull terriers I've ever seen. I had a brindle bitch at home. So that gave us something to break the ice with. They told us a bit about the constant harassment they'd suffered since the junkies moved in. It turned out they'd moved into not just one house, but two places right alongside each other, directly over the road.

'The police say they can't do anything unless they catch them in the act.'

It got my blood boiling. Fricking useless coppers.

'Bull and Wack,' I said. 'How about youse go over the house straight across. Snake, Shadow and Chop take the place to the right.' We had a rule where we didn't go into private houses. And we stuck to it. So the brothers stood out the front calling these blokes every name they could think of to get 'em out. We knew they were in there. We could hear the music and we saw the odd movement behind the venetian blinds. But no one emerged. Houses were one thing, but cars were another, and seeing as how they'd smashed Harry's car, my brothers set to work on theirs.

As Snake's chain ripped into the duco of a beaten up Valiant and as Chop's boot went through the windscreen, the doors of the house suddenly flew open and all these scumbags came pouring out with baseball bats and bits of wood, the odd knife. 'We're not scared of you, you bikie scum.' There must have been a dozen of 'em, all dirty long hair and skinny white arms. It only took a few seconds.

Whack, bang, bash, and my brothers had blitzed them. I wasn't required. Snake kept belting 'em long after it was over.

'Youse cunts have got three days. You're gunna be out of this house and out of the neighbourhood. We've got your car regos. If Harry and Barbara so much as lay eyes on you again, we'll find you.'

They didn't argue.

Nevertheless, Barbara and Harry were worried about reprisals, so Snake, Wack and Chop spent the night there. For the next three days, we made sure we always had someone at the house. We set up camp, with two in the spare bedroom and one on the couch. We sat around and watched TV. We listened to their stories and of course they wanted to hear ours. We told them a few yarns, but had to water them down. We could hardly tell old Barb what we did up the Cross. It was like being with your grand-parents. Harry was into his beer, so Bull and Snake were happy chugging down a few KBs with him. Barb cooked up wonderful big breakfasts. She made me milkshakes, so I brought over a tin of protein powder and asked her to put some of that in too. I would leave early to go to training, but at least two of us always hung around.

They were nice people and they appreciated what we did for them. The junkies snuck out on the third night without so much as a whimper.

Soon after, I got a call from Dr Ted. 'Caesar, you and your brothers have changed my whole outlook on bikie clubs.'

'They're not bikie clubs. They're outlaw biker clubs.'

'Well, you've changed my whole outlook on them whatever they're called. For you fellows to go over there and do that, when the police were so useless, was just marvellous.'

'It's our pleasure, Ted. This sort of stuff never gets into the paper. You never see "Gladiators Help Old Lady" in the headlines. We've only gotta run a red light and you'd think we'd murdered someone.'

'Well, I'll spread the word. You and your brothers will never pay for orthopaedic treatment again. Thank you so much.'

We continued to drop in on Barbara and Harry every few months to check that they were okay. We kept seeing them till Barbara got crook and they moved north to be with their kids in Queensland. But before they went, Harry bought us all expensive buck knives and had our names engraved on them. The knives took pride of place in the cabinets in all our lounge rooms.

It ended up being a bad deal for old Dr Ted, though. My brothers got a lot of injuries. They were always getting hit with baseball bats and getting cracked bones here and there. For the next 15 years before he retired there was always a line of Campbells going up to Dr Ted's door.

CAESAR'S LAW

VII

MY HERO

Achilles. He's meant to have been the best warrior ever. I would have loved to have fought him.

I think I first learned about him at the Marist Brothers at Hamilton. I read up on him and a lot of the other Greeks. A lot of bikers think the Vikings were the toughest blokes going around. They were pretty rugged blokes, but the Greeks took on the whole known world at the time and won. And Achilles was their almost invincible warrior. It took a bloke with a bow and arrow to take him out. That was a bit of a sneak job. He was killed when he got shot in the heel – his only weakness, like kryptonite for Superman.

No one's found mine yet.

14

THE ICEPICK AND OTHER WAYS TO COLLECT KNIVES

Still yakking on at the pub in Cooma, the conversation turned to blues we'd been in. Crikey, there'd been a few. It was a long conversation. At some point, PJ asked: 'Were any of you blokes there the night Caesar got into it with Icepick?'

'Was that over the ton?' Scotty asked, referring to $100 that Icepick owed me.

'Nah,' I said. 'I wouldn't fight anyone over a hundred bucks. I only ever got into with Icepick once and it was over Lenny Baker.'

'Yeah, fuck, I was worried about you that night you went looking for him,' Chance said. 'If it had just been a fist fight I wouldn't have worried, but with that pick thing of his it made him pretty dangerous. He was pretty good with that.'

Icepick was a standover man and cut-price hitman. The sort of bloke they might get to deal with a runner who lost their money or was dumb enough to be shooting it up his arm. He was about six foot four, maybe a bit taller than me, similar build. Not quite as big in the shoulder and chest. He got his name from the custom-made icepick that he always carried. The tip and about the first third of the pick were like a normal icepick. The middle third had four miniature blades, like razors, built in. And the last third was a beautiful pearl-shell handle. It was very good for stabbing and slashing, and he preferred it to a knife. I was right into collecting knives, so I'd paid particular attention to his little toy.

Now, Lenny Baker was a tough little bloke, 50 years old, small and strong like a Jeff Fenech or a Kostya Tszyu. Lenny was a runner for just about everybody because people knew they could trust him. Icepick was in his late 20s. I can't remember what their blue was over, but he'd taken to Lenny with that pick of his and sliced him up pretty bad. When he was younger, Lenny might have held his own with Icepick, who'd been in 20 martial arts competition fights for 18 wins and two disqualifications. Icepick was pretty good with his hands and his feet. I couldn't understand why he always pulled the pick out every chance he got. And I couldn't forgive him for going Lenny, who was almost 30 years his senior. Back in them days, if you were in your 20s, you didn't go a bloke 50 or over. So that, combined with the fact Lenny was my good mate, meant I was obliged to go looking for Icepick.

In those days, if you wanted to find someone, all you had to do was sit outside either the Carousel Club or the Manzil Room and sooner or later they'd pop up. I sat outside the Manzil Room and I soon saw Icepick come out and head down the little lane at the bottom of Springfield Avenue.

I followed him and it was on.

Like I've said before, I like a good knife fight. Nothing else gives you the same life-and-death thrill. At that time,

I was using a US Marine Ka-Bar. It was one of the best knives I'd ever owned. And when that thing came out, the blackness descended on my brain and whatever happened happened.

Sitting at the pub 40 years later, PJ seemed to remember more about it than I did. He told me that other bikers had seen me standing around outside the Manzil Room for a long time and when they saw me following Icepick down the lane, word went around about what was going down. 'There must have been blokes from 12, 15 clubs there,' he said. 'There were Angels, Jokers, Executioners, the whole lot.'

PJ and Chance were talking over each other trying to describe it. 'When you'd finished with him, you couldn't recognise the bloke,' PJ said.

'His nose was hanging off, his lips were hanging off. You took off one of his ears. His chest was cut right open,' Chance said.

'I was looking at blokes who were founding members of their clubs and they're chucking up at what they're seeing,' PJ said. 'And I wasn't far from chucking up myself.'

Now PJ is a pretty hard man. He was both the sergeant-at-arms and the enforcer for his club. I saw him get into a lot of blues for his club and he could really handle himself. 'It was funny seeing such tough men chucking up,' he said. 'Some looked like they were going to pass out. I couldn't recognise Icepick, he was such a mess. I saw him stick you in the chest first, so he's started it. It was like you let him have first go. But boy did you finish him off.'

'Yeah, I tried to warn Icepick,' Chance said. 'Not that we were mates or anything, but I know what you're like, Caesar, once you get going. I didn't want to see you inside. It surprised me that Icepick had the balls that he did and didn't dob you in to the coppers. I would have laid any odds that he would have dobbed, but you've got to give him that. He didn't.'

'Yeah, I never said that Icepick never had balls. He just picked on the wrong bloke who happened to be a good mate of mine. And he went against the code. You know back in them days you didn't go after blokes who were 50 or over, not unless they came at you with a shiv or a baseball bat or something.'

'Yeah, I knew where you were coming from,' Chance said. 'I was just worried you might get hurt, and if you weren't, that you'd end up killing him or he'd give you up. But I was wrong on all counts.'

Icepick got carted away and spent six or seven months in hospital being put back together. Someone from Satans Slaves scored his icepick. I wouldn't have minded having it for my collection. I've never seen anything like it before or since. Whoever made it for him was a real craftsman. Whoever you are, if you're reading this book and you're still making knives, I've got a knife in mind that I wouldn't mind having made. Get in contact with me and we'll talk terms.

*

I'VE GOT knives from a diverse range of sources. One of my favourites came to me after we'd been having a few problems with Sons of Satan. Must have been about 1976. There were about 19 of them in the club, which was based at Punchbowl. That's why we decided to head deep into their territory, the Sundowner Hotel, this Friday night when the pub had a couple of good bands on – might have been the Ted Mulry Gang. If we got lucky and ran into Sons of Satan it was going to make a good night better.

We got to the ranch-style pub about 7 pm and as usual my brothers set about making themselves right at home. They were rooting just about every sheila in there.

And I must admit I wasn't doing too bad either, but come 10 pm we figured the Sons of Satan weren't going to show up and it was time to head into the Cross.

We were walking through the car park back to the bikes when all of a sudden car doors all around us burst open, and big blokes started jumping out. We had their entire club coming at us with baseball bats, pickhandles and chains. They weren't wearing colours, but a few of 'em had T-shirts with their funny-looking devil on it, so we knew who it was. One of their hang-rounds must have spotted us earlier and tipped them off, because this was an ambush.

Without speaking, my brothers instinctively formed up into our tight circle formation and we gave Sons of Satan a hell of a good stomping – all except three of them who hit the toe. During the fight, I'd felt a slicing sensation in my middle but I hadn't taken any notice of it. Afterwards, as we surveyed the carnage, Shadow came over to me. 'Caesar, you've got a knife sticking right into your gut.'

I looked down and sure enough there was a buck knife coming out of my black T-shirt.

'You gunna pull it out or you want me to?' he said.

'You can.'

'Fast or slow?'

'Slow.'

'You're sick,' he said. 'You just like the pain.'

So he pulled it out real gradual and, shit, maybe he was right. Maybe I do love pain.

'How'd that feel?' he asked.

'Like a long, hot, wet kiss,' I said.

'You *are* sick.'

He gave me the knife and it was a nice-looking thing with a fancy handle, so it went in the cabinet right alongside the knife Harry had given me.

15

HOW TO GET AWAY WITH MURDER

One day I was in Abe's office above the Pink Pussycat with JR and my stripper friend Sandra Nelson. Abe wanted JR to do a job for him in Melbourne, but JR wasn't too keen. He knew that in New South Wales he operated with near impunity, because Abe had so many coppers and politicians in his pocket. In Victoria, JR felt more exposed.

'You don't think I can protect you down there, Johnny?' Abe said, opening a drawer in his desk. 'Take a look at these.' He pulled out a manila envelope and threw it across the table.

JR opened the envelope and pulled out two large-format black-and-white photos. I leaned in for a peek. Each picture showed a different middle-aged man, going hammer and tong up a big-titted blonde.

'Yeah, nice pics. So what?' JR said.

'Don't you know who they are?' I said.

'Nah. Should I?'

'Yes, you should.' Let's just say they were two Victorian politicians who were famous enough for me, a biker from Sydney who didn't read the papers that often, to recognise.

'Really?'

'Yeah, really.' Sandra grabbed them off us so she could examine them more closely and have herself a good old laugh. Both girls appeared to be above the age of consent, but the politicians were of the usual goody-goody family-man type and so Abe had them over a barrel and was rooting them up the arse, so to speak.

After we'd all calmed down and wiped the smiles off our dials, Abe broke in, 'So you see, boys and girls, I've got a green light in the Garden State too.'

JR did the job and returned home untroubled by Victorian law enforcement.

None of this should come as a surprise to anybody who has been paying attention. In his book *Mr Sin: The Abe Saffron Dossier*, journalist Tony Reeves documents the systematic blackmailing of Sydney's power elite by Saffron. If he didn't have someone he needed under his thumb, he set honey traps with young girls, big-titted strippers, boys, musclemen. Whatever it took to get them into a room and fucking, he did it, preferably at Lodge 44 Motel in Edgecliff, where he had a studio-quality television camera set up behind double-sided mirrors. I got shown through it by one of Abe's staff. They said Abe got the gear from a mate of his who was high up at Channel 9. You could see the entire room from behind this mirror, so they captured everything.

Reeves claims that the woman who ran Saffron's black-mail operation in the 1960s, Shirley Bega, was murdered when she attempted to steal a portfolio of photographs from him to use to blackmail the clients directly herself.

She was gunned down on the street, according to Reeves, yet the murder went unreported and unsolved and does not exist on the record. I'd never heard of Shirley Bega, but I can attest to the fact that the blackmail files were real and that it was routine for Saffron to arrange for deaths to go unreported and uninvestigated.

The power that these files gave Saffron put him higher up the organised crime tree than George Freeman or Lenny McPherson. He was the one who could make the cops disappear from a neighbourhood when I was round-ringing. If one of Abe's mates – including Lenny or George, but also a lot of allegedly straight businessmen – wanted a favour from the government or a council when they were trying to do a real estate deal, they'd go and see Abe. Abe would have a word to the relevant mayor or relevant minister. Maybe he'd give them a couple of still shots and let them know he had the whole reel. Maybe he'd give them a sling. With his carrots and whips, it would be payday all round.

While Abe's go was to blackmail the rockspiders, he also had Chance offing some of them. Now maybe Chance was given the ones who didn't play ball, but the way I understand it from Chance himself was that there was some bloke high up in the entertainment industry who had a passionate hatred of paedophiles. Every time this bloke found out the identity of one, he'd see Abe and pay for the person to be taken care of, whether they were high up in business or politics or the police force or whoever they were. Chance would be given the job.

So while Abe was using some of the kiddie fiddlers to his own advantage, he was also having others taken out. I think it was two sides of the same coin.

I'd also like to point out that, to my knowledge, in 50 years of outlawing there's never been an outlaw biker locked up or even charged with being a paedophile. In that time, there have been politicians, businessmen, scout-masters, priests, coppers. All sorts of people from public life, but I've never heard of an outlaw biker even being accused of being a paedophile. If there had been, they wouldn't have got to trial – their club would have taken care of them first.

16

PICKING OVER THE BONES OF THE VULTURES

While the foundation of the Bandidos was the high-light of my biker career, the best years for being an outlaw biker were from the late 1950s through to the '70s. I can't really comment on the late 1990s or the 2000s, because I haven't been able to ride with my club for those years, but the '50s to the '70s were a rocking time to be an outlaw. There were fistfights and parties and hard riding. Especially the hard riding.

I don't see a lot of outlaw clubs out on runs these days. Back in the old days, it was nothing to see three or four clubs at the one service station waiting to fill up. They were heading out with their own destinations. All tents and sleeping bags and freedom. In winter, there was nothing better than having your old lady with you to cuddle in the sleeping bag. We'd get one of those big blue tarps and stretch it over two bikes, leaving enough room for four people to sleep between them. If it rained, your bike didn't get wet and neither did you. If you left your bike in the open in winter, your speedo, seat and tanks got covered in ice in the morning. You had a mighty job of wiping your bike down before you could ride it.

I can remember about 1977, when seven of us Gladiators and three prospects all headed off on a two-week run out through Windsor, Scone and Armidale, stopping all the way at little towns – going off the main road, camping in paddocks, sleeping around a bonfire and just having a great time. We stopped at Inverell and spent two or three days there before cutting across through the mountains on some pretty rugged dirt roads before we hooked up with the Pacific Highway and headed south, stopping at Kempsey, Port Macquarie, Taree and Bulahdelah, picking up women everywhere we went. Every one of us was getting a girl. They loved us. We headed into Newcastle and stopped there for a couple of days, because that's where most of us grew up. I went down to Hannebery's gym to have a look at where I boxed as a young teenager before I got into *muy thai*.

The run made my brothers and me even tighter. We worked the prospects pretty hard collecting wood for the bonfires, keeping watch on the bikes, but they had a good time too. They got their share of the women. When we got back to Sydney, it took us three days to recover, but it was worth it.

Around the time we got back, I was up the Cross on a Friday night and as usual it was packed full of bikes. Even more than normal. They were parked around the corner into Macleay Street and Springfield Avenue. There was a new club called the Vultures that had been going for six or seven months. Their president's name was Buzzard, very original. They, along with some other small clubs, had parked in Victoria Street and were using the lane that came up beside the Manzil Room and into Springfield Avenue to get into the main drag.

Out the front of the club, three of the Vultures had got into an argument with Chance and said some things they shouldn't have about his club. I was there with JR and I'd noticed that Chance had no colours on, so I knew he'd done a job or was on his way to do a job. Anyway, he told these three Vultures to fuck off, which they did. They started walking down the lane and Chance followed them. So JR and I followed him to back him up. Now, remember, this book is three per cent fiction. We thought there was going to be a punch-up, but as Chance came up behind these blokes, he pulled out his Walther .38 pistol, and *Bang! Bang! Bang!* Three shots to the back of three heads.

I thought, *You prawn. If you'd wanted 'em knocked out or friggin' taken out, why didn't you just tell me? You didn't have to go firing off a bloody gun.*

But he had. I scanned the lane for witnesses. Saw the coast was clear. I wasn't that worried about being done for accessory. I knew Chance and JR wouldn't dob me in. And I knew Abe had ways of helping out his staff. If we did things right, we wouldn't cop any heat.

And we didn't, so we must have done something right.

If the surviving Vultures had any inkling of what had happened, they never did or said anything about it.

If a gun was fired in the back streets of the Cross, windows would shut, blinds would be drawn, lights would go off. People just would not report anything. If the coppers ever questioned them, it'd be, 'I was asleep', 'I wasn't home'. They knew if they went witness against any of the hitters up the Cross, they'd get hit. So there were a lot of people whacked in those back streets and wrapped up in tarps and buried at Kurnell or taken out through the Heads and dumped.

I saw JR about two nights later at the Carousel Club. He hadn't heard a thing about any investigation. 'I thought

THE OUTLAW AND THE HITMAN

you were bad-tempered,' I said. 'You'd put a bullet in anyone, anywhere, but I thought Chance was a lot cooler, headwise. He surprised the shit out of me plugging those blokes the other night.'

'You're not the only one,' JR said. 'I was expecting to end up in a blue, or at least see you knock the three of 'em out, but Chance just sort of . . . God, it was all over in a split second and the three of 'em were just lying there. Next thing I know, you're picking these blokes up like they're sacks of potatoes and hauling 'em over the fence. I'm going to have to find out who got rid of those bodies. It's been annoying me, not knowing.'

'Well, good luck to you.'

As usual we spent three or four hours together yakking on. We had a couple of strippers come over after a couple of hours. They were sitting there talking to us and we both ended up with a root for the night. JR was like a magnet to the sheilas and I always did pretty well, so whenever we were together we always had a pack of them wanting us to take 'em home. I wasn't with Donna at the time. I still didn't take strays home, but always went back to their joint. That way, people didn't know where I lived.

About three weeks after Chance had dealt with the three Vultures, the 20 or so of them who were left were still causing a lot of trouble. They'd seen too many bike movies. They were the sort of blokes who'd ride up the footpath and carry on, surrounding cars and booting them, hitting them with chains. So my brothers and I decided we'd visit their clubhouse at Alexandria.

We checked the place out for a couple of weeks, watching who came and who went. We established that Wednesday was their meeting night, so we got there early on Wednesday afternoon. We broke in and waited. A few of the blokes might have helped themselves to a beer. When the first two Vultures arrived, we tied up one and told the other he'd get his head bashed in if he didn't do what we said. So he was the bunny who opened the door as the rest of the club arrived in ones and twos.

The really staunch outlaw clubs from those days were the ones that are still going now. With the exception of the Sydney Gladiators – we retired our colours undefeated – all the others were more social clubs. They pretended to be outlaw clubs but, when the hammer came down, they crumbled. A really staunch bloke wouldn't have opened the door. He would've yelled out 'Ambush!' or something and copped a smashing in the back of the head or a knife in the ribs. He would've taken it and let his brothers know. He would've saved his club.

We beat 'em up and took their colours. It's no small feat to pull a petrol tank straight off a bike, but Bull ripped the tank off one of theirs, uncapped it, poured petrol over all their colours and lit them. When the adrenaline was running, you had to watch Bull. Snake and I were out in the yard with him. Shadow, Chop and Wack were inside making sure none of the blokes called the cops or fucked off till we did. Wheels was out the front making sure no one got out the front door. After the colours had turned to ash, we smashed up all their memorabilia and ripped down a flag with a vulture on it, tearing it into shreds and throwing it on the fire. Wheels came inside and was just going around wrecking the whole place, hitting the walls with his shoulder, making them collapse.

A couple of the Vultures watched him from the floor, not game to get up. Wheels, six foot five and 23 stone, was like a bulldozer, just bouncing into the walls and bringing them down. Chop, who was a little ball of powerlifting muscle, decided to do the same thing but he had to leap off the ground to do it and even then would mostly just bounce off. The Vultures had started renovating and had partially knocked out a wall. Wheels picked one Vulture up straight above his head and threw him through the wall, completing the renovations for them.

Most of them were just moaning, the few of them who were conscious or not playing dead were, like, 'Don't hurt us', and that sort of shit. Shadow and Chop told them that, if you want to be an outlaw, you shouldn't go fucking whingeing when something goes the wrong way. This is what you cop.

We went out the back and all got on our bikes. The brothers kicked 'em over and as usual I waited till everybody else had their engines roaring before I got mine started. I gave the signal and we took off, heading to the Palace Hotel at Darlinghurst, a little triangular, tiled pub that had bands. My brothers had a drink and played pool.

As usual, the girls flocked around. There was this one black-haired chick who'd been a Miss Australia entrant. I think she'd won the Miss New South Wales part of the contest. She tried to crack on to me, but I wasn't that interested so she tried with Shadow, but he already had two sheilas hanging off him so she bounced back to me, and she must have grown on me because I let her have her way with me back at her flat at Elizabeth Bay, down where all the posh houses are.

It was a good night.

*

SATANS SOLDIERS and Satans Slaves (not to be confused with Satans Council or Sons of Satan) had a bit of an animosity going that soon blew out into outright war. Unlike what happens these days, they took their blue out to a footy oval somewhere out the back of Richmond and tore into each other there. I was out Penrith way at the time and

I remember hearing the parade of ambulances bringing in the wounded. Talking to one of the Slaves a few days later, he said it was brutal: chains, fists, some knives, but that's the way it was in the '60s and '70s. When clubs were at war, it eventually ended out in some paddock away from the public. Well, 80 per cent did it that way, so you didn't get the public involved. It was just between the two clubs.

If things had stayed that way, we wouldn't have all the trouble going on that there is today with governments breaking the constitution to get rid of all the outlaw clubs. It's something that we always talk about when me, Chance, PJ, Irish, Scotty, Bear and Witch get together. If clubs could settle their differences out in a paddock, there wouldn't be the pressure on cops and politicians to close them.

I know that might sound a bit hypocritical coming from me after what happened on Father's Day 1984 at Milperra, but I never knew that was going to happen. No Bandido knew that the Comancheros were going to be there. We went there that day for a swap meet and for the band that was supposed to be on. If you've got nothing else from this book, you will have noticed that I'm not afraid to tell you about all my blues and about how, with some of them, I went and actively chased the blokes and belted shit out of them, and some.

I would have happily done it to the Comos too, but I would never have taken my club to do it in a crowded car park full of civilians – guns or no guns. As it turned out, they were waiting with guns and walkie talkies. We were unarmed except for two of Snoddy's hunting guns. And the rest is history. You can get the full story in our first book, *Enforcer*. But don't get your history from that book *Brothers In Arms* (by Lindsay Simpson and Sandra Harvey) – which is more about the court case – and especially not the TV series about the bikie wars. That was all made up.

Anyway, a great example of how clubs should go to war occurred around the end of 1977 early '78. The Undertakers and the Gravediggers were at each other's throats. With names like those, it was a formula for conflict and they went out to settle their little demarcation dispute on a soccer field at the back of Campsie.

They got stuck into it with chains and iron bars and baseball bats – the old Louisville slugger was a favourite back in those days. It went on for quite a while and the story goes that there were half a dozen coppers sitting in the dark in their cars watching as all these bikers beat the living shit out of each other. The cops couldn't have cared less, because the bikers weren't hurting anyone except themselves.

Both clubs had been infringing on our turf. We didn't like either of them, so we were almost as happy as the coppers to see them go for it.

The only club we didn't have a problem with in our home turf was Corporation of Sin. They didn't cause us any trouble and they seemed to be a staunch little club. And their president Les Markham was a tough man. I met him years later under difficult circumstances, but he turned out to be a top bloke.

These other two clubs, though, the Undertakers and the Gravediggers, they caused us nothing but trouble. Like the Vultures before them, they'd seen how bikers acted in the movies and they figured that was what you did. The Gravediggers had even named themselves after the club in the Australian biker movie, *Stone*. So that showed you where they were coming from, doing all the car-kicking and wheelies in shopping centres on their Jap-crap bikes. They generated a lot of bad press and caused us a lot of grief. And on top of that, we'd heard they were mouthing off about us.

We decided we'd had enough of both of them.

17

BURYING THE UNDERTAKERS

Chance had become a regular for dinner over at JR's place too. We'd be at Arncliffe a couple of nights a week. JR's old lady, Cheryl, would do us up a big feed of stroganoff or goulash, because she knew I loved beef. We were over there one night when JR decided to show us another surprising feature of his house. He pulled a little lever next to a grandfather clock and the thing swung out. He did something else that made the whole section of wall swing out, leaving an opening not much more than a metre high. We crouched down through it and found ourselves in a room that was about 3 metres by 3 metres. My head just about touched the ceiling. Our eyes shot around to see guns and ammunition and other valuables. A bulletproof vest was hanging from a hook. It was this big cumbersome thing, like an old air force flak jacket. He had some sawn-off shotties and – Chance picked up on it straightaway – a nice little Walther P38.

That was Chance's pick in guns. James Bond's too, in some of his flicks.

'Why don't you buy a couple of H&Ks?' I said.

'You like them don't you, Ceese?' JR said.

'I just reckon they're a good gun.'

'I thought you were a .357 Magnum man.'

'I am. But I just think that out of the nine mils, the H&Ks are the better choice.'

'Let me guarantee you, Berettas are the best,' JR said. 'Get the chambers ported [where you have small holes drilled in the barrel to let gases escape and reduce recoil]. Get a bit of work done to the extractors. You can't have a better gun. That's why I use 'em.'

So we yakked on a bit and Chance mentioned what a great space it was. JR agreed. 'Sometimes when I'm having someone over here I don't trust, if Cheryl's in the house I'll put her in here. That way I know she's safe.'

Little did Chance and I know that the secret room was to play a crucial role in the JR and Cheryl story a few years down the track.

But back on this night, JR pointed to a black Ruger .357 revolver with a nice wooden handle. 'I bought it because I knew you liked them,' he said, handing it to me. Chance picked up the Walther .38, JR grabbed one of his Berettas and we went downstairs into the converted bomb shelter to put up some targets. We must have spent three or four hours doing what boys do – having a good time, shooting things up and bullshitting to each other – before I decided to call it a night.

Me and JR had our usual big hug. I rode home and The Woman told me that Snake had just called. He was at an address in Lakemba and he wanted me out there. So I had a quick look at the Gregory's street directory and got back on my bike and rushed over. It must have been a bit after midnight when I pulled up at a run-down old brick joint. There was no sign of Snake. No bike. Nothing. I knocked on the door.

Snake answered, looking a little worse for wear. 'Come in,' he said, with just a hint of a smile.

I walked in and it was like a tornado had gone through – followed by a threshing machine. There was blood on the walls. And blokes that looked like bikers lying all over the floors. And there in the middle of the laundry floor was a neat pile of leather vests with the colours of the Undertakers on the backs. Snake had poured petrol on them and was just waiting for me before setting them alight.

'What have you done this for?'

'They were going round running our club down,' he said.

'Yeah, I know that. I thought I told you to go and see where they hung out.'

'That's what I did. And then I thumped 'em.'

'Why didn't you get me or some of the other brothers?'

'You're not the only one who can do things by himself.'

I counted seven of them lying on the floor, all still unconscious but none of them looking too seriously wounded. And then there was Snake with a grin bigger than his great heavy chain.

'What are you going to do with 'em?' I asked.

'That's what I called you over for. You're the president!'

I looked through the bodies and, as far as I could tell, the Undertakers' president wasn't there. So we splashed some water into the face of the guy we thought was their sergeant-at-arms. I had a talk with him. He gave me his word that no club member was mouthing off about us. That it was just a couple of prospects.

'All right. You give me your word that you'll take care of these prospects and that no Undertaker will ever disrespect the Gladiators?'

'Yes.'

'Are the prospects here?'

'No.'

'Well, you take care of 'em and we'll call it quits.'

'You got me word on it, Caesar. You've got me word . . . Fuck, your brother's a mad man.'

'Well, if you upset Snake you're gunna get bitten.'

Snake and I headed out to go home. He had his bike parked down the side of the house. That's why I hadn't seen it when I'd rolled up. So I waited for him to come out and we headed home. I remember us pulling up at a red light and looking across at each other with the bikes rumbling and we had a bit of a cackle. It was pretty funny how easy he'd done them. A couple of the Undertakers were big blokes.

Unfortunately, they weren't so big on keeping their word.

I didn't like people who didn't keep their word.

I lived by a code. My father used to go on about this thing he called the 'old code'. He and his father and all my grandfather's nine brothers were all into this thing going back to the Highlands of Scotland. I was always getting pounded with the Campbells of Argyll, the Campbells of Cawdor and all that. Dad said that if you gave your word, you kept it no matter what. Even if it meant chopping off your arm. The old man pounded it into me: 'Never give your word lightly. It could cost you your life.' He believed that much in keeping your word and your honour that you'd die for it.

So you can imagine how disappointed I was when a couple of months later we heard that the Undertakers were going round to the places we drank, mouthing off and telling people how they'd bashed Bull and others. They weren't very bright, because they moved to a new clubhouse and held a big party there. Even though we didn't get an invite, just about every bike club in Sydney now knew their address.

We watched them for a couple of weeks after the party, learning when their club night was and what time the first blokes arrived to open up. So, on the night of the attack, I got Bull and Shadow to go in over the top of the bloke unlocking the door. They knew not to bash the guy, but just to hold him there while the rest of us came in. We turned the lights on and put on some music nice and loud.

We had our bunny completely convinced that if he so much as let out a squeak about what was going on we were going to tear him a new arsehole. When most people used that expression, it was more of a metaphor. When we used it, though, people understood that we might be thinking more literally. So, as the Undertakers arrived in ones and twos, we had the bunny open the door for them. As each one entered, we thumped them and tied them up, till we had the entire club.

Before we burnt the colours, we searched the place for guns, because we didn't want anybody waking up and trying any heroics. But there were no guns there. There rarely were in those days.

We covered the Undertakers colours with petrol for the second time in a few months and I let Snake drop the match onto them. He pissed on a few as well, so then Chop decided he wanted to do the same. I thought, *Fuck me, next thing they'll be wanting to take a shit on 'em.* It smelt bad enough as it was, with all that steaming urine. I got the club out of there before things got real smelly.

We headed back to the Illinois Hotel at Five Dock feeling pretty happy about things. And as we sat around debriefing, the events of the night started to get exaggerated to the point where I wasn't even sure we were talking about the same thing. I just sat back and listened to my brothers enjoying themselves. That was what made me happy. I didn't have to drink to have a good time.

After the bullshitting was all done, they got up to play some pool. Chop was over at the jukebox looking for his Beatles songs. He loved the Beatles. And I was sitting in the end booth, feeling a bit peckish. I saw Gladys the barmaid. She was like a grandmother to us. She knew all our names and if the cops came in she was always on our side. So the cops had a hard time trying to set us up there, with old Gladys as an independent witness.

I asked her if she could rustle us up a couple of hot dogs, which she did. So I was sitting in my booth with my back into the corner – which I always did no matter where I was – scoffing my second hot dog when this local chick Julie came up to me. Julie hung around the pub and was into bikers. She really liked Shadow and Snake, but this night she decided she wanted to go for a ride with me. 'C'mon, Ceese, if you take me for a ride I'll take you for one.' She was a pretty hot sheila and twelve months earlier I would have happily ridden her, but I'd recently met Donna, so I wasn't interested. Since I'd been with Donna, I hadn't rooted any other chick.

Donna was the best thing to ever happen to me and still is. We've been together for 38 years now and I just thank the Lord that He gave me the honour of having this special woman in my life.

I told Julie it was a no-go. She got the shits and said, 'Well, I'll get Shadow to take me for a ride.'

'Well, you get Shadow to take you for a ride.'

Which she did – along with the rest of my brothers except Bull, who stayed with me. He ordered some hot dogs and we played pool, waiting for our brothers to get back from the clubhouse, where they'd taken Julie. I think it was about three hours before they came back in with big smiles on their faces and Shadow said that Shultz, Lurch, Rhino and Peaceful had been up at the clubhouse and they all went through her too. So she pulled a bit of an onion that night.

That was all part of biker life.

CAESAR'S LAW
VIII

THE PERFECT
ROMANTIC EVENING

For me it used to be taking Donna out to either Doyles at Watsons Bay or one of those fancy places on the water at Rose Bay, depending on which one she wanted to go to.

After that we'd drive from there to a place at the Royal National Park near Sutherland. There's a spot out there called Love Rock. It's a big boulder about 100 feet back from the edge of the cliff and the ocean. It's roughly shaped like a heart. You go down a fire trail for a couple of Ks and you come to the edge of the cliff. You park there and look out over the ocean and see all the stars and the lights from the boats in the distance. I'd put on a snazzy tape I'd had made up and listen to the old songs like 'Teen Angel' and 'Don't Be Cruel'. Perfect.

18

EARNING
YOUR WINGS

Shadow had this sheila knocking around the club called Jade. There's a thing with outlaw clubs called a Dirty Mary. Not many sheilas can do it well. Jade was one of the rare ones who could pull it off, so to speak. It entails one bloke going up a sheila's arse, another going up her pussy, while she sucks another bloke off and pulls off two more – one with each hand. A lot of 'em try it, few succeed. It takes a lot of co-ordination to do it so that all five blokes have a good time.

You wouldn't believe the money that Shadow was offered for her. He was even offered a Harley from blokes from another club if he'd give them Jade as one of their club mamas. We had a couple of chicks around the club who could do a Dirty Mary almost as well as Jade, so it left me wondering why Shadow never took the money or the bike.

Not that Shadow ever took part in the Dirty Marys. He'd trained Jade and he liked to watch her in action.

Especially if we had blokes over from another club who'd never been in one before. They'd be blown away by what Jade could do. And Shadow wasn't backwards in coming forwards in letting them know he'd taught her everything she knew.

Sex is a big part of an outlaw biker's life. A lot of clubs have the red wings and the gold wings award system, but the Gladiators never went in for any of that. I could have earned them both plenty of times over but I couldn't see the point in going down on some sheila with her rags on in front of me brothers just to prove something. But I must admit I did like it every time I notched up a cop sheila. It mightn't seem much over 50 years of being an outlaw biker, but I would've earned my gold wings 11 times over. It'd be 13 if you counted head jobs. But the rule is that you have to have fucked 'em, so 11 it is.

We were riding down Victoria Road one night in 1977 when we pulled up at a set of lights. Shadow had this sheila on the back called Betty Sue, who was wearing a real short skirt. We noticed people in cars staring at Shadow more than the rest of us, so I manoeuvred my bike up alongside him and saw that Betty Sue must have just got her monthlies. There was blood everywhere down her leg and with the short skirt on you could see it something fierce. All over his seat. She must have put her hands down there, because there were red finger marks on his T-shirt too.

I told Shadow at the next lights and he pulled over at the Ermington pub. He got all cranky at Betty Sue and sent her inside to clean herself up. When she came back, he got her to go into the kebab wagon in the car park and get some napkins. He made her clean the seat and wash the bike. And he made sure there was a thick wad of paper under her legs before she got back on the bike, which we all thought was rather funny.

We were on our way to a party at the Demons' club-house in Parramatta. It was in Brickfield Avenue, which years later would be the same street as the Bandidos club-house when I got out of jail. When we got to Parramatta, instead of going to the Demons' clubhouse we swung into Parramatta railway station. Shadow was going to put Betty Sue on the train. But when we pulled up, I said to Shadow, 'Nah, don't put her on the train, bring her up the clubhouse, you might be able to do yourself a deal. There might be some blokes looking to earn their red wings. The Demons go in for that sort of thing.'

So Shadow changed his mind and took her with us. There were three or four blokes wanting their wings, so Shadow bargained himself a carburettor, a couple of tyres and half a front end in exchange for Betty Sue. All so these blokes could go down and stick their tongue in her bloody pussy.

The Demons weren't a big club. There were about nine of them and they didn't have any real good bluers. They had a bloke called Crazy Larry who'd sneak up behind people and stab them in the back or belt them in the head with an iron bar. When it was face to face, he wasn't much chop. The Demons survived by not spending too long in the one spot with their clubhouse. They'd move every four or five months and not settle into any one part of Sydney. That way they didn't step on any of the tougher clubs' toes.

Other clubs that were there that night were the Pagans, the Headhunters, some blokes from the Executioners and a few down from the Devils Dozen in Newcastle. They had a side of beef on the spit, so no one went hungry. And I think everyone there had a good night. Even Betty Sue.

One time, me and all my brothers went to a party at the Gargoyles' clubhouse. When we arrived we were greeted by the president, Buddha, who welcomed us and we paid him our due respect. The sergeant-at-arms, Grizzly, showed us into the lounge room, where there were these two sheilas in the raw with their legs spread wide and a light smear of blood over their lower regions. Two blokes had their faces buried in the sheilas' crotches, with two lines of about five blokes stretched out behind. Watching these blokes earn their red wings was kind of like the party starter. Certainly broke the ice. I was watching one bloke and he wasn't licking her out, he was putting his finger in and pulling out these blood clots and eating them.

We moved into the bar. The music was good and a band was setting up out in the backyard, where there was a pig on a spit. More people started rocking up and the two sheilas got moved into another room as the queue of blokes trying to earn their wings got shorter, but there always seemed to be someone there giving it a slurp.

Anyway, it was a top night. There were plenty of other sheilas there and Bull and I sat back and watched as our brothers went about cracking on to as many strays as they could muster. I reckon Snake rooted five sheilas that night. He must have had a good brekkie.

19

A BIG DAY OUT

There was one day back in about 1977 that pretty much covered the gamut of a biker's existence. I got up, got dressed, made breakfast – orange juice and a litre of protein drink made up of yoghurt, skim milk, chocolate protein powder and a banana whizzed up in a big industrial blender. I drank it, then gave it a half hour to settle down before I put the colours on and went out and kicked the Panhead over.

Even when I got a bike with an electric start, I still used to like kicking it over. The bike I've got now is a top bike, a '91 soft tail with a 100-cubic-inch Revtech motor. The heads have been polished and bench-blown. The whole motor's been blueprinted (where they take it apart and put it back together with superfine attention to detail) and balanced. It goes like a blur. But it hasn't got a kickstart, so it just doesn't feel the same.

Anyway, this day I rode to a chopper shop at Homebush where a mate of mine, Greenie from the Nomads, worked. I wanted to get a bit more performance out of the Panhead. Greenie was one of the best Harley mechanics ever in Australia, so we sat down and had a bit of a yak and he told me what he thought I should do to the Pan. I thanked him for his advice, hopped back on my bike and was riding down Parramatta Road towards Parramatta where Bull was now living.

As I got towards Granville, I got pulled over by the coppers. They wanted to search me. I said, 'I'll clean me pockets out for you, but you aren't putting your hands on me . . . I don't do drugs and I don't carry them. You've got my word. If my word's not good enough for ya, let's go down to Parramatta cop shop and we'll talk to the station sergeant. I'll betcha he takes me word.' I'd known the station sergeant there for years and he knew I wasn't into drugs.

'Yeah, right. Well, who's the station sergeant at Parramatta?' asked one of them.

I told them.

'How long have you known him?' asked the other one.

'About seven years. If you want, get on your radio, but there's no way you're getting me to strip off here in public. I'm not some young kid you can harass. The first one of youse to put a hand on me, I'll flatten.'

'We can arrest you for that. That's intimidation of a police officer.'

'Well, if you're that big of a girl that that intimidates ya, go ahead.'

One of them went back to the car and got on the radio and there was an uncomfortable minute or two where I just stared at the other one until the first one came back. 'He's all right. Let him go.' He turned to me. 'Why didn't you say who you were?'

'Why didn't you ask? I thought that'd be the first thing you'd want to know. But you weren't interested. You just wanted to show how tough you were to the people around here by pulling over a biker and harassing him, but this biker don't get harassed.'

Little did I know that one of these coppers would years and years later have a relative in the police force stationed in the Snowy Mountains and when this copper found out that I was down here and had a son with me, he had his relative and the other coppers down here harass the shit out of my young bloke who's done nothing.

I continued my trip out to Bull's and went in. Chop was there having a beer with him. So I went into his fridge and pulled out a Tab cola. Bull always kept a few in there for me. We sat out in the backyard. Bull pulled out his air rifle and put a few pegs up on the Hills Hoist. We'd shoot 'em off with the air rifle. Chop was a bit on the hopeless side, but me and Bull were pretty good. We'd hit a peg most times. We did this till it got boring and we decided it was time to go for a run.

I went out the front and waited while Chop and Bull rolled their bikes out and put their colours on. We rode down to the Rosehill pub, played some pool and were having a good time when, wouldn't you know it, in came some Phantom Lords wanting to know what we were doing in the Parramatta area, which they considered to be their territory.

Chop told them to get fucked. One of them picked up a pool cue and gave Bull a good whack on the side of the head. He just stood there and looked at this Phantom Lord like he didn't feel a thing. Bull picked him up and slammed him into the jukebox, while Chopper and I got into the other five.

Chopper was like a little tank with all the powerlifting he did. He picked up whole tables and tossed them 6 metres down the pub at some Lord who was hiding behind a pole. Bull was using bodies like tenpins.

'The manager's called the cops,' the barmaid yelled out from behind the bar. 'Youse wanna get going, Caesar.' We left the Phantom Lords lying on the floor for the cops – or ambulance – to collect. We got on the bikes and, knowing the cops would be coming from either Parramatta or Granville, we headed north towards Harris Park and cruised around in a loop and back to Parramatta, where we ended up at the Tollgate Hotel to continue playing pool. Chop picked himself up a babe and left to take her up to this little flat that he and Shadow rented nearby. So Bull and I headed to our homes. It was still just mid-afternoon.

*

WHEN I got home, The Woman told me I'd had a call from Dr Ted, our orthopaedic specialist, so I gave him a ring and he asked if I'd come up and see him. So I got back on the bike, rode up to Lewisham, went in and told his receptionist that he wanted to see me.

I was ushered straight in. Dr Ted gave me a warm handshake and, after exchanging brief pleasantries and asking how my brothers were, he said there was another elderly couple he hoped we might be able to help.

'We love helping people out, Ted. What's the story?'

'I'll let them tell you themselves.' He picked up the phone and dialled. After speaking briefly to the old guy, he passed the phone to me. 'Here, Caesar, this is Bill.'

Bill told me that his son owed some people money for drugs and had taken off interstate to get away from them, and these blokes were harassing him and his elderly wife to come up with the cash.

'There's eight of them,' Bill said. 'They come a couple of times a week in two cars. They throw things through the window, scratch our car and just vandalise whatever they can get their hands on.'

Again I got on the blower and called up my brothers. We went over and met Bill and Dell. They lived in a beautiful old Federation-style cottage with fancy ironwork and stained glass. A little run down. They were a lovely couple and we were keen to help. Bill said the hoons usually came at night, so me and the brothers made a plan that we'd gather there each night at dusk and wait. Dell didn't mind having us around. She managed to whip up a little dinner for us and we sat around and watched the television.

Shadow asked if he could have a shower and Dell went and got him a towel. But he walked into the bathroom and took one look at this enormous claw-footed iron bath and decided he had to try it out. A while later, Chop came and grabbed me. 'You gotta have a look at this.'

We found him there with all these bubbles overflowing the top like he was in the ad for Cussons Imperial Leather. We went diving around the house trying to find a camera. Unfortunately, Dell was out of film.

On the first night, sadly, nobody showed up. So we left, telling Bill and Dell we'd be back again the next night. Again, nothing.

It was on the third night, I think it was a Thursday, when we heard horns blowing and engines revving. We'd parked our cars a little way down the street, so we started them up, pulled out from the gutter and eased in behind the hoons' cars. The street was lined with a lot of trees, so when we parked behind these blokes, they were trapped.

We could see they were just your usual Leichhardt/Annandale hoodlums, flannelette shirts, desert boots and prison tatts. They might have been a bit on the big side for that era. Nobody did weights back then. Blokes were smaller, except for me and me brothers. But we knew half of them by sight and we knew they were all mouth. Nobody bothered getting weapons out of the car.

None of us spoke as we rushed their cars. We had this thing where we didn't talk during fights. We all knew what was required. They were all still in the cars when we got to them. We started dragging them out through the doors. The ones that were fast enough to push down the locks had their windows smashed. My brothers used to love smashing car windows. Elbows were the easiest, but if you hit hard enough with a good straight wrist you could do it with your fist.

So we dragged these yobbos out and beat the shit out of them. Then we turned to their cars, an FC Holden and a Torana. We lifted the bonnets, ripped out the wiring, the spark plugs, smashed the distributors and rolled them into the gutter.

'Now you pricks are going to fuck off.'

'What about our cars?' said one who could still talk.

'You send a tow truck. If you pricks ever show your face in this area again, we'll put you in wheelchairs for the rest of your lives.'

After it was all over and the dickheads had scarpered, old Bill came out wearing his brown cardigan and slippers. He pulled out $500. 'This is for you, Caesar. Share it with your brothers.'

'Bill, we're not doing this for money,' I said. 'I hope that if my dad and mum were in this situation someone would help them. What about your neighbours? Why haven't they helped?'

'Most of them are as old as us. The ones who are younger just aren't interested. They just pull the blinds down and stay out of it.'

'Well, you keep your money, but do us a favour and let your friends know that outlaw bikers aren't like what you read about in the papers and see on TV. We're just a bunch of blokes who love our bikes and our clubs and love being together. Not just our club, but all clubs. I reckon if you'd gone to any outlaw club and explained what was going on, I guarantee they would have helped you.'

'Well, thanks Caesar.' Bill went around and shook all the brothers' hands and we got in our cars and headed off well satisfied.

Me in 1972, around the time I started doing the round-ring fighting.

Bulldog Brower was a nutcase. A 120 kilogram ball of muscle, he came looking for us up the Cross in a spiked dog collar.

Tex McKenzie was a six foot nine man mountain. Didn't do him much good when my boot hit his knee and my elbow jolted his jaw.

ABOVE: Wrestler Brute Bernard. He held Bulldog Brower back, saving him from a flogging by my brother Chop.

RIGHT: Mark Lewin, 'master of the sleeper hold'. I thought I could match any sleeper he put on, but he backed down so he never let me test him.

Abe Saffron enjoying the pleasures at one of his clubs. He liked to be called Mr Saffron. The rest of us knew him as Mr Sin.

Me, about 1975. The hair's getting longer. The money bags in the secret wall cavity are getting heavier.

My brothers: Snake, Bull and Wheels, aka the Sydney Gladiators, aka the Wrecking Crew. Whatever you wanna call 'em, you'd have to be crazy to take 'em on.

Terry Clark, 'Mr Asia'. To me, he was just a big-noting sadistic drug dealer, taking credit for hits that were done by my mate Johnny Regal.

Lenny McPherson, 'Mr Big'. He was always geeing me up, telling me I was in for a hiding. I'm still waiting, Lenny.

George Freeman, or 'Mr Las Vegas', and Lenny McPherson at the funeral of 'Paddles' Anderson at Waverley Cemetery, 1985.

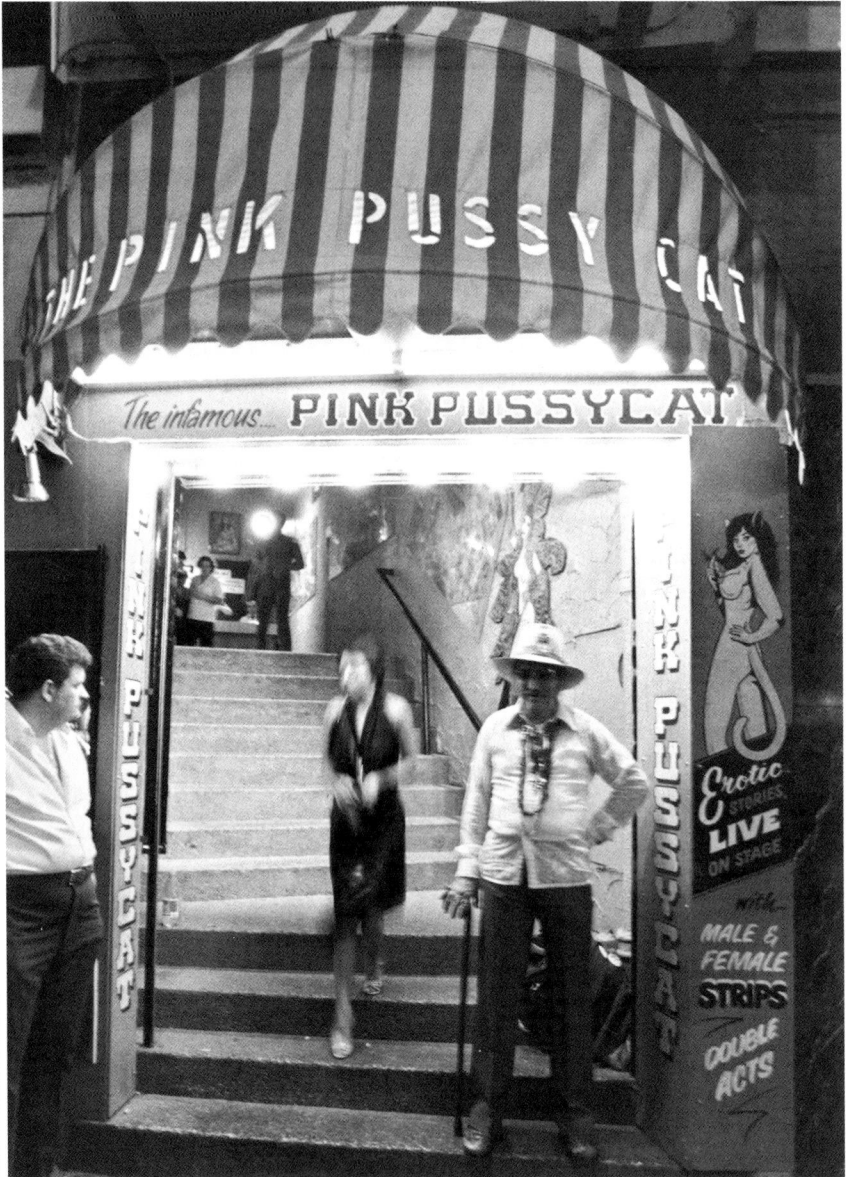

I met the famous stripper Sandra Nelson at the Pink Pussycat.
I loved Kings Cross for the girls and the bikes. I always found it
easy to pick up.

After I got out of jail in the early '90s. Abe's power was waning. My peak earning years were behind me. The biker world would never be the same again. Hence the smile.

Me and The Woman at home in Cooma. Donna is the best thing that ever happened to me. We've been together 38 years.

The outlaw life is a hard life, but a good life, and it's one I'll never give up. I was born to be an outlaw. And I'll be an outlaw till the day I die.

CAESAR'S LAW
IX

MY MODERN HERO

Fred Hollows went around the world helping people with their eyesight. He gave up so much of his time and went to so many dangerous places, and put his own health on the line to help other people. He's a real Aussie hero.

20

A COUNTRY ESTATE

The next night, I was sitting on my bike up the main drag of the Cross, talking to Haystacks from the Jokers and Cub from the Angels, when JR and Chance rocked up and asked me if I wanted to go over to Sweethearts. So I went over to the café with the two triggermen.

Now, the legend of the Widowmaker had continued to grow in the couple of years I'd known who it really was. Some people thought it was JR, but no one guessed it was the sergeant-at-arms for an outlaw bike club. It was rumoured all around the Sydney underworld that JR and the Widowmaker had made trips interstate to take care of crims and some paedophiles. Chance in particular loved those rockspider jobs. A lot of well-known people from a couple of states were taken out due to the talents of JR and the Widowmaker.

I was the only one wearing colours this night, so I knew Chance was working. Chance and JR got their coffees and I ordered a passionfruit shake. We were sitting there yakking when JR said, 'You notice anything new?' He opened his fancy brown leather coat far enough for me to see he'd had silver conchos put on his twin holsters.

'Fuck me. Are you a two-bob lair or what?'

'If it was anyone else but you, I'd put a bullet in 'em for saying that.'

'Just as well it is me, then, because if you went for your piece, I'd grab you by the throat and rip it out before you even got the gun out.'

'I know that. I'm only mucking round.'

Chance jumped in: 'Yeah, Ceese, don't be so serious. What's got your goat?'

'Oh, I was just talking to Haystacks and Cub about how hard a time our clubs get in the media. We've only got to jaywalk and it's a major criminal offence, but we do work for charities. Just about every club in Australia does charity work. They raise big money with their bike shows and that never gets in the papers or on TV. It's just pissing me off.'

'Come on, big feller, calm down,' Chance said. 'I want you to do a bit of work for me in a couple of nights time.'

'What do you want?'

'I want you to come on a trip with me. It ain't charity, but we'll be doing the world a favour.'

'Hmmm.'

'There'll be one less big-noting crim who's also a big give-up. He's gone and given up the wrong person this time and our friend wants him taken care of.'

See, Chance wasn't one of these blokes who just went out and shot people indiscriminately. He made sure he got his target, but if they had bodyguards he wanted them taken care of without killing them. That's where I came in. The minders were just doing a job. A lot of them weren't bad blokes. That was the funny thing – as I did a few jobs for Chance over the years, I found out that I was sometimes knocking out blokes I knew and was on good terms with. So I was glad Chance had his code.

A few days later, we got into a rental car and drove a long way out into the sticks. I won't say where. It was a country estate. Chance had been there before to check it out. He'd sat up on a hill with his big binoculars and watched the place for hours, observing the six bodyguards and security guards and how they moved around the place. He'd heard that some of them were ex-military blokes who were pretty crash hot, so that's why he wanted me along.

'They'll be nothing for you,' he said. 'You'll murder 'em.'

'I'm not going to murder them,' I said. 'I'll take 'em out for you.'

'Yeah, Ceese. It was just an expression.'

Around dusk, he parked the car on a quiet bush track and we got out. There was nothing but trees in every direction.

'Come on, we're walking from here. It's about two miles.' He led the way west, bush-bashing through the scrub. Eventually we came to a clearing and hopped a Cyclone fence. Unusually for me, I was wearing joggers – black – because Chance had warned me we'd have to jump this fence.

I was wearing black jeans, a black shirt. My hair was tied back and, as always, I had a black bandana covering my forehead. Chance was done up like a friggin' ninja, all in black with a black balaclava. We sat and watched the house and the guards walking around for an hour or two before I moved in.

With the *kyite* – the Korean martial art which I practised – I'd been taught how to move around quietly. I'd noticed how the guards had a pattern to their rounds, coming out to a point about 30 metres from their post, so I got myself into a dark pocket on that route, stuck my head down and waited. Speed was crucial. I got the first guy with my hand over his mouth and a hard punch to the liver, which stunned him. He moaned as I got my hand over the top of his head and bent his neck back. I stuck my thumb up under his hyoid bone and he was out cold. That was one of my sleeper holds. I kept the pressure on the hyoid for 25 seconds, knowing that would keep him out for ten to 15 minutes. I tied his hands and his feet with black cable ties, then pulled out one of the gags Chance had given me – a ball stuck onto the middle of a strap. I jammed the ball into his mouth and tied the strap tight around the back of his head.

I ran crouching to the next post. I grabbed the guard and this time I just pulled him down and got my knees in his back, choking him into unconsciousness. I moved through, closer to the target, knowing that the nearer I got, the more highly trained the guards were likely to be. And more highly armed. But they just weren't expecting an attack like this, so they weren't on their toes. I knocked the six bodyguards out without any of them so much as getting their hands on their guns. I flashed a little green light to Chance. He flashed a red one back. That was my cue to get out.

Chance came in and did whatever it was that he was there to do and I waited for him at the Cyclone fence.

He returned in three minutes flat. Job done. The whole thing was over in about twelve minutes. Now, remember, this book is three per cent fiction and 97 per cent fact.

The target in this case was a crim. They're like outlaw bikers. They won't talk to the cops. His people weren't going to give anyone up. They'd either just let it go or try to even up themselves, but when two blokes come in balaclavaed up it's pretty hard to know who to get even with. So Chance and I never heard anything more about this one. We were sweet.

We got back to town in the early hours of the morning and Chance paid me off with a tidy sum. 'You'd be making some big money up here, wouldn't ya?' he said. 'I'm paying you a good wage and I know you're getting a fair whack when you bodyguard these couriers.'

'I hope you don't think I'm bodyguarding drug couriers,' I said. 'There are a lot of diamonds and important documents that get moved from state to state or suburb to suburb.'

'Nah, I know you don't have nothing to do with drugs,' he said. 'You seem to be the flavour of the month to be the bodyguard or the courier.'

'Yeah, that probably comes from people who saw me doing the round-ring fighting. They've seen me beating the best blokes in the world, so they figure their stuff's going to be safe with me. Not that I'm patting meself on the back. It's a fact.'

'Yeah, I know Mr Sin is quite happy with your work.'

'Well, that's good to know.'

＊

LIKE I'VE said before, JR was a spiffy sort of bloke. A lot of the time he wore a fedora. When he wore his brown leather coat, he'd often match it with brown leather pants, pointy brown shoes. One night, I was sitting in the Manzil Room with him and Chance. Lenny McPherson was there with his crew, George Freeman was there with his and even Joe Meissner had popped in for an hour or so. It was a Who's Who of the Cross. It was interesting to watch them. Freeman's blokes were like their boss – more expensively dressed than Lenny's blokes, who were more knockabout.

Meissner didn't have a crew. He was a hard man in his own right, a former world karate champion, and didn't need anyone to take care of him. (A few years later, in 1982, Dolph Lundgren got a job working for Meissner as a bouncer. He was a big unit who was the current European champion in *Kyokushin* karate. He and I had a go one day. Since he's now a movie star, I won't dint his image by going into detail other than to remind you I've never been beaten.) Meissner ran a strip club and a couple of other clubs. He wasn't into drugs or anything else like that. Nothing really illegal. He was just Joe Meissner and you didn't mess with him. People respected him.

Anyway, JR got up and swaggered straight at all these blokes to get to the bar. As they saw him coming, they just parted like the Red Sea for Moses. So our leather-panted Moses came back with a round of drinks and hadn't he enjoyed that show.

'Wouldn't you like people to step aside for you the way they do for me?' he said to Chance. 'All you gotta do is let people know you're the Widowmaker and they'll be falling over 'emselves to get out of your way.'

'Mate, I like it just the way it is,' Chance said. 'If it was any other way, I wouldn't be doing what I'm doing.'

I butted in: 'But he doesn't have to go around telling everyone he's a hitman to have people step out of his way, JR.'

'Yeah, I know they step out of the way of you and your brothers, too. I just reckon they'd do it a lot faster,' JR said. 'Sometimes I get sick of hearing about this Wrecking Crew of yours.'

'Hey, it wasn't us that called ourselves the Wrecking Crew,' I said. 'That was Jimmy Anderson. And I can't help it if people step out of the way when me and me brothers walk down the street.'

We were yakking on about this when my brothers walked in. But they didn't come towards us. They were at full steam, heading towards a far corner of the place, all chests out and steam coming out their ears. They didn't even stop to say hello to me. Something was going on. I got up and saw that there were some Jackals over in the far corner. I hadn't even noticed they were in the joint. A pillar had blocked my view.

I got up, turning to Chance and JR. 'You fellers stay out of it.'

My brothers were swinging before they even reached the Jackals. Snake leapt over a table to land right in the middle of them. It was a mess. I ran over and clocked a couple, but pretty soon I realised that this wasn't the time or the place to be squaring up. With all the top blokes from the Cross here, there was too much opportunity for things to spill over and for us to find ourselves bluing with all these blokes we had no quarrel with. I didn't want my brothers belting any of Lenny's blokes or George's blokes. We would have smashed them, too, but we didn't want those guys for enemies. My brothers didn't give a fuck about who was who, though. If they wanted to get someone, they got 'em and on that night it was the Jackals' turn.

I had to drag them away. 'C'mon, we'll wait for 'em outside.'

So we left. And as we stood a little bit down the road, my brothers explained that a few days earlier, a bunch of Jackals had tried thumping Wack in the Carousel Club. Wack decked about four of them, but copped a pretty good gash across his left eye with a buck knife.

We waited and waited for the Jackals to come out. It ended up that the bouncers threw them out and as soon as they hit the footpath it was back on. Again, it was down into the little lane on the side where I'd beaten up Icepick. They got stomped to the shithouse.

The Cross might have been neutral territory, but the Jackals had broken the rule by going Wack, so we were only getting payback. As far as the other clubs were concerned, we were in the right.

JR rang me at home that Sunday and told me that Big Lenny and George were going on about it. 'Lenny said: "Those Campbells are friggin' maniacs." They were both wishing they had youse working for them.'

'Well, that's not going to happen,' I said. 'Well, not as a family anyway.'

About five days later, I got a call. It wasn't hard for anyone to get my number. Just about everyone up the Cross had it. Not that I handed it out, except to some strippers and a few of the other girls. But they apparently handed it out left, right and centre. I picked up the phone and it was the Jackals' president, Grizzly (just about every club had someone called Grizzly or Bear). He wanted to have a chat about what had happened. He asked if I'd meet him at their clubhouse in Gladesville. I got into my gear, put on my cut and rode straight over. As I pulled up, this big bloke came out of the clubhouse. He hadn't been there on the night of the blue and I didn't recognise him. He turned out to be their sergeant-at-arms, a guy called Monster, who my brothers had told me was the one who'd started it all. 'You Caesar?' he said.

'That's right.'

'The prez will see you inside.'

'No, if your president wants to speak to me, he can come out here,' I said. I wasn't walking into the clubhouse without knowing who or what was in there. I wasn't that stupid. So Grizzly came out and he wanted to know what it was all about.

'Apparently, the night before the blue your sergeant-at-arms here kicked over me brother's bike to impress some sheilas up the Cross,' I said. 'Then he took off with a few of your other members, so me brothers went looking for him.'

Monster was standing there listening to all this. He stepped towards me and growled: 'Well, you tell your brother any time he wants to, I'm ready.'

'Really?' I said, stepping towards him. As far as I was concerned, if you wanted to fight my brother, you wanted to fight me.

As quick as I could, I lifted my boot and side-kicked him in just the right spot on the knee. As he was going down, I hit him with an elbow and broke his jaw.

I'm protective of my brothers, but we're all protective of each other. It would have been the same if he'd told Snake or Bull or Wack that he wanted to fight me. So now I had the rest of the Jackals standing outside the clubhouse looking at their president to see what the next move was going to be.

'You can consider this thing over,' I said, staring them down. 'Otherwise, you can step out here onto the footpath. I'll take all your colours.' I stared at them some more, daring them to come down. They stared back. And I did something I don't normally do. I took my shirt off. At that time I was built like I was working out with professional bodybuilders . . . because I was. I was training with the Australian heavyweight champion. I had a bigger chest than him. He had 20-inch arms and mine were 21.5 inches.

I'm not sure why I took off my shirt, but when I did, there was a 'Whoa' kind of thing came back at me from them. I think it's why blokes, especially these days, build themselves up and wanna look like Arnold Schwarzenegger.

They think their bodies impress people and scare them. Probably they do, but as a fighter I knew the best bluers weren't the muscle men, they were the ones with rock-hard bodies like boxers. I'd never think much about taking on some big meathead who struggles to fit through a door. It's probably true that the bigger, musclier blokes are harder to hurt, but there are still places you can hit them – under the side of the ribs, or in the throat, or the medulla in the back of the neck. You can cripple them there.

Anyway, the Jackals weren't game to come down and test out whether I was all show and no go. I gathered up my gear and rode off.

21

WHAT HAPPENS TO PAEDOPHILES

A couple of years after my little run-in with Mr Asia, Terry Clark was getting himself a big rep for taking out those who annoyed him. Even though he and Mr Sin had got off to a bad start, they must have come to some sort of arrangement because they started doing a bit of business. And when JR, Chance and I were sitting up in the Manzil Room or the Venus Room we'd hear people talking about all the blokes this Clark was meant to have put in the ground. I noticed that it really peeved JR.

'Why do you get so pissed off when you hear about Clark knocking someone off?' I said. 'You know it's probably bullshit. Why does it upset you so much?'

'Well, the main reason is that 95 per cent of the blokes Clark's supposed to have put in the ground, I did 'em.'

'You did 'em? You worked for Clark?'

'No, Abe took on these jobs that Clark wanted done, like a subcontractor. I went and did 'em for Abe and then

146

Clark's gone and taken credit for 'em. With some of them he'd wanted to know where the bodies were, and he'd go out and cut 'em up and mutilate 'em after I'd already wasted 'em. He's a sick motherfucker. I just don't like people taking credit for the jobs I do.'

'Don't blame ya,' said Chance.

I told him a joke and he had a bit of a giggle. 'That's better,' I said. 'The JR smile.'

'Yeah, JR, Caesar's right,' Chance said. 'Don't worry about it. You're the one who's pulled the trigger. Look at me. I've got this big reputation – "The Widowmaker" – and no one's got a clue who I am. Only you, Caesar and Mr Sin and that's it. And that's the way it's gunna stay. I don't give a fuck about people knowing whether I was the one who pulled the trigger. I get the job done and get paid. That's all that interests me. Not having people think I've killed 20 or 30. Don't worry about that fuckwit Clark.'

'Ahh, youse don't understand,' JR said.

'Yes we do,' I said. 'You want to be JR, King of the Hill. You like it when everyone's stepping out of your way. You like it when you walk up to the bar and blokes move away.'

Chance chimed in, 'But what about when you get some big footballer who doesn't know who you are, JR? You walk up to the bar and start being a smartarse and they beat the shit outta ya.'

'C'mon, Chance,' I said. 'It's not JR's fault that he can't fight.'

'Who are you saying can't fight?' JR wanted to know.

'Now, come on. How long's it been that I've been trying to teach you how to do it and you still can't fight your way out of a wet paper bag?'

'That's a bit harsh, Caesar,' JR said, his feelings hurt.

'Now, think about it, JR,' Chance said. 'With all this Widowmaker stuff, what's one of the things that scares people? The stories that the Widowmaker puts some of his victims through an industrial meat mincer. Clark's heard those stories, now all of a sudden Terry Clark puts some of his victims through an industrial meat mincer. But does that worry me? No, I couldn't give a fuck. If he's stupid enough to go around telling people that he does that, it just shows what a dick he is.'

Chance and JR were professionals, and as far as they were concerned, Clark was just a big-mouthed sadist who got his rocks off by hurting women and people who couldn't fight back. To them, what they did was a job and they did it as quickly and pain-free as they could.

Unless of course it was Chance with a paedophile. Then he did go out of his way to cause the bloke some distress. And who wouldn't?

*

CHANCE HAD a good friend, Barbie, who was a stripper up the Cross. She lived at Surry Hills and one afternoon around 1978 while she was getting ready for work, waiting for the babysitter to arrive, she heard a noise outside the door of her terrace house.

She went out the front and looked left and here was this bloke with her little girl under his arm, running down the road. She screamed out and a young bloke – about 13 or 14 – heard her and pushed his dragster bike in front of the guy. The bloke fell over, dropped the girl, got up and ran to his car. By the time Barbie got there, he was just pulling away in a blue sedan before she could get a look at the numberplate.

Barbie picked up her little girl and was giving her a great big hug when the young bloke tapped her on the shoulder. 'Here. He dropped this.'

He handed Barbie a wallet.

Barbie lived in our world, so she knew the cops would be useless. Didn't even report it. She got on to Chance and told him what had happened. Chance took a look at the wallet and got on to me.

Now remember, this is three parts fiction, 97 parts fact. Chance and I went and visited the address on the driver's licence, a place at Mascot in Sydney's south. We saw the blue car, we saw that the bloke living there matched Barbie's description. He was about 45 or 50 – ordinary sort of fellow with a Yugo or Polish accent.

He ended up in the boot of Chance's you-beaut V8 Falcon, bound up with tape and cable ties, and with a ball gag stuck tight in his mouth.

There was another bloke called Scrooge McDonald who ran the Cockatoo Club – a gambling joint in one of those huge old terrace houses down the end of Victoria Street, Potts Point. Scrooge also owned a property out the back of Windsor up towards the mountains some-where near a river. I'm not going to give the exact address. Chance got the keys to the place from Scrooge. He wanted somewhere private.

So Chance drove up to this property a good two hours north-west of Sydney with another sergeant-at-arms, let's call him Chains. I know I said it was me, but I think it was another sergeant-at-arms.

The way I heard it, they drove nice and steady, not wanting to attract any attention with this rockspider bumping and moaning in the boot behind them.

They arrived about 4 pm on a Thursday, already wearing overalls, latex gloves and the cheapest runners they could find. Chance got the bloke out of the boot. Car boots don't have good air flow, so the bloke was soaking with sweat as they carried him into the cabin – some shipping containers that had been converted into a basic little weekender – and decided what to do with him.

'Well,' Chains said, looking at the squirming rodent at his feet, 'you know, are you squeamish, Chance?'

'You know I'm not.'

They had a look around at what was available. Scrooge had cots and beds and tools everywhere. They noticed a welding machine and wondered if that might come in handy.

They found some plastic that was lying around that looked like it had been used as a drop sheet for painting. They laid it on the floor. Chance got the spot welder going and put four anchor points onto the bottom of the container. They tied him down, spreadeagled, to the anchor points.

Chance had brought an IV line with some water bottles and salt. Chains had brought along some sugar. They wanted this bloke to suffer. They got the IV line into a vein on the bloke's wrist, taped it on tight with some electrical tape and set to work on him.

They had a wire saw, like a surgeon's saw, a scalpel and a heap of medical tools. The bloke started going right off when he saw them get laid down next to him, wriggling and screaming these muffled screams. Chains put his weight on the guy's body, picked up the wire saw and started cutting through his leg just above the ankle, through the tibia or the fibula or one of those bones. When he cut clean through that first bone, he used the wire saw to then cut upwards, splitting the two bones apart from the ankle up to the knee. The paedophile was screaming his head off through the gag as Chains got a firm grip of the shin bone at the bottom and pulled it up through the skin all the way to the knee, ripping and crunching all those knee ligaments and cartilages.

The bloke's body shook and went limp.

Chance went outside and chucked up. He'd thought he was going to be the one doing all the damage, but when he saw what Chains was up to he realised it'd been taken to a whole new level.

Chains packed the sugar into the wound. Apparently it was an old remedy for stopping bleeding. Soldiers had used it in the Napoleonic wars.

They took the gag off, because the bloke was vomiting and unconscious. They waited for him to come around and when he did he was just screaming that he'd never do it again. 'I'll make it up to the kids,' he said, dobbing himself right in that he'd done it more than once. Didn't do himself any favours there. Those sorts of blokes don't let the kids go. They use them, kill them and dump the bodies somewhere out in the scrub. Chains had no sympathy. He was determined to make this last as long as he could.

Chance would pop his head in from time to time to see how it was going.

Chains set to work on the other leg, doing the same thing, ripping the bone through the skin nice and slow until the bloke went into convulsions again. This went on. They had to remove the gag every now and then because they didn't want him to choke on his own vomit. Chance changed the IV bottle to keep the guy's fluids up and more sugar got packed into the wounds.

They gave him some water to drink and cooled him down, getting him back to a fit state to cop some more.

They started on his right arm. Chains cut through the skin with a scalpel, then used the surgical wire to cut through the radius bone and pulled it out slowly. Left arm, same thing. Then they got a syringe and Chance went out to his car and opened the bonnet. He unscrewed a couple of lids off the top of his battery and sucked up the acid. He came back and that got injected into the rockspider's eyeballs. You can imagine what happened. They exploded.

The bloke was virtually dead by this, so Chance took the surgical wire and cut off his cock and balls. He bled out around about this time and stopped moving. After that he was dismembered: legs, feet, hands, head. They all got buried in different holes with plenty of lime thrown in on top to aid the decomposition process.

Neither sergeant had any regrets about doing what they did to a paedophile – a bloke who picked up a little girl off the street. Who could tell what horrors she would have suffered if he hadn't fallen over the young bloke's bike.

Both sergeants cleaned up the place. They'd brought plenty of bleach to wash down the whole area. They built a big hot fire and started throwing all the evidence into it. The groundsheet, the surgical gear, the bleach bottles. They stripped down and threw their blood-splattered overalls and runners into the fire. So they were standing there naked except for the latex gloves watching the fire burn. They tossed the gloves on last, then walked back to the car, changed into their regular clothes and drove back to the Cross, where they arrived about 3.30 am on the Friday. It had been a long night. Barbie was still working, so they went in to see her.

'The problem's been taken care of. You'll never have to worry about him again.'

She gave them a big hug and went back to work.

I never heard about there being any investigation into the paedophile's disappearance. I suppose his relatives put out a missing-persons report, but I never saw another thing about him. Thousands of people go missing every year. Hundreds are never found.

The only other bloke who ever heard the story was JR and, like me, he gave both Chains and Chance a big pat on the back and a hug. 'That's me boys,' he said.

22

DINNER AT CHERYL'S

When I got home one night, Donna told me that Cheryl had rung and invited us over to her and JR's place for dinner the next night. 'Who else is going?' I asked.

'Cheryl thought you'd want to know that. She said Chance and a couple of Cheryl's girlfriends and that's it.'

'Give her a ring back and tell her we'll be there.'

We rocked up about 7 pm. Cheryl had roast beef with all the goodies. Another great feed. Us fellers were yakking away. Sometimes we couldn't hear ourselves over the girls' cackling. After we'd finished, the girls took all the dishes and that out to the kitchen and Donna helped Cheryl with the washing up. JR, Chance and I disappeared down to his bunker and let off a few rounds. In between our shots, we'd sit on one of the lounges and he'd get drinks from the fridge he had down there.

Chance and JR were talking shop when Chance turned to me. 'Caesar, do you know the spot on the body where coroners hardly ever look for puncture marks?'

'Let me guess. The belly button.'

'How'd you know that?'

'I saw it on a TV show about three months ago.'

'What show?'

'I don't know. *Quincy*, or something like that.'

'They had that?'

'Yeah.'

'Well, I'll be fucked. But it's true. They hardly ever check belly buttons for a needle mark. That's my favourite spot to put 'em. I used to have a problem getting it in there when the patient was squirming, but since you showed me that sleeper hold with the pressure point on the neck, it's been a lot easier.'

He was talking about the artery and nerve on the left side of the neck. If you put your thumb and forefinger in and pull them out and squeeze hard, it knocks a person out in eight or nine seconds. The longer you hold it, the longer they're out. You've just got to watch that you don't hold it too long and kill them.

The more high-profile people that Chance got rid of couldn't just be dumped out at sea or put through the mincer. Their disappearances would have created too much of an uproar. The cops would have been all over it. So he had to make them look like accidents, or, his favourite, the injection of potassium chloride to make them look like heart attacks. Potassium chloride has been used in the States for lethal injections in death-row executions. The heart muscles just stop working, so it looks like a heart attack to investigators because it *is* a heart attack.

We got back to the topic of guns. Both JR and Chance knew more about how to pull a gun apart and put it back together than I did. I could do it, but not like them. I was just as good a shot, however, and we had a few competitions going until Cheryl came down the stairs saying the girls were getting bored.

When we went back up, Cheryl's girlfriends weren't too interested in what JR had to say. They were over at me and Chance wanting to know what outlaw bikers did and would we take 'em for a ride. Donna was quick to jump in, 'Well, Chance might take you for a ride. But Caesar isn't.' Chance's old lady jumped in just as quick. 'And neither will Chance.' So that shot the two girlfriends down.

23

GUITAR AND WHAT HAPPENS TO GATECRASHERS

I was down the local shops one day, talking to the butcher, Bob. We were pretty good mates. He was telling me he was up our pub, the Illinois, a couple of nights earlier. 'Some of your brothers were in there. Just how many of you Campbells are there?'

'Brothers?'

'Yeah.'

'Eight. Would have been nine but I had a brother, Stephen, who died when he was three days old. Does that answer your question?'

'Yeah, that's a big family. You've got a heap of sisters, too, haven't you?'

'Yep. That's enough of being nosy for one day. How much do I owe you for the chops?'

I paid him and left and cranked the bike over and headed home. When I got there, I pulled into the driveway and there was another bike sitting there with the death's head on the tank. I recognised it straightaway as belonging to Guitar. He was sitting on the front verandah with Donna having a cup of tea. Guitar preferred it to coffee. And everyone knew the rules with the Campbells and their old ladies. No one went in the house unless we were home. Whenever I went out, my big red and white bull terrier, Buck, was put inside. I'd trained him so that if anyone went near Donna, he'd rip 'em to pieces. She was always safe.

Guitar had just dropped around for a chat. He did that a fair bit. The Woman took the meat inside. She brought me a Coke and we sat out there exchanging biker-world gossip until it got a bit cool.

'You wanna roll your bike into the garage and stay for dinner?' I said.

'I'd love to.'

So we both rolled our bikes in and went inside. Buck wanted to take Guitar's leg off at first. He was so protective of me that he just wouldn't cop other people getting near me. I had to tell him to sit in the corner. Buck obeyed and sat there, but he wouldn't take his eyes off Guitar, who was a bit uneasy about it all. Buck, however, was that well trained he just stayed where I told him. After a while, Guitar hardly even noticed he was there. I put on a Roy Orbison record, followed by some Buddy Holly.

We had a great meal and Donna had made a pavlova, so we sat back and spent the night talking. Guitar was always good company, full of stories about the biker world and his brothers over in the States. I don't know why they called him Guitar. I never saw him play one. I used to call him Banjo to stir him up. 'My name's Guitar, not Banjo,' he'd say.

'But you're built more like a Banjo than a Guitar.'

'I'm Guitar, okay?'

He was quite proud of his name.

In the wee hours of the next morning, Guitar decided he'd better head home.

'You can crash here for the night if you like.'

'I'd love to, Caesar, but if I don't go home the old lady will kick me out.'

'Yeah, well, you do spend a lot of time away from home.'

'You know what it's like.'

'That I do.' We went out and took the padlock off the garage and wheeled his bike out and got it started. He took off out of the driveway and I walked up to the letterbox to check for mail. As he was hurtling up Liverpool Road, I watched as everybody coming out of the RSL club at closing time stopped to watch this big Hells Angel roaring up the road.

*

THE NEXT week, I saw Guitar up at the Illinois. He was one of the very few bikers that me and my brothers let into our pub. We were sitting there with Snake, Shadow, Wack, Chop and Bull when he told us about a big party at Macdonaldtown the next weekend. Snake was interested, so Guitar gave us the address. I ended up going with Snake, but all the other brothers had something else on. It was quite a rocking little party. There were only about 50 people there, but a ton of sheilas and they had a local band of young blokes who pumped out some good music.

About 1 am, though, everything changed. All of a sudden there were all these cars rocking up, fancy horns blaring out Dixie like the *Dukes of Hazzard*. Yobbos in flannel shirts and lumber jackets were pouring in. They must have all left a pub at closing time together. There were 70 or 80 of them, and they were just straight into it, smashing up things, hassling the band. Snake said to this sheila he was getting friendly with, 'Come on, I'll take you and we'll go.' We were walking out, but the yobbos gave us the whole look-at-the-big-bad-bikies thing.

It was on. We hit one or two out near the front gate, but I saw the yobbos start surging out through the front door towards us.

A block away, there was a footbridge across the railway to a train station. 'We're going to have to get to that bridge,' I called out to Snake. 'Get the bikes.' We ran to the bikes and kicked 'em over and these blokes ran to their cars. They screeched out behind us but we darted in behind some cement blocks where they couldn't ram the bikes. We hoofed it up the footbridge stairs. The yobbos thought they had the big tough bikies on the run. 'Look at the poofters.' 'Stand and fight, ya gutless wonders.' They were pretty brave when they were chasing us in a big pack.

When we got to a landing, halfway up the stairs, we turned.

Snake got his chain off. I got my fists up. And as these blokes came up the stairs we were into 'em. Most of them had just run down the street and on the way they picked up whatever they could lay their hands on. They hit us with wooden fence palings and those iron spikes that terrace houses have on their fences. They threw bottles at our heads and the gamer ones came at us with their fists.

I don't think any of them landed a punch, but we copped a lot of wood and metal. Snake had blood pissing out the side of his face. I had it pouring out the top of my head and from a cut in the chin where a bottle had got me. But we just kept pounding. Kicking. We never back down from no one.

We belted that many blokes and left so many of them lying on the stairs that the other blokes couldn't climb over them to get to us. They were stumbling and slipping over the bodies, yelling out what they were going to do to us.

'Well, come on, we're standing here, ya cunts,' Snake yelled back. 'Come and have a shot. See what we've done to your fucking mates. Me and me bruvver. We'll take the fucking lot of youse.'

I usually try to calm things down, but we'd gone way past that. I let loose. 'C'mon, you cocksucking wimps, c'mon.' We were at boiling point, but our opponents had lost their fire. We started stepping down over the bodies ourselves, coming right back at them. We had to dodge the odd bottle flying through the air that would go smashing down onto the tracks behind us. And now it was our turn to pick up the palings and iron bars that they'd dropped, swinging wildly at them. But their most staunch blokes were already out cold and the rabble that remained soon decided it would be better to fuck off. They jumped into their cars and sped away, leaving their mates in a big pile on the stairs. Quite a few cars remained. Their drivers must have been the blokes having a snooze.

We went back to the bikes, which fortunately hadn't been touched. Snake and I, though, were covered in blood and bruises. It was a mad fight. We had trouble starting our bikes because our legs were so weak from exhaustion and wobbly from the adrenaline. We eventually got them going and headed home. We lived pretty close to each other in Ashfield at that time. I made sure Snake got into his joint before I headed home. I rolled my bike into the garage and hauled my aching body into the kitchen where The Woman, who'd heard me come in, had put a toasted cheese and tomato under the griller.

Two nights later, Guitar walked into the Illinois. 'I heard you and your brother had some fun over at Macdonaldtown.'

'Yeah, thanks a lot. It was a good party, but you coulda given us a clue there might have been some gatecrashers coming.'

'Caesar, if I'd a known that was going to go on . . .'

'Anyway, what happened to you?' I asked.

'Well, I had some club business and by the time I got to the party, there was coppers everywhere. I never seen so many ambulances. Fuck, which brother was with ya?'

'Snake.'

'I shoulda guessed. Fuck, youse made a mess of 'em.'

'Yeah, well whaddya want? There were 60 or 70 of the cocksuckers.'

'I know. I got told. I just can't believe you two did that much damage to that many blokes.'

'You better believe it.'

'No wonder nobody wants to mess with you Campbells.'

HOW TO TRAIN A DOG TO ATTACK ON COMMAND

It's all repetition. I'd get my brothers to come in and whack me with a newspaper and I'd say 'Help!' and I'd urge my dog onto my brother, who would whack the dog on the nose. So the dog starts to see that me getting hit and the word 'Help!' are the same thing as him getting hit.

When I first got Cougar at six weeks old, I was the only one who fed him. He slept on the bed alongside me, then on the floor next to me. I got it so that he saw the two of us as one and the same. He was happy to spend the whole day sitting at my feet, save for half an hour to have a crap and lie in the sun. If anyone came near me, like if my daughters gave me a hug, he'd stand up and grab them by the arm, really gently, and he'd pull them away till they were about six feet from me. Then he'd walk back and sit down between me and them.

When all my grandkids came down, they'd sit on him and bounce on him and ride him through the house. But if one of my mates came in and gave me a bear hug, he'd drag them off. He got Witch by the arm one time and dragged him into the hallway, then started baring his teeth and growling when he came back.

'Just sit down for a few minutes,' I said to Witch. Then I said to Cougar, 'Friend.' And patted him on the head. He was cool after that, but he never left my side or took his eyes off Witch.

I got into a blue in the back of the Aussie hotel in Cooma one time. I had Cougar in the car with the window half down, and I'm punching on with about five of these blokes so Cougar's gone bang and busted the window to get out, and he got this bloke down on the ground ripping the shit out of him. 'Fuck this is going to be nice,' I thought. I could see the headlines. 'Pitbull attacks pub patron.' And I'd be fighting for his life, but nothing came of it fortunately.

He was the quietest dog going around. He never barked unless someone was at the front door. I don't know why people say pitbulls are savage. They are the most loving, affectionate family dogs.

24

BRANDY SNAPS

About 18 months after we'd had our run-in with the Jackals, I saw Guitar up the Cross. 'I hear the Jackals have closed down because you and your blokes have been hunting 'em down,' I said.

'Yeah, the fucking wimps,' he said. 'We've been looking for 'em for three or four months. They kept moving and we kept missing 'em and now they just seem to have disappeared. We got hold of some bloke who was a hang-around, and he told us they'd closed down and gone their own way. Some interstate, some to the country. A few of 'em kept their colours, but the rest had burnt 'em.'

It didn't come as any surprise to me, having seen the way none of them would front me after I'd smashed their sergeant, Monster. That's the way some blokes are. They open these pretend outlaw clubs. They get the sheilas and they scare civilians, but when it comes down to it they turn to jelly.

'Well, you'd be feeling good, wouldn't you?' I said. 'Another club youse have closed down. If they're that easy to scare, they were never going to make it in our world anyway.'

'You're not wrong, Caesar. I still remember the time you walked into our pub to face up to us when those pricks from the Phoenix told you we were looking for you and were going to bash ya.'

'Yeah, and I remember the first time you walked into our pub. Chop was going to bite off your ear.'

'So do I. I'm glad you spotted me, knowing you and your brothers . . .' He paused for a bit, then turned to me. 'That bloke you hang around with, JR, are the stories about him true? About him being the number one hitman in the country?'

'They certainly are,' I said. 'You wanna tell your blokes if they ever mess with him, he's always tooled up and he's a firecracker. If you get him wound up, he'll pull 'em on ya and he'll use 'em. He doesn't care where you are, who you're with, what time it is. If there's a dozen coppers standing around, he'll still put a hole in ya.'

'Yeah, that's what I heard. I wasn't sure whether to believe it or not.'

'Well, you can believe it. I know him real well.'

So the next time I was up the Cross with JR, I spotted Guitar and called him over. 'Guitar, this is a really good mate of mine, JR. JR, this is Guitar, the sergeant-at-arms of the Hells Angels, who's also been a mate of mine for years.'

JR gave me a funny look, as if to say, 'So what?'

'Calm down. Be nice,' I said, like I was talking to an overexcited pitbull.

Guitar, who was a lot bigger than JR, gave him a funny look until JR smiled and patted him on the shoulder.

'Nah, I'm just geeing you up, big feller.'

Guitar had a bit of a chuckle. We wandered over to Sweethearts and they had a coffee while I had a shake. JR started telling Guitar stories about me and him, and Guitar told a few about him and me. This went on for about three hours. I'm listening to 'em both rattling on like it was an episode of *This Is Your Life* when we heard a huge roar of Harleys hooning into the Cross. It was Metho Tom and the Nomads. Tom saw me and nodded. I nodded back. The Nomads did their big lap and parked. Tom wandered into Sweethearts and said g'day. He knew Guitar, but he didn't know JR, so I introduced them. The four of us were sitting there. I ended up stirring the pot by reminding all three of them how many times I'd pulled them out of a fight or stepped in to save their bacon. 'Especially you, JR.' Both Metho and Guitar were good with their fists, but there had been a few times where I'd had to back 'em up. 'But there's been a few times where you've stepped in to back me up too, Guitar and Tom.'

'That's true, Caesar,' Tom said. 'That's true. Us Newcastle boys have got to look after each other.'

We were sitting there talking about the different clubs coming up the Cross of a Friday night when Sy and Arm from Lone Wolf came in, as did Matchie from the Angels. The whole place was filling up with well-known outlaws when JR motioned to me that he wanted to have a word, so we moved outside.

'What's up?' I said.

'I just got a message,' he said.

'What, from Lenny?' I'd just seen Little Lenny Baker slip out of the café.

'Yeah. He just handed me a note. Mr Sin wants to see Chance straight away. Have you seen him around?'

'Well, it's Friday night, he'll be out there somewhere.'

'Can you run him down for us, Caesar? If anyone can find him, it's you.'

'Yeah, I'll find him for you.'

So I went cruising around all the usual haunts until I pulled him out of the Rex Hotel, where he was having a beer. I walked him around to Abe's office and went upstairs.

'You want me to wait outside, Abe?' I said.

'You can do something for us, Caesar. You can watch the door. Make sure no one comes in. And I mean no one.'

So I left him and Chance talking and I could hear virtually everything. My ears pricked up though when I heard the name of a prominent politician, let's call him 'Wayne Kerr', and then I heard Mr Sin tell Chance that Wayne Kerr needed to take a long, long holiday.

Just then the phone rang and Abe put his hand over the mouthpiece and told Chance, 'Come back in half an hour, will you? I've got to take this call.'

Chance and I wandered off down the street. 'Did you hear any of that?' he asked.

'A bit.'

'Surprising the people who turn out to be paedophiles and child bashers and people who rip off old people's funds and do all this nasty stuff to good people,' he said.

'Well, it sounds like you'll be taking care of one part of the problem.'

'Yeah, I'm looking forward to it. Wouldn't you?' he asked.

'No, no. If you need some blokes thumped or put away for a few hours, I'll give you a hand, but the rest I'll leave up to you. I was an altar boy. Being a Catholic and an altar boy, I don't know that I can be friendly with a hitman.'

'You're being a bit of a hypocrite, Caesar. You're looking down at me for what I do.'

'Nah, what are you carrying on about?'

'It sounds like you think what I do is the wrong thing. Yet I've been to every one of your round-ring fights and there's been quite a few, and I mean quite a few, where blokes that you've fought have gone off for the long holiday.'

'Yeah, but I don't know where you get the idea that I'm looking down at you, thinking that you're doing bad things. You're taking care of paedophiles and these blokes who are doing the wrong thing. I think it's great. But don't get too stroppy. You might be good on a dark night, but if you want to push, don't push too hard or you'll find yourself not fitting it up.'

'You'd really have a go at me?' he said.

'If you wanna be fair dinkum, you'd last about 30 seconds.'

Chance just looked at me. It was like looking at a mirror. We were both toey when our honour was being questioned. He thought I was doubting his honour, but then I wasn't going to be spoken to as if I was frightened of him because he was the Widowmaker. He didn't scare me one bit, so it was a quiet, frosty 20 minutes until Chance broke the ice.

'You wanna come over the cake shop?'

'Yeah,' I said. 'I wouldn't mind a cake.' The bakery in the middle of the strip made great stuff.

So we went over and Chance ordered himself two big chocolate eclairs. 'What are you having?' he asked.

'I'll have a dozen of those little brandy snaps.'

'Ooh, brandy snaps,' he said, and looked to the woman over the counter. 'Actually, can I cancel my order and have the same as him?'

So we were sitting on our bikes eating the brittle rolled up biscuits filled with cream when Little Lenny came down and said, 'Abe'll see you now.'

'Well, best you trot off and see Mr Sin,' I said.

'Yeah, but don't forget you work for him too,' Chance shot back at me as he walked off.

'Yeah, I know that. There's no need to get your shirt in a knot.'

I sat back to finish my brandy snaps as Sy and Arm from Lone Wolf came up. I'd known them for that long it was hard to remember when I'd met 'em. We'd all started outlawing around the same time. It was as if there was a whole bunch of us who were just born to be outlaw bikers. Anyway, they were looking at my bike. I'd just got a new Panhead and Sy had done a lot of work on it to bring it up to speed. Sy was one of the two best Harley mechanics in Australia.

It's a shame that Sy is no longer with us. He passed away in 2015. I felt really bad about not making the funeral. I was in Canberra Hospital in a coma. I hope his old lady and daughter know that I meant no disrespect.

But getting back to Arm and Sy, they spotted my last brandy snap. 'That looks good,' Sy said. So I broke it in two and gave half to him and I was holding the last half.

'Nice,' Arm said. 'You could have given me a piece.' Arm had a big bushy beard and a bald head with the Lone Wolf colours tattooed on the back of his skull. He looked as sad as a rained-on cat watching us eat. I was waiting for Sy to give him a bit of his, but he didn't, so I gave him a bit of mine. Sy ended up going over to the cake shop and bought out every brandy snap in the place. He came back with this dirty great box of 'em. He gave me and Arm a couple and there were Lone Wolves coming from every-where to get theirs.

So I was yakking on with Sy and the rest of the Wolves when we heard a rumble coming up the street and all the bikers in the Cross stopped doing what they were doing and waited to see who it was. A big and well-established club rumbled down the street. They and the Wolves didn't have a good relationship at the time, so Sy and Arm did the smart thing and got all their boys back around their bikes. Even though it was neutral ground, it was best to keep everyone in tight. That way there was less likelihood of blokes bumping into each other and causing trouble, and if there was trouble, you were all close and ready. But after about half an hour, everybody could see there wasn't going to be a problem, so everybody went back to what they were doing.

I wandered up Darlinghurst Road and ran into Guitar. We went round the corner and down to the Manzil Room to have a drink. Soon, JR and Chance turned up and joined us and we spent the next hour or so bullshitting, with everyone telling everyone else how much better they were than the rest of the blokes at the table. I got a bit sick of it, so I made my goodbyes and wandered back to my bike. My brothers were chatting up some strippers who'd just come off work.

I told them I was heading off. Each one of my brothers had got a girl for the night, except Bull. He was like me. He was happy with what he had at home, but he decided he was going to stay up the Cross a bit longer, so I rode off and did a Uey and went down William Street and out along Parramatta Road, thumping along at 100 ks and that was it for the night.

Or I thought it was. When I got to Leichhardt, I ran into four blokes from the Road Barons riding Jap bikes. Three of them were on 750 Honda K1s, and the other was on a 900 Kwaka. Normally, they would have left a Harley for dead, but my Panhead was a 93 cubic inch. Sy had had all the parts imported from the States and the Baker brothers had ported and polished and bench-blown the heads. The motor was blueprinted and balanced and it had an S&S carby on it, the same as the rest of the parts in the motor, so she had plenty of grunt. When I got up alongside the Road Barons, we all sort of looked at each other and one of them I knew by sight gave me a nod and it was on. We tore down Parramatta Road at over 150 ks. No helmet. The speedo had wound off, but my Panhead was still accelerating. I don't know what speed we got to, but I was in front when I slowed down at Ashfield Park because my turnoff was coming up. I gave a nod to the bloke I sort of knew and they kept on down Parramatta Road.

I turned into Frederick Street and pulled into the driveway. I rolled her into the garage and The Woman had a toasted sandwich under the griller and a can of Coke out for me. And thanks to Donna, the night just kept getting better.

*

I saw Sy about a week later and told him about the drag with the Road Barons.

'So you're happy with the work I done?' he said.

'More than happy. The thing goes like a bat out of hell. For a Panhead to blow off three 750 K1s and a 900 Kwaka, she's gotta have some grunt. That was up top. If it had been off the mark, I don't know who would have won, but I know I was pulling away as the needle bounced off. Nah, she's got some real grunt in her. You did a top job. It'd be interesting to see you and Greenie each build a bike and see who could put together the fastest and most reliable road-going Harley.' When I said Sy was one of the two best Harley mechanics in the country, Greenie from the Nomads was the other one.

'Who do you think'd win?' Sy asked.

171

'I don't know. That's why I said it'd be great if someone gave you some money and let youse loose to build a bike without any money restrictions.'

'Yeah, it would be interesting. You seem to have a bit of money whenever you need it,' he said.

'Get out of it. I'm not paying for it, but I might be able to get someone to come up with some sort of contest where they could make money and youse two could build your bikes.'

Over the next month I thought about what I'd said to Sy and in the meantime I'd run into Greenie and told him my thoughts. He was all for it too, so I went up the Cross looking for an SP bookmaker I vaguely knew. We'll call him 'Slim'. Slim didn't mind taking bets on all sorts of contests, so I started asking around to get in touch with him, but didn't have any luck.

I was sitting in Sweethearts when Chance came in.

'Have you seen Slim around?' I said. 'No one seems to have seen him for the last three or four days.'

Chance leaned in closer. '... And no one will be seeing him.'

'You haven't?'

'I have.' The smile on his face was like he'd just pulled off the best practical joke ever but wasn't ready to tell anyone yet.

'Why?'

'Because.'

I told Chance what I had wanted Slim to do and Chance said it was a top idea. 'Probably every outlaw biker in the country would turn up to a contest like that. Slim could have made a lot of money running a book on it, but you won't be getting him to back it.'

'Good on ya,' I said a bit sarcastically. 'You couldn't have waited a couple of months?'

172

'Nah. It was a rushed job. Actually, I didn't want to do it because I like to take my time and scope out a job before I do it, but this one was a special. I got double my usual rate. What do they say? "He sleeps with the fishes."'

'Yeah. Good on ya.'

'Well, why don't you ask Abe to back it?'

'Nah, Abe wouldn't be interested in doing something like that. Unless he can make mega bucks, he's not interested in doing anything.'

'You never know.'

'Well, you get on with him better than I do,' I said. 'You ask him.'

'All right, I will.'

For the next week or so, every time I saw Chance I pestered him about asking Abe. Eventually he got back to me. 'Nah, you were right. He's not interested in getting mixed up with the biker scene.'

'Well that's pretty funny since you're his number one hitman and I'm his number one collector . . . and he doesn't want to get mixed up with the outlaw scene?'

'Yeah, when you look at it that way, it is a bit ironic.'

So we sat on our bikes and chatted and watched the traffic on Darlinghurst Road.

'I heard that Wayne Kerr died in a car crash,' I said.

'Yeah, very sad,' he said. 'So young. You just never know when the reaper might come knocking, do you?'

'Or the Widowmaker,' I said.

He left it hanging there like Ronald Ryan. And we watched the girls go by.

25

STONE

About a month later I was up at a motorcycle dealership and I was talking to the owner Phil. We were pretty good mates. He was huge. About six foot ten. He'd just bought a big job lot of all the bikes they'd used in the movie *Stone*. All those dark Kawasakis with the mad paint jobs. He had the star of the movie, Ken Shorter, there doing PR work for him. They were telling me about the impact that the movie had had, so much so that a club had started up called the Gravediggers just like in the movie. 'Yeah, I know,' I said, 'but they're not going anymore. Me and me brothers took their colours about three weeks ago.'

'You did what?' Ken Shorter said.

'He means that they no longer exist,' Phil said. 'That he and his brothers shut them down.'

Ken Shorter didn't have any idea what we were talking about, so we took him through it slowly and he finally got it. He looked at me suspiciously while I was looking at these Kwakas. They were all stock bikes with loud exhausts and lairy paint jobs. Shorter said all the fancy riding in the movie was done by stunt riders, which I'd already guessed anyway. He asked what I thought of the movie.

'Not much,' I said. 'You know, whoever made it, he might be a nice bloke and all that, giving a patch to the Vietnam vets, but he's obviously read too many *Easy Riders* and *Biker Lifestyle* magazines.' There wasn't much in the movie that rang true for an outlaw biker.

I think Ken Shorter took an instant dislike to one Caesar Campbell, which didn't worry me. He was an ex-copper.

He left and Phil turned to me. 'I think you upset him.'

'Well, shit eh.'

'I mentioned that I knew you and some of your brothers because we were talking about outlaw bike clubs and he said he'd arrested one of your brothers when he was about 15.'

'Yeah, that's when we were living in at Surry Hills. He picked up Shadow for getting into a blue. Brought him home and Shadow copped a good whacking out of that from the old man. But, yeah, he did know us.'

'Hang on, the phone's ringing,' said Phil, excusing himself.

So I walked around the shop and he had a couple of second-hand Harleys there and one of them wasn't a bad bike. It was a near-new Low Rider.

I waited for Phil to get off the phone and asked him what he wanted for the Low Rider, because Bull was looking for a new one. Phil gave me a good price and we did a deal, so Bull ended up with a near-new Low Rider. I took it around to his place and he was pretty happy about that.

We sat down to watch some TV. His old lady, Chris, was cooking us up some steak, eggs and chips. It was a good relaxing afternoon till a fight broke out in the backyard between some of Bull's seven hunting dogs. Some of the great dane–pitbull–Rhodesian ridgeback crosses were in pens, but others were roaming the backyard and they got into it. Big, solid dogs, they were going at it hammer and tongs. Bull and I ran out and tried to grab them by the collars to pull them apart, but with four of them there'd always be one getting a bit of leeway. Bull's wife, Chris, had the hose on them and us. We got them apart eventually, but both of us ended up with bites up our arms. So what had started as a good relaxing afternoon had ended as one where I was soaking wet with dog bites, saliva and shit all over me from these bloody great mutts.

*

YEAH THE '60s and the '70s, they were the years. Outlaw clubs had twenty times more runs than they do these days. The clubs were tighter because they were smaller. Clubs didn't want to own Australia. You just had clubs that were there for the brotherhood and the fun of riding. If you had two dollars in your pocket, you'd give your brother one. You shared your women, except your old lady. If you had a spare tyre and your brother needed one, you gave it to him. You didn't sell it. If a brother's bike needed fixing, then everyone would throw in parts they had lying around.

Back in 1963 and 1964 when Dad moved us down to Victoria, there were already outlaw clubs down there. There was Bad Blood, which I think started in 1951. There were the Vigilantes, the Outlaws. I'm not sure if that's the same Outlaws that are still going today. There were Black Angels and a couple of others. Just seeing these clubs made me want even more to live the outlaw lifestyle.

When I was wrestling down there and I won the state championship, I was hanging around more with Bad Blood than I was with my own family – which was unusual for me, because our family was really tight. When we moved back to Sydney at the beginning of 1965, that's when I decided to start the Gladiators.

A lot of people always wondered why the Gladiators from Newcastle and my club never got into it. I don't really know why. We both started up about the same time. They didn't bother us and we didn't bother them. I know it was unusual to have two clubs with the same name, but I always figured if they wanted to be the only club called the Gladiators, we weren't hard to find. And my old man used to say, 'Always remember where you come from.' I was a Newcastle boy and I didn't want to start having trouble with a club from Newcastle, because there was a good chance they'd have been blokes that I grew up with.

It couldn't happen these days. There were two clubs called the Vikings in Sydney. They went to war and a lot of shit happened. Arthur Loveday, who later became well known as the spokesman for the Bandidos in Australia, was in one of the Vikings clubs. He'd gone and got the full club patch tattooed on his back when he was still a prospect. The president of the Vikings came around with his vice-president, Lucifer, asking me if I'd chastise Artie for having the tattoo on his back before he'd become a member.

'Well, that's your job isn't it?' I said. 'You got a sergeant-at-arms, Mousie. He's three times the size of Artie.' Back in them days, before Artie hit the 'roids in jail, he wasn't a very big bloke, but he had a reputation as being pretty vicious.

I did them a favour and had a yak to Artie. I explained to him that it was the wrong thing to do, but it wasn't my place to tell him off. 'Go talk to your president or your sergeant. Sort it out. I'm pissed off that your blokes are that worried about you. You're a pipsqueak. Look at Mousie, he's three times your size. I know you've got a reputation for being a bit of a crazy, but crazy only gets you so far. If you were in my club, I'd have kicked the shit outta ya, and I'd have burned it off your back. It would have been the end of you with my club.'

Artie wasn't too happy with that. Anyway, he stayed with the Vikings then, but he later had the good fortune to join the best club in the world and I'll just say, Artie, I hope you're with the Ride Forever chapter and you're having a good time.

BIKERS IN HOLLYWOOD

I don't think any movies have got the biker world right. Not one. I thought the television series *Sons of Anarchy* might be going to do it after watching the first four or five episodes, but then they went off the rails. The gun violence, the drugs and paying off coppers were all off the mark. And the drive-bys and shootings in main streets were ridiculous.

Having said that, I would have loved to have had a chapter as staunch as the blokes in *Sons of Anarchy*. You'd have the toughest chapter going around. In the last season, they had a bunch of real Hells Angels in the cast. If they'd asked these blokes about what really happened in their clubs, *Sons of Anarchy* could have run for another ten seasons.

While they overdid the gun side of things, some of the stuff that goes on in outlaw clubs – the violence and the women – would make *Sons of Anarchy* look tame.

The worst biker movie was the 1974 Australian flick *Stone*, and a 1991 American effort called *Stone Cold* was pretty bad too. Then there's been a few things like zombie bikies and werewolf bikies. I don't know whether to laugh or cry, so I just cringe.

The miniseries about Milperra, *Bikie Wars: Brothers in Arms*, was pathetic. They had me on a Sportster. I never rode a Sportster in my life. It's a girl's bike.

The best documentary was put out by the Hells Angels themselves. It was called *Hells Angels Forever* and it follows them from the time they started. I think you can still get hold of it. It's the best one I've seen.

26

CARBONARA MAGGOTONI

One day at Sweethearts I was talking to Chance about the whole secrecy thing surrounding the Widowmaker. He told me he had no idea where the name came from or who gave it to him. He just started hearing about himself on the grapevine. And he didn't mind it that way. 'People know that the Widowmaker's around and if you get on the wrong side of certain people he'll pay you a visit and you'll cease to exist,' he said. 'No way would I like people to know who I am, like JR does. I love JR like a brother, but I don't like the way he flaunts what he does. One day it's going to be his undoing. All those namby-pamby wannabe hitmen that he hangs around with like the Sattler brothers and Popeye Wilson (not their real names). He's not keeping good company and it's going to be his undoing.'

While I kind of agreed with Chance, I had no idea how spot-on his prediction would prove to be.

And JR didn't mind taking a few unnecessary risks. Besides being Australia's number one hitman – a title which Chance could have laid claim to if he had been at all interested in titles – JR was a real practical joker. One time, I was at his place when Cheryl told me about the time he put some rancid meat out in his backyard. She was wondering what he was doing, but knew better than to ask. After a few days, the meat was riddled with maggots. He collected them all and put them in his freezer to kill them.

There was a smack dealer up the Cross called Giorgio the Whale. JR had done a job or two for him, but he didn't have much respect for him. Giorgio surrounded himself with guys from Sicily for bodyguards and he thought he was a real Godfather. I'd been in a blue with one of his blokes and knocked him out, so Giorgio wasn't real keen on me, but he thought JR was the best thing since sliced salami.

So JR got these maggots out of the freezer and got Cheryl to make up a spaghetti carbonara, only, instead of using pasta, he had her put the maggots in there instead.

He took this carbonara maggotoni up to Giorgio the Whale at the Carousel Club and greeted him with the big Italian hug, handing him the pasta in an insulated container. Giorgio tucked into it and scoffed it. Thought it was the best meal he'd ever eaten. When he'd finished, he said, 'Your wife a good cook. You must be a happy man.'

'I am. And now you've had a good Australian dish.'

'What do you call it?'

'This is what we Aussies call maggot salad.'

The Whale didn't get it.

Telling the story later as we sat back after one of Cheryl's more edible feasts, JR said the situation got a bit dicey because all of the Whale's blokes were getting real toey. 'They'd understood straight up what I'd meant when I said he'd had the old maggot salad. Next thing, he was spewing his guts all over the floor of the club.' If it had been anyone else, Giorgio would have had his balls, but JR just sat there laughing his head off.

Apparently, after the Whale came up for air, he walked up to JR. 'Why you do such a thing to me, Johnny?'

'It's a compliment, Giorgio. My wife she make-a this all my best friends. It is tradition. You know about tradition.' Giorgio thought he'd been complimented by JR, having his missus make up this maggot salad. JR walked out of the club thinking, *Dumb fucking wog.*

I said to JR, 'You're a cheeky bloody prick. What if one of Giorgio's blokes had pulled a piece on ya thinking you'd poisoned the boss?'

'I'd have put air in his head. Drilled him a few ventilation holes.'

'You're one of a kind.'

'Thanks, Caesar. That's a nice compliment coming from you.'

'If you don't watch your practical jokes, JR, someone's going to put air in your head.'

'Never.'

CAESAR'S LAW

XII

MY FAVOURITE RECIPE

I haven't cooked for a couple of years, but my speciality when I did was a pretty hot chili.

Donna was a great cook who used to do a lot more than just the toasties I've mentioned in this book. All the roasts, steaks and stews, six days a week. But on Saturdays I'd give her a break and do my speciality. I'd cut up some tomato, onions, carrots and potatoes, throw them into a pot with some blood beans and four jalapeno chilies all diced up with the seeds left in. I'd add between one and three tablespoons of Tabasco, a teaspoon of wasabi, three bay leaves and then just let it cook for about three hours.

I'd end up eating most of it myself because it was too hot for everyone else.

When I got shot in the stomach about four, five years back – a drive-by in my front yard – it did something to my duodenum and I can't handle the real spicy foods now. That's a bummer.

27

COMANCHERO

While the Gladiators were the most feared club in the state – the tightest band of brothers you could get – to be a successful club we needed more than that. It had to be more than me and my brothers. I wanted to bring in new blood, but my brothers were deadset against having anyone new who wasn't a top bluer, comparable to themselves. Those sorts of blokes were hard to find. To me, if a bloke is staunch, if he'll back you up no matter what the odds, if he loves riding his bike and loves the colours, well then he's going to be a good member even if he can't fight so good.

The Gladiators were stagnating. I never wanted a big club, but the other clubs were starting to expand and get real big and we were stuck with just seven or eight members. As a result of this debate with my brothers, I ended up leaving the Gladiators in 1978 and not long after that they decided to fold the club.

As I described in the first chapter of *Enforcer*, there was an outlaw biker called John Boy who'd caught some blokes putting my bike on a truck and helped me to beat the shit out of them. I gave him my word that if I could ever do him a favour I would.

I don't regret much about my life, but if I had my time over again, the one thing I would definitely take back would be giving John Boy that promise. John Boy was a good bloke and all, don't get me wrong. But soon after I left the Gladiators, John Boy asked me to return him that favour and join his club, the Comancheros.

The last thing I ever had on my mind was joining the Comancheros. I'd been talking to Guitar and it looked like I might have been going over to the Hells Angels. As it happened, Guitar was away for a couple of weeks when all this went down. Otherwise, that's where I would have been and all the shit that followed would have been avoided. Like my old man had pounded into me: 'Never give your word lightly.'

Having said that, I found four or five really good blokes at the Comancheros – blokes like Sheepskin, Mousie, Davo, Charlie and Opey. All a pleasure to be around and I knew they'd back each other up. And to be truthful, the club president, Jock Ross, wasn't so bad either. Jock persuaded me to ask my brothers to come over too, with the promise that they'd do their prospect time with a minimum of shitkicking. They all agreed, except Wheels, who didn't like Jock. Our addition made the Comancheros the most feared club in Sydney and that didn't hurt our ability to recruit more good blokes like Lance Wellington, Leroy and the McElwaine brothers – Knuckles, Gloves and Dukes – who were elite-level boxers.

It was only a small club when I joined, 13 members, but over the next 18 months we increased it to about

25 and had something like 15 prospects on the go. Eighteen months later, we were up to 42 members. We ruled the whole of Parramatta and all the surrounding district. If you weren't a Comanchero, you didn't drink at any pub in the area unless we said so.

The increase in numbers was all due to my brothers and I changing the club culture to being more about partying and riding. Before that, they just used to drink at their pub in Ermington and play pool. They rarely went anywhere or did anything else. Jock didn't like his club members talking to other outlaws for fear that, if they ever went to war with the other bloke's club, they might not want to punch on against their mate. So we'd rarely seen them up the Cross.

Jock made me sergeant-at-arms soon after I was patched up and I did my best to change a lot of that and to make the club more about getting out there and having fun. You've just got to look at the numbers. The club had been going for 12 years when I joined and it had 13 members. Five years later it had 42 or 44.

This was too many, I now realise. But that wasn't so clear to me then.

When I first joined the Comos, we were down the Melton Hotel in Auburn one night. There were still only 14 of us and I hadn't really seen them in action, so I didn't know who could handle themselves. A fight started with some members of the Executioners. Jock was up against this bloke who was six foot five. They went at it, punch for punch. Jock was holding his own when little Charlie walked up behind the bloke. Charlie had a fondness for pool cues and he got this bloke a beauty across the temple and down he went. Jock blew his cool because Jock reckoned he had the bloke's measure, and from the way the fight was going, I think he was right. But Charlie was only doing what

I'd brought to the club, and that was that you look after your brother no matter what. Even if it meant you took the knife or the bullet for them. That's what Charlie was doing – protecting his brother and president.

Sheepskin and I took on the rest of the Executioners by ourselves. We looked over at each other as we dropped them. I saw Sheepie using a backswing elbow. He was very good at it and I thought he must have trained pretty hard in martial arts, which I later found to be the case. I went to his home one night and one of his young sons, Ryan, dragged me over to look at something. He opened a large cupboard door to reveal a jumble of martial arts trophies piled high. It would have taken me two days to count them all. I knew then that we had one bloke in the club who would always have my back.

I got on well with the president, Jock, for a long time. One time early on he and I went for a run up to Wisemans Ferry with just the two of us. We sat up at the pub there and yakked on about bikes and sheilas and blues we'd been in. It was a good day.

He told me his plan for building the club and stretching it out to different states and I thought that was a good thing. I wasn't thinking of chapters in every second suburb. I was thinking one chapter in every state. I liked the idea of having national runs and having clubhouses in all the states where you could crash.

So we were sitting at the pub this day getting on real well, with him telling a yarn about his days in the British Army, sipping on his spirit, when nine hefty blokes came in with their sheilas. You didn't need your crystal ball to know that these types of blokes were going to want to show the girls how tough they were by picking on the outlaws. The afternoon changed in an instant from convivial chatter to extreme violence. Jock and I stood shoulder to shoulder, punching the shit out of these blokes. We decked the lot of 'em. The whole nine.

We walked out with our arms over each other's shoulders. We got outside and gave each other a big hug and told each other we loved each other. We rode back to the clubhouse. It was club night. Jock couldn't wait. He set himself up near the bonfire in the backyard, and started rolling out the story.

Roger, Sparra, Snowy and Mousie couldn't take their eyes off him, soaking up every word, like they knew they were hearing the first reading of a new folklore. By the time Jock had finished, we'd fought about 30 blokes. But I wasn't gunna interrupt him. He was happy.

Part way through, he broke off the story to say, 'I told all you men I made the right choice when I made Caesar my sergeant-at-arms. The man's got a hit on him like Thor's Hammer. Hey, Caesar. We gave it to those buffoons.'

'That we did, Jock. That we did.'

Roger turned to me. 'Did Jock really knock down that many blokes?'

'Hey, he's your president – would he lie to ya?'

Roger went back to soaking up Jock's aura. Jock got about two or three hours out of it. I sat back and enjoyed the story as much as the other blokes. He was a good yarn spinner. It ended up being another great night at the clubhouse, with, as usual, the prospects out the front watching the bikes. We also had a couple of prospects up on the factory roofs around us with 12-gauges making sure that no one snuck up on us.

I know I've been critical of Jock's militaristic ways in the past, but I must admit that I was involved in the idea to put them up there. I can't just lay that on Jock. The clubs from the suburbs surrounding Parramatta were getting restless because we'd got so big and were throwing our weight around.

There were rumours in the air that one of our larger rivals was going to challenge us by coming and drinking at one of our pubs, or by hitting the clubhouse. If you want to take on another club, both of those moves would be reasonable.

One thing I can't stand in the biker world is clubs condoning their members going to blokes' private houses to do club business. Up to the early '80s, there was a warrior's code that you never went to a man's home. If you were looking for him, you waited 100 metres down the street and ran him off the road. Pounded him. Did whatever you wanted to him. You got him at his local pub. Got him at a set of lights, in the park, but not with his kids. They were the two rules. You didn't touch him at home. You didn't touch him if he had his kids with him.

These days a lot of clubs let their members go to people's homes, whether they have kids or not. It's especially bad if the kids have to watch their dad getting punched to the shithouse by blokes who have got no honour. I don't care if blokes from clubs that let their members do this think I'm full of shit, or that I deserve a kick in the head. There's no honour in going to a bloke's house where you know you've got him cornered or belittling him in front of his old lady and kids. Be a man and get him by himself. If it's just business, do it by yourself. If it's club business, take some members with you, but either way, get him away from his home.

I know some clubs like the Jokers and Lone Wolf still live by the old code and, if you don't, I just say to you that you've got to be able to look at yourself in the mirror.

Anyway, nobody attacked us and our hold over Parramatta and surrounds remained secure.

CAESAR'S LAW
XIII

HOW TO BE A GOOD LEADER

Put your club and members first, before yourself.
Make sure you've got time for every member who's got a problem and go out of your way to help them with that problem, whether it's family matters or financial. If it's a club problem, it's important to have the strength to know when to say no to them and having the authority to keep people in line so they don't end up doing stupid things.

If you've put their needs first, they respond better when you give them an order.

28

MORE BRAWLS, MORE SEX

The 1980s dawned and they proved to be just a continuation of the 1970s for my brothers. They drank hard, fucked hard, rode hard and definitely fought hard. And now we were doing it with a new, much larger, band of brothers.

I remember one Saturday afternoon I was at the Tollgate Hotel in North Parramatta with Charlie and Dukes. They got a game of pool going while I sat back at the bar having a lemon squash. A bunch of about 20 park footballers walked in. They had some sheilas with them and, surprise surprise, as soon as the chicks saw the colours they were over flirting with Dukes and Charlie. Again, no crystal ball was needed to see how this was going to play out.

The boyfriends didn't like it. They started on Charlie and Dukes. Dukes was a top boxer – even though his old man used to call him 'Canvasback'. Charlie whacked into them with his pool cue. He was only a little bloke, but he had a big heart. I rushed over and got into it, knocking 'em down as they came at me. I saw Dukes drop three onto the canvas and Charlie had dropped two with his cue before five of them jumped on him. I worked my way through the rest of them to get over to Charlie. I pulled three of them off and Charlie turned around and said, 'Leave these two cunts to me.' He broke the cue and started stabbing them in the guts with the splintered part. The two blokes pleaded with him to stop.

I ended up pulling him off so he didn't kill anyone. Dukes had decked another one or two by this, so that when we left – and we left quite quickly – there were blokes lying all over the Tollgate floor. We headed straight back to the clubhouse and I congratulated Charlie on how well he went. 'I didn't think you were that good, Charlie.'

'Only when people get me mad, Ceese, and those pricks got me mad.'

*

ANOTHER TIME on a club night this Hillman Minx, one of those old-fashioned British cars, pulled up outside the clubhouse with three sheilas in it. Opey and Davo soon disappeared with two of them in the Minx until, not long after, Davo came running back: 'Caesar, we got a problem.'

'What?'

'You're gunna have to come around the corner and see for yourself.'

I went out and walked around the corner and here was Opey with his pants down on top of this sheila but he couldn't get off her because his boot was stuck in the glovebox. Once we'd stopped laughing and called a few more of the fellers around to analyse the problem, we ended up cutting his boot down to the heel so we could pull his foot out. He got himself a good root but lost himself a good boot. Poor old Opey didn't hear the end of it for the rest of the night.

*

SATURDAY NIGHT was club night, but as part of my plan to get us on our bikes more, showing off the colours more, I'd instituted a weekly club ride before we settled in to party at the clubhouse. When you saw something like 40 Harleys boring down Parramatta Road, it was a sight to behold. We'd go all the way into town, do a circuit of the Cross to let everyone know the Comancheros were still ruling the roost, then over to Bondi, back through Randwick and on to Victoria Road, because we used to like racing along next to Rosehill racecourse. Everyone liked to see who could get over the railway tracks the quickest and who'd be first back to the clubhouse. It was always between me, Lout and Shadow.

Suitably pumped up, we'd begin the partying. We had some rip-roaring nights at Granville. The music was always cranked up, there was always a big bonfire in the backyard, plenty of food. All the old ladies were there, plus the strays. All our old ladies knew the rules. If a member turned up with a stray, they treated her as if she was the old lady and didn't cause any trouble by dobbing to the real old lady. Otherwise they'd be banned from the club for anywhere from six weeks to life. The old ladies had to live by a code too.

*

ONE NIGHT, my brothers and I were cruising through Earlwood on our way to a party when we spotted these sheilas with tiny dresses and huge tits out waving balloons on the street. We saw a sign saying 'Penthouse Club' and there was a screech of brakes, the bikes were spun around and parked and we walked into this club that was virtually empty. It had something to do with *Penthouse* magazine and they had their girls parading around in different costumes.

We'd been there for a while with Bull and I sitting back enjoying the show, him having a beer, me sipping on my orange juice, when we looked around and noticed that we hadn't seen the rest of our brothers for a while. I looked out to the bikes and they weren't there. We wandered around the club looking for them but the place was pretty empty so it was obvious they weren't there. I asked a barmaid if she'd seen any Comancheros. 'Yeah, a bunch of 'em went out the back,' she said. So we went down this corridor into a back room and here's Shadow, Chop, Wack, Snake and Wheels all rooting these *Penthouse* sheilas. The ones from the magazine. You had to laugh. It was quite a scene.

Bull and I spent the rest of the night back out in the bar area while my brothers went to town on these models. I was bored as all get out. Every now and then one would emerge: 'Come out the back. You won't believe what's out there.'

I was fine where I was. But there was also another sheila there who seemed to be the most important one. She came over for a chat and it turned out she was a celebrity centrefold from *Penthouse* in America or one of its sister publications. Whoever she was, they thought she was important enough to give her four huge African–American bodyguards. She started cracking on to me, but I told her I wasn't interested. I knew Donna was all the woman I needed.

Maybe I didn't tell this centrefold politely enough, or maybe she wasn't used to dealing with rejection, because she sicced her four black beefcakes onto me. 'You're gonna get your heads kicked,' she said, as they came at me smiling with all their glistening muscles and gold chains.

These guys were enormous – 130 kilograms of pure fast-twitch bulk. And I could tell by the way they moved that they knew what they were doing. I reckon they weren't used to rejection either.

Bull was standing alongside me and, as the first one came nearest, he's gone *Bang!* Dropped him cold. Things didn't get any better for the bodyguards. There were only about six punches thrown and the four guys were lying at our feet. We'd dropped two each. Bull and I looked at each other like we knew we'd just done something special. We gave each other a hug.

'I wonder how they'll tell the story when they get back to America?' he said.

'I reckon they'll be telling their buddies they kicked the shit out of us. It's too bad we didn't have a camera here,' I said.

'Either that or they'll claim they got ambushed by a gang of bikers with baseball bats.'

We went out the back and told our brothers it was time to go. As we got on our bikes and started the engines, we heard sirens coming from Campsie way. So we headed the other way, towards Marrickville. We cruised on there, then up to the Cross to our usual haunt, the Venus Room.

Bull and I sat there quietly satisfied by our night, while Wack, Chop, Wheels, Snake and Shadow were noisier about theirs. They bombarded us with stories of all the different ways they'd rooted these centrefolds. Me and Bull were looking at each other smiling. As long as your brothers were having a good time, who cared?

I was thinking of gathering the brothers up at about three or four in the morning when this big Maori walked in. He got into an argument with Snake so, as usual, we're all getting up to go over but, by the time we got there, Snake had headbutted him and split his nose, and was stomping the shit out of him. It took four of us to pull him off. I think the Maori bloke ended up in hospital. Snake is one bloke you don't want to get angry, because he gets real nasty.

We went out, got on the bikes, kicked 'em over, went down through the main drag of the Cross, down William Street and onto Parramatta Road and headed off to Ashfield, where most of us lived. I pulled up at my place and switched the bike off and rolled it into the garage all quiet. We had a block of flats next door. I didn't want to get the neighbours offside and Daniel was just a young bub.

The Woman came out and asked if I wanted anything to eat. She was the best thing that ever happened to me. I covered the bike up after it cooled down and she had some sandwiches on the table for me and a can of Tab. I sat down and started to eat and thought how good life was.

HOW TO PICK UP CHICKS

Get a Harley.

You can put a 50-year-old 140-kilo biker and a 30-year-old businessman with a Porsche in a club and the one that's going to be leaving with the hottest chick is the biker. That's a fact. Don't believe me? Try this. If your wife or girlfriend has a good-looking girlfriend, I'd say that whenever blokes hit on her, 99 per cent of the time she shuts them down, right? Next time you see a bike show advertised, take her to it. I'll bet you your wife's girlfriend leaves that show on the back of a Harley. Put money on it.

There wasn't a night went by when a bloke sitting on a Harley up the Cross wasn't hit on by some sheila. 'Take me for a ride and I'll give you a root.' Even these old blokes in their 50s and 60s who used to sit near Sweethearts would crack at least one a night. That's what a Harley will do for you boys if you're struggling to make it with the ladies.

Beyond just forking out for a Harley, the recipe for being able to pull chicks totally at will is to start hanging round with a bunch of outlaw bikers for a few years. Show them you're staunch, do your year or so as a prospect, get patched up, never back down from no one in defence of your club, be prepared to be hit by baseball bats and bullets. Make sure you shower.

You'll be in like Flynn.

29

THE ICEMAN

I was sitting at home one night when I got a call from JR. He wanted me to meet him up the Cross. So I put my colours on, jumped on my bike and rode to the Manzil Room. Chance was there too and he asked what JR wanted.

'Mr Sin's got a job for ya.'

He told me the details.

I screwed up my face. 'You can tell Abe I wouldn't get out of bed for that sort of money.'

'You're joking!'

'I'm not joking. If he wants something collected, he knows the go. Everyone else round here might charge five to ten per cent but I charge 35 per cent and that goes for everyone.'

Chance interrupted: 'Caesar, you oughta come into our line of business. You'd make a fortune, and we've both seen you shooting. You're as good as we are.'

'Maybe, but shooting targets is a lot different to what you and JR do.'

'Let's change the subject,' JR suggested. 'How's your mum going, Ceese?'

'She's doing pretty good.'

JR turned to Chance. 'If you ever get to meet Caesar's mother, you'll meet the best woman ever put on this planet. She raised 14 kids. Caesar's dad died at 46, so Caesar had to help raise his brothers and that. That's probably why they're so tight. My mum, god bless her, she died a couple of years ago and I was a real mess. If it hadn't been for Caesar, I probably wouldn't have pulled it together.'

'Yeah, you only get one mum,' Chance said. 'You gotta look after 'em.'

'Caesar, tell Chance that story about you and your mum when you went to the pictures when you was a kid. That's a crack-up.'

'Well,' I said, 'my old man was known around New-castle as the best street fighter and pub bluer there was. He was known as Big Frankie C. I saw him in a lot of fights. I used to always hear him say to other blokes and sometimes us kids, "Hey sport, if you don't watch it, you're going to get the thrashing of your life."

'This day, me and me mum have gone to the pictures at the Strand up at Newcastle. We were watching *Robin Hood* with Errol Flynn. He was Mum's favourite. We came out at interval for a choc-top ice cream and this bloke pushed in front of her. He looked like a big bloke to me, but I was only about ten. I said to him, "Hey sport, don't push in front of my mum. Are you looking for the thrashing of yer life?" He just started laughing at me and gave me a bit of a shove. And then I heard the bloke say, "Oh, Big Frankie." The old man had come out of nowhere and was standing there. Next thing the old man's given him this big backhander and floored the bloke. Dad's standing over him saying, "Don't you ever put your hand on my son."

'Anyway, we didn't get to see the second feature. The old man took us home and on the way he gave me the big lecture: "You might think you're going to be something special when you grow up, but till then, stick to kids your own age. Don't go taking on full-grown men." And I said, "Yeah, but he pushed in front of Mum." "I know you were trying to stick up for your mum, but no one would have touched her. Everyone knows she belongs to me."'

'So your old man had a bit of a reputation up there, eh?' Chance said.

JR butted in: 'Not only Newcastle. In the '50s, Big Frankie C was as well known up the Cross as he was in Newcastle. Not many people wanted to mess with him. You know who he used to knock around with, don't ya? Blokes like Ces Rolls.'

'Really?' Chance said, his ears pricking up at the mention of the old-time hardman.

'Yeah, Ces was a mate of the old man's,' I said.

'Your old man did travel in some heavy company,' Chance said.

'And it wasn't just Ces Rolls,' JR said. 'He drank with Chow Hayes and Darcy Dugan and Jockey Smith. Caesar's old man got around.'

'I never knew this,' Chance said.

'Well, you know now.'

I told the story about how he would come down to Sydney and go to the Tradesman's Arms Hotel in Darlinghurst – now yuppified and renamed the East Village – and he'd always have a beer with Paddles Anderson, who was the first real Mr Big of Sydney, but on other days he'd be inviting senior coppers and/or the mayor of Newcastle over for dinner at our home.

'I remember one night he brought me down to Sydney when I was ten or 11. He went to take me into Chequers nightclub and these bouncers told him I couldn't go in. They wouldn't budge until this really big bouncer came out. "Oh Frank, come in." The other bouncers said, "You can't let him in with a kid." The big guy turned to Dad and put his arm on his shoulder. "Sorry about these fellers, Frank. They're new." As we went through the door, he turned to the other blokes. "You know who you're talking to, don't ya?" They're looking at Dad blankly. "This is Frank 'the Iceman' Campbell." All of a sudden they were all looking at him very respectfully and maybe a little scared, and I'm standing there wondering what's going on.

I hadn't heard the Iceman bit before, but suddenly these blokes are trembling and I'm wondering, *What the flip?* We get taken to our table and the singer Bobby Limb comes over and he's shaking the old man's hand. (A while later, Dad ended up with Bobby Limb's E-Type Jag. What that was for, I don't know, but he got it.) On the way home, in his great big Yank-tank Ford Customline, I'm quizzing him on the Iceman thing, and he's going, "I'll tell you one day, son". I pestered him about it for weeks, but he wouldn't tell.'

'So, did you ever find out?' Chance said.

'Years later, I got him to the point where he told me he'd tell me on my next birthday. But he died before I got there. That was in 1969.'

'That explains a lot of things about you, Caesar,' Chance said. 'Sounds like he was a tough customer but managed to spend his whole life out of the limelight and out of trouble. It's a bit like JR and me.'

So we sat there for another few hours bullshitting to each other and said our adieus and each of us went our own ways. I headed home and as usual The Woman was sitting up waiting, wanting to know if I needed something to eat. As I was tucking into my food, the phone rang. It was Dukes. 'You've got to come up to the Illinois.'

*

So I GOT my colours back on and rode over. There was a ton of sheilas there and a whole heap of Comos, all having a rocking good time.

One of the bouncers up there, Terry Regan, was a young bloke down from the country playing first grade for Balmain. Regan was a real hard-tackling forward and a good friend. When it came closing time, Dukes and some of the other Comancheros had told him that I wanted him to keep the pub open, or the back part at least, because we had a lot of sheilas rocking up. So Terry did this for them, but he was waiting for me to arrive so I could keep an eye on them. Dukes was worried he was going to kick 'em out if I wasn't there.

Terry had unlocked the jukebox. Everyone was playing their songs for nothing. People were dancing on the pool table and on the dance floor. It was what the life of an outlaw biker was really all about – when you're with your brothers and a ton of women, letting it all out. It's when the blokes bond and get that feeling of brotherhood. I sat back and had a great time just watching.

This went on from about 1.30 am through to about 4.30, when Terry said to me, 'You're going to have to get 'em out of here and get a few of 'em to help me clean up.' So I got some of the prospects and sent 'em to work for Terry. And I said to Dukes, 'You're the one that started all this, you can get in and give 'em a hand too.' He helped straighten the place up so everyone was happy.

But Terry was worried that the boys were doing this sort of thing a bit too often. He pulled me aside. 'We're going to have to quieten this down a bit, otherwise the coppers are going to wake up to what's going on and I'll be in all sorts of shit. I'm surprised they haven't busted the joint yet.'

'Yeah, thanks for doing it for us, Terry. I'll have a word to the boys and tell 'em that no one's to stay here after closing unless I've given you a tingle and cleared it first. So, unless you get a ring from me, don't open the place up.'

'Thanks, Caesar.'

*

THERE WAS a Tuesday night when Donna and I, plus Chance and his old lady, rocked over to JR's for our regular meal. We went there about twice a week, but it turned out this night was going to be special. While we were eating our roast lamb with loads of mint sauce, JR kept hinting that he had a surprise for us. So, after we'd polished off the bombe alaska, we left Cheryl and the old ladies to yak on while we went downstairs.

As soon as we got into the bomb shelter, JR turned on the light. Sitting there in front of us was a Tommy gun, like we'd all seen in the gangster movies.

'How'd you get that?' I said.

'That's for me to know and you not to find out . . . Watch it go, man.'

He picked it up and started firing and boy did it make a mess of the target. The .45 bullets smashed into the sandbags at the back of the range. I had my hands over my ears, and by the time he'd emptied the circular magazine, the bunker was thick with smoke. Me and Chance couldn't wait our turns. Because JR and I were best mates, he gave it to me first.

I held it in my hands, thinking about Babyface Nelson and Eliot Ness and all those old gangster movies. My hands slotted nicely into the wooden finger grooves on the handle at the front. And then I pulled the trigger, *Rat a tat tat*.

I didn't hear the noise or smell the smoke. It was like starting a really loud Harley. It might have been a god-awful racket to some people but to have it under your control and to just let it rip was beautiful to experience.

It had a bit of a kick to it, though. You really had to hold it down.

Chance got his go and he was in love with it as much as I was. But the ventilation in the shelter wasn't up to all the gunsmoke and nitrates in the air. As we retreated up the stairs for a breather, he was hassling JR, 'I'll buy it from you. How much did you pay? I'll double it.'

'No way,' JR said.

We had quite a night that night. We spent about three hours down there, taking regular breaks for the smoke to clear and for the barrel to cool down. But it also got hard to talk after a while. Our ears were ringing too much.

CAESAR'S LAW
XV

BEST ADVICE I EVER GOT

My old man told all us kids, 'You treat others as they treat you.' I told my kids the same thing. I told my girls if they were with any bloke and the bloke was showing them respect they should give respect back, because my girls tend to be a bit hot-headed. With the boys, it was always, 'Make sure when you go into a pub or a house that you don't know, you check it out, find the ways in and the ways out, and the best spot to defend yourself. Always stand and sit with your back to a wall.' That's what Dad taught me and I've never forgotten it.

30

BLOWING THE HOUSE DOWN

I was yakking to Guitar one day at the Illinois and he got on to my round-ring fighting and also about how he'd seen me in a few fights for my club. 'You were always up front. I've been in a few fights with you and I know what you can do.'

'Yeah, well, you're not too bad for a tubby little bloke, either.'

'Enough of the tubby-little-bloke business,' he said. 'That's all muscle . . . and I'm not that much shorter than you.'

'Come on, you're like a great big teddy bear.'

'And the girls love it. Anyway, I wanna have a talk.'

'All right, come up to my booth.' We went up and sat down. 'What's up?'

'Any chance of you leaving the Comancheros?'

'No, I don't think so. Why?'

'I'd still like you to come over and ride with me and me brothers. And bring your brothers with you.'

'Nah, everything's going along quite smooth at the moment,' I said.

'Yeah, fuck, youse have built that club up. I remember when there was only ten or so of 'em and then you and your brothers join and now there's about fucking 40 of youse.'

'Forty-four to be exact,' I said. 'I don't mind telling you because you're a mate.'

Most clubs don't like giving out the exact number of members. And if they do give a number, they usually up it by a third. But with Guitar, we'd been getting around the traps together for years and doing a lot of riding together, so I trusted him. He was only looking out for his club.

'Guitar, we'll stop talking about that anyway, I'm not leaving the Comos.'

'No worries. There's something else I gotta ask you about,' he said.

'What?'

'About Matchie and Max from the west chapter. Apparently they were at your clubhouse not long back and there was a bit of trouble there. I've heard Matchie and Max's side. Do you wanna tell me yours?'

'Ahh, you know what Jock's like. There were a few sheilas come in and he wanted to impress them. He said, "Get those Angels out of here." I don't know why Jock wanted me to do it. He was quite capable of doing it himself. Matchie, Max and me were having a bit of a yak and I said to them, "It's best if you leave." Matchie told Jock to get fucked and I more or less ushered them out of the clubhouse.'

'That's not how I heard it,' Guitar said. 'Matchie said you practically carried him out.'

'Oh, I don't know about carry. I mighta picked him up a little bit, but it all ended up good. I left with them. We got on our bikes and went down to the Rosehill pub. Matchie and Max carried on drinking. I ran into Shadow and Wack down there with a couple of sheilas.'

'When isn't Shadow with a sheila? Every time I see him he's got a different one. Hasn't he got an old lady?'

'Yeah, he does, but you know . . .'

'It's that way, is it?'

'Yeah, if it wasn't for the kids he wouldn't be there. But, yeah, we had a good night at the pub with Matchie and Max. We played a bit of pool and they had a yak to all my brothers. You know what me and Matchie are like. We're like me and you. The best of mates. So that was all.'

'Yeah, I was just wondering.'

'Well, now you've heard both sides, you can make up your own mind.'

'Are you coming up the Cross tomorrow night?'

'When aren't I up there?'

*

I WAS still getting plenty of work from Abe, but I'd sometimes work for other people if the money was there.

One time, I went out to Galston on the north-western edge of Sydney, collecting for a mate who was owed some dough for some coke.

I spoke to these blokes who were living in a garage on a large rural block. They said they didn't have the money, but they could get it for me in three days. So I let them off the hook. 'All right, you've got till Friday.' I turned to walk back to my car when next thing I heard, *Ping, ping.* They were shooting at me with a .22.

You pricks.

I went down to my XR Falcon. Nicest car you ever seen. I'd spent 20 grand on the brakes, suspension and a crate motor out of a Nascar. I happened to have a 12-gauge shotgun in the boot, so I pulled it out and pumped it. I started firing at the roofline of this fibro garage and I kept firing and reloading, working my way along until the whole side of this garage collapsed.

I heard a pathetic voice from inside.

'We've got the money. We've got the money.' They handed it over, plus they had more, so I took that too for my trouble.

*

NOT LONG after I met Donna I was at the Manzil Room when a good mate of Abe's, Barry Bath, found me there. He was owed some money and was facing a lot of shit if he couldn't get it back.

'I've sent four blokes to collect this money,' he said, 'and they've all come back either bashed up or told to go fuck themselves.'

'I'll give it a go,' I said. 'You know I take 35 per cent?' He shrugged as if to say, 'What else can I do?'

'Where is it?' I asked.

'He's on a yacht down at the marina at Double Bay. His name's Enrico. He's a tough little prick. Portuguese or Brazilian or something.'

I walked up to the boat, and stepped on board. I heard someone moving down below, so I went straight down the little wooden stairs and saw a bloke there in the galley.

'Enrico?' I asked.

'Yes, that is me.'

'You owe Mr Bath.'

He let fly with a kick and caught me under the left arm. He was spinning round and kicking like he was doing

Capoeira, that Brazilian martial arts dancing. Jumping and spinning. I could hardly move, the space was so confined. He was right in his element.

I was still in hard training then and was built like the proverbial shithouse, but I was all bent over and squashed while the little prick was going to town on me – *Boot! Bang! Boot!*

'Fuck me roan.' He landed more kicks than I copped in my entire round-ringing career.

So I just walked in on him, cut down his space and crushed him into a corner with my weight. I got the cable ties on him and asked for the money. 'Things can be nice,' I said. 'You've had your little bit of fun. Hand over what you owe and that'll be it.'

'You go fuck yourself.'

Here we go.

So I broke his pinkie. Nothing.

I broke the rest of his fingers, one at a time. Nothing.

I pulled out the needle nose pliers and ripped out his fingernails. Nothing. He looked at me with his black eyes, staring hatred.

'I give you nothing, you motherfucker.'

Motherfucker? Enrico was clearly the toughest bloke I'd ever collected off and maybe the stupidest.

I found an icepick in a champagne bucket on his bar. As I came towards him with it, maybe his eyes faltered a little, wondering what the fuck I was going to do with it, but still they just stared me down with contempt. I stuck the icepick in under the back of his ear and started pushing. I knew how painful that pressure point could be. I got it in about a centimetre before he started yelling.

He was beaten.

He took me aft and showed me a barrel of oil. He put his arm in and started pulling out plastic bags full of money, which was pretty difficult for him with his hands so badly busted up and bleeding, but there was no way I was sticking my hand in there. I made him get me another plastic bag to put all these slippery bags into. I didn't want to count the money there, with all the mess, so I broke my usual rules and didn't count it on the spot.

'If it's not the right amount,' I said, 'I'm coming back to put you in the fricking barrel.'

I took all the money up to Barry. We counted it out and it turned out to be enough with $30,000 left over. 'All right,' I said. 'That's mine. Now count out my 35 per cent.'

Barry was quite happy to give me that.

'Caesar,' he said, 'I thought I'd done me dough there. I've had some blokes breathing down my neck and if I hadn't got this much back I'd have been fucked.'

'Glad I could help you, Barry.'

31

SHARPIES

One afternoon, Sheepskin came round to my place asking if I'd go for a ride with him to Town Hall.

'One of my girls got thumped by this Town Hall sharpie,' he said. Sheepie had girlfriends everywhere. 'He won't be hard to pick out,' he said. 'He's got a swastika and an Aztec sun tattooed on the side of his head.' So we went for a ride. The sharpies used to hang out at a pool hall behind Town Hall. So we went down there and this joint was full of these blokes with homemade tatts, bald heads and hardware-store chains around their necks. Pretty much the first one we saw when we descended the stairs into the smoky room was this bloke with the swastika and the Aztec sun on the side of his noggin. Sheepie went over and had words with him and gave him a flogging. Didn't need my help for that.

But a few more of them there decided to jump in to help their mate. Can't blame them for that. So we flattened them too. We were just starting to leave, satisfied with a job well done, when about 20 of them came down the stairs ready for a blue. Somebody must have gone and got them. Well, Sheepie and I stood there, back-to-back, pounding the shit out of these blokes. Pool cues were swinging at us, chairs flying. All of a sudden I got this massive hit to the cheek. I thought some bloke had blindsided me with the quickest, hardest punch ever. I wobbled a bit, dazed, wondering what had hit me. Took me a few moments to realise it was a pool ball. Whoever threw it, I reckon they could have played for the New York Yankees.

I recovered enough to finish the job and we limped out of there with bodies all over the floor and about eight of them hotfooting it down the street. Sheepie had the biggest black eye and my cheek was all swollen. My mouth tasted of blood. We jumped on the bikes as sirens started drowning out the other noises of the city, getting close. We figured we'd shoot over to my mum's place at Woolloomooloo and lie low there for a while.

We pulled up outside the modern four-bedroom terrace and she came out, 'Now, what have you two been up to? As if I can't guess. Sheepskin, you're as bad as Col.' Mum never stopped calling me Col. She was the only one who didn't call me Caesar.

'Oh Mum,' Sheepie said. (Everyone in the club called her Mum.) 'We couldn't get out of it. We were minding our own business sitting on the bikes having a hot dog when all these blokes jumped us.'

And they reckoned I could talk shit.

So he was talking to Mum and I looked in the mirror at the lump on my cheek getting bigger and bigger. Mum put some ice on Sheepie's eye. 'Well, whatever happened, Sheepie,' she said, 'it looks like you came off worse.'

'He always comes off worse, Mum,' I said.

It turned out that Sheepskin and I were practically family. We were talking about our dads one time and I mentioned some of the old-time gangsters that my dad used to know, and wouldn't you know it, Ces Rolls turned out to be Sheepskin's stepfather. As we talked about it and the people our dads knew, we realised Sheepskin knew a lot of the same people, and he'd fought a lot of the blokes I'd fought. So that made us even closer.

A bit later on, I was talking to Sheepie about our dads and where we grew up and all that. Sheepskin grew up in Rockdale, so I mentioned JR – Johnny Regal.

'Yeah, I know Johnny,' he said. 'Him, Brian Mason, me and a whole lot of others used to hang around together when we were young blokes. How long have you known JR?'

'Since the early '70s,' I said. 'All the way through up to now. I still see a lot of him.'

'You'll have to give me his number,' Sheepie said.

'I will next time I've got The Woman with me.'

'Why would you need The Woman to give me the number?' he said.

'Because Donna's got just about every number I ever need in her head. She's like a computer. Once she sees one, she never forgets it.'

So a couple of weeks later, on club night, I gave Sheepie the number and he caught up with JR and had a good yak about old times. Then one night, Donna and I were over at JR's place when Sheepie turned up. JR hadn't told us he'd invited Sheepie, which didn't worry me because we were club brothers and I wasn't going to tell Sheepie what JR's business was.

After a meal – lamb, because Cheryl knew Donna loved lamb – and a yak, we all ended up down in the bunker. And the four of us spent a couple of hours shooting. Sheepie turned out to be a pretty useful shot. JR gave him one of his Berettas and he improved a lot as the night progressed. He wasn't up to our league, though. JR and I had been shooting down there up to twice a week for almost a decade, so we had a lot of practice under our belts.

With a little tuition, Donna had become quite a good shot too. We made up all sorts of team games with them and always had a laugh. JR had a little fridge there with his beer and my soft drinks. He used to go on about that. 'Would you believe it. Me, JR, the number one whacker in the country, with soft drinks in his fridge. All because of this big girl.'

'Who you calling a girl, you fucking spiv?'

We used to love heaping shit on each other, but he was real easy to wind up.

We'd be sitting there at Sweethearts and I'd go, 'Is that a bit of lip rouge you've got on tonight, JR?' He'd fly straight off the handle. I'd get him going to the point where he had veins sticking out on his neck and the side of his forehead. I'd sit back with a big grin on my face and he'd go, 'You bastard.'

So the girls came downstairs for a shoot this night with Sheepie and we had a boys versus girls shooting match. It was a lot of fun. Then Chance turned up and came downstairs.

JR was just in the middle of reorganising the teams to fit Chance into the games when Chance said, 'Nah, sorry. I've come to see Caesar. Can I have a word with you, Ceese?'

So we wandered into a corner of the bunker. Chance lowered his voice. 'I got a job on tonight. There's a couple of blokes I want you to put to sleep. As soon as you knock 'em out, you can take off and I'll finish the job.'

'Are you sure you don't want me to hang around?'

'Nah. Once they're out cold, everything will be sweet.'

'How long's it going to take?'

'You'll probably be gone for about two hours.'

We rejoined the group and I told Donna I had to go. 'Do you want to stay here or do you want to go home?'

'How long are you going to be?'

'About two and a half hours.'

'I'll stay, then.'

'JR, you look after Donna.'

'With me life,' he said.

'Looks like it's Donna and Cheryl up against Sheepie and JR.'

Cheryl, being the cheeky one, said: 'And we'll shoot the arse off you.'

'Will you now?' JR said.

So Chance and I left. The job went smoothly and we were back in under two hours. JR and Sheepie were straight over asking what I'd been up to.

'You both know I can't tell you that.'

'Come on,' JR said, 'I'm your best mate.'

'Yeah, and we're in the same club,' Sheepie said. 'We wear the same colours.'

'I don't care what you say, I can't say nothing to ya. If you want to know anything, you ask Chance, so don't bug me or I'll belt the both of youse. Now, let's get back to this shooting match.'

We must have been there till three in the morning. There were shell casings everywhere. We helped Cheryl and Donna pick them up. JR had his own bullet press down there, so he kept all his casings and reused them.

It was a good night. We'd had good fun. I'd made some money. It felt good taking out two so-called ex-special-forces bodyguards. It always got the adrenaline pumping doing something like that. When you do it right, it feels extra special.

While JR lifted the roller door, Donna and I went to get on the bike. She was in some leather pigskin jeans I'd bought her, but she put on the little voice: 'Ceeeeeeese, I'm cold.' So I took off my Brando jacket and she put it over hers. She snuggled in behind me out of the breeze as we thundered through the early morning streets. I was just in my cut and black T-shirt, gloves, no helmet, fully alive to the biting wind on my face and arms.

CAESAR'S LAW

XVI

TO TATTOO OR NOT TO TATTOO

If you can't fight, don't get a tatt. Once you put on a tatt, you can't get 'em off and there's a lot of blokes out there who consider that tatts should only be worn by blokes who can back it up.

A lot of blokes think tattoos draw the women and makes them look tough, but you've got to have more than that. Take that Justin Bieber. He thinks that getting himself covered in ink is going to harden up his girlie image, but it ain't. If he was to wander into a pub with a bunch of outlaw bikers, he'd go out on a stretcher. Although I suppose he'd have half a dozen body-guards. But he'd need them.

I haven't got many tattoos. Something like 49.

32

MR POTATO HEAD'S CAR

One night we were up at the Prospect Hotel having a good time as usual. My brothers were picking up a lot of strays. There was rooting going on in the male and female toilets. Any spare room that could be found. At closing time, we adjourned to a kebab stand out the front, all in pretty high spirits. Two cop cars pulled in as we were queuing to order. We must have just about cleaned him out of kebabs and chips and everything else he had. All that drinking and rooting had built up a healthy appetite in the boys. But they weren't finished having fun yet, either.

Snoddy, Wack, Chop and Shadow got in on a plan and asked the bloke behind the counter if he had four whole potatoes. The bloke handed them over without asking for payment.

So they snuck over to the back of the cop cars while the cops were chatting up some sheilas in a Celica.

They jammed the potatoes up the exhausts of the cop cars as far as they could get them.

We waited there, innocently chewing on our kebabs until the sheilas in the Celica left, and the cops went back to their cars, eyeing us off. One of the cars started for a few seconds, then coughed, farted, and conked out. The other one wouldn't start at all. We sat there with big grins on our faces while they got out and had a look under the bonnets. Every now and then one would get back behind the wheel to try to turn it over, but it was no good. They couldn't figure it out. And all the while they were looking back at us, knowing we must have had something to do with it, but unable to figure out how we could stuff up two cars without having lifted the hoods.

Snoddy gave it away by almost falling off his bike with the laughing. I had to put me hand over his mouth to stop him. I got the blokes on their bikes and we hooned illeg-ally straight across the road, because there was no way they could chase us. I heard the boys laughing even over the roar of the engines.

*

ONE SATURDAY afternoon there was a bunch of us at the clubhouse early when we got a phone call from the Vauxhall Inn telling us there were a few Angels there.

Snoddy said to me, 'Let me handle this one. I know most of the Angels from around here pretty well.'

'All right, but if you're not back in 15 I'm coming down.'

He took Chop, Wack and Shadow with him.

It turned out to be Skippy from the Angels. Even though Snoddy was good mates with him, he was obliged to challenge him. 'What are you doing drinking here?' Snoddy said.

'We didn't think it would hurt. We're mates of yours aren't we?'

'There's no such thing as mates between our club and your club. If you wanna drink here, you ask first. Otherwise don't come to our pubs.'

'How can every pub in Parramatta be yours?'

'Well, they are. If you wanna dispute it, get your boys and do it.'

With that, Skippy got his guys and left and that was the last we heard of it. Snoddy was back in about 12 minutes. That was the difference between the Angels Snoddy knew and the Angels I knew. My mates, like Little Billy, Guitar, Jerry, Pancho, Matchie and Max, they would have told Snoddy to go fuck himself. There's always a mixture of blokes at outlaw clubs. Some have just got more balls than others.

Here's a point in question. One Saturday night the whole club was drinking at the Vauxhall Inn when who should pull in but Guitar. The entire Comanchero club was there, but he wanted to see me and he didn't give a fuck about the rules. He was just coming to see me. He walked in and everyone gave him the big stare. I went over and we gave each other a big hug. We walked outside and had a yak. Anyway, a prospect came out to me with a message: 'Jock says he's got to piss off.'

'Fuck off,' I said to the prospect. 'I'm talking to a brother ... You tell Jock we'll be up the Rosehill pub.' So Guitar and me went up there. Within the next half hour, three-quarters of the club were up there with us and there was no problem with Guitar. They just wanted to be where their sergeant was.

Me and Guitar were like brothers, even though he was an Angel. When I first met him years earlier, he had told me straight up that if we ever got into a blue he wouldn't back me because he only backed other Hells Angels, but about six months later he turned to me and said, 'Caesar, if you ever get into a blue and I'm there, brother, I'll back ya.'

*

ONE SATURDAY, the club decided we'd spend the night at Berowra Waters and have a big bonfire and party around it. Everyone had sleeping bags and other bits of gear. Leroy had a couple of blankets on the back of the Harley Sport he was riding. One of the blankets came loose and got wrapped up in his wheel. All of a sudden his bike was dragging all over the road and I got in next to him to try and steady the bike while he eased the brake on. When we'd finally stopped his bike, I got some of the blokes to stand out in the road, facing back the way we'd come with the headlights on so people coming down the road could see us. I had a couple of others shining their lights on Leroy's bike while we took to the blanket with our buck knives. We got rid of it and chucked it over the guard rail and made sure the other blanket was secure.

We continued to Berowra Waters, crossed the ferry and set up in the big parking area with a bonfire. Got the music cranked up, with plenty of spare batteries for the stereo. There were loads of snags and steak. The old ladies all started dancing around the bonfire while the blokes sat back and bullshitted about their latest conquests. It was a top night.

Even though I hadn't been that keen on joining the Comos at first, we had some really good times with some really good blokes. If it had gone the right way, it would have been the biggest and strongest club in Australia, but it didn't.

*

SNAKE AND I pulled into the Empire Hotel at Annandale. He had some business with a bloke there. We did a lap of the place but couldn't find him, so we got a drink and waited. All these footballers rocked in. They were only reserve-graders or park footballers, but there were about 30 of 'em.

As usual, someone looked at Snake the wrong way and it was on. Snake belted into this bloke and all the others got up and so it was really on. I rushed out to the door and yelled to Snake, 'Up to the lounge.' You had to go out onto the street to get to the narrow staircase up to the lounge bar. So we ran up the stairs and maybe these blokes thought they had us on the run, but as soon as we got to the top step we turned and gave it to them.

Once again, Snake and me struggled to get back down a staircase because of all the bodies lying on it. A few of the steps were so awkward we had to kneel down on the blokes to get across them. When we got to the bottom, there were about ten of their mates still standing at the bottom. Snake was going, 'Come on, you cunts. Come on. There's still only the two of us. Come and take me and me brother on.'

'No, mate, we don't want anymore trouble.'

'Yeah, that's what you get when you mess with the Campbells.'

One bloke said, 'But you've got Comanchero on your vest!'

'I might be a Comanchero, but I was born a Campbell.'

The next night, Shadow came around to my place. 'Snake told me about the fight you were in yesterday,' he said.

'Yeah, it was a good one.'

'That was sort of what I wanted to talk to you about.'

'What, last night's fight?'

'Nah,' he said. 'The fights we're always in. I love being in this club, I love the blokes. Well, most of 'em. This fallacy about you having to love every bloke in the club, it's all bullshit. You can love a lot of 'em but you can't love everyone.'

'I know that,' I said, 'and I think everyone in every outlaw club knows it. You just respect the colours. As long as you respect the colours and the bloke who's wearing 'em, you don't have to love him. But you back him up and look after him the same as the ones you do.'

'Yeah, I go along with that,' Shadow said, 'but me and a few of the other brothers are getting sick of being the ones who are always out in front. Every time there's a fight. Usually we're outnumbered and it's always us Campbells going straight to the front, doing the heavy fighting, taking the brunt of the best fighters. It's only when we've got over them that the rest of the club starts getting in.'

'Nah, there's a few exceptions,' I said. 'Like Sheepie and Davo and Mousie.'

'Yeah, a couple, but the bulk of the club stands back and waits for us.'

'And the McElwaines,' I said.

'Yeah, but they're more second-string,' he said.

'Well, they might not be right up with us, but they're not far behind. Give 'em their due. They're boxers, not street fighters like us. We were brought up to fight on the street. We've all done martial arts and different sorts of stuff. You know, we've done it hard all our lives in the fight scene and these guys have always done it with a referee to stop the fight as soon as things get nasty. They'll get there. Anyway, what are you getting at? Are you thinking of leaving the club?'

'Nah, not leaving, but what do you reckon if I bring it up at the next meeting that for the next few fights we're in, the Campbells are taking a break? That we'll be at the back of the pack?'

'Come on, Shadow, really? If a fight started, would you stand back and let the other blokes get belted? I know you. As soon as it starts, you'll be up front thumping on.'

Shadow never brought it up at a club meeting, but I always knew there was an undercurrent with him and a few of my brothers not being happy with always being the battering rams. Didn't worry me! I loved it. And so did Snake. But even battering rams get worn down.

Inside the Comancheros, my brothers and I made a lot of the blokes feel inferior because of the way we fought. If we had to get out of a pub fight, like if the cops were coming, it would be us fighting on the footpath, guarding the retreat while the others got on their bikes and kicked them over. We were doing it for them, yet it made some resentful.

And the blues kept coming. There was one blue up at the Bridge Hotel in Rozelle. It was all pretty routine. We cleaned up a few blokes and the rest of their mates backed off. Suddenly someone says, 'Roger's been shot.' I've run around the bar and there was Roger with this big red stain on his white T-shirt. I looked at these blokes we'd just been punching on with and one of them was backing away, guilty-like, so I grabbed him and twisted his arm up his back until it snapped. He had a little .22 pistol in his hand. It turned out Roger had been shot during the fight but hadn't even noticed.

Anyway, we all went back to my place. They wanted Donna to pull the slug out. She had a go, but couldn't get it. Another couple of members wanted to try, so they had a bit of a poke and prod. Poor old Roger was lying there sucking it up as everyone had a dig. When no one could get it, we took him up to Western Suburbs Hospital. I saw him the next afternoon. It looked like a white pointer had taken a chunk of him. It turned out he'd only been shot with a .22 cap, not a full bullet, but the scar went from his heart down below the rib cage and round his belly to under his right arm. The doctor had got it, but he'd opened his whole body to find it. What a butcher! The Animal could've taught him a thing or two.

*

EVERY SO often the Comancheros would go on what they called a bucks run. I hated them. The idea was to pick up sheilas. But when there's 30 or 40 of you going out to a place like Dunedoo where there were already 50 blokes for every sheila, how they expected to pick up chicks was a bit beyond me. I used to say if you're having a bucks run, go up the coast.

'Nah, nah, if we go out west, we can do some shooting too.'

'What do you wanna do, go shootin' or shaggin'?' I'd say.

'Both.'

So we'd head west and you'd see 35 bikes rolling down Parramatta Road all with rifle scabbards strapped to the bikes. The coppers wouldn't do a thing because there was never any trouble with guns and bikers in those days. There were no drive-bys. We all had gun permits. None of us had been to jail. The cops just didn't worry about us. When we got out west, I'd see the local copper and tell him we had the guns and we were here to do some shooting and I'd ask where the best pigging was. He'd say, 'Out such and such, there's a tank where they come in at sunset to drink.' But the blokes would head straight to the pub as soon as we got to town and that'd be it for the hunting.

They'd be lucky if they even fired their guns once. And even then it would just be at beer cans set up on a fence post. Bull and Shadow were the only ones who ever went and had a look for pigs. They'd chat up some bloke in the pub who had a four-wheel drive and they'd get him to take 'em out. They'd buy him a carton for his trouble. But that'd be it. For the most part, the guns were all about show, having them on the bikes.

I couldn't be bothered sitting in the pub all day and all night. So I'd make Shadow or Davo temporary sergeant and I'd go cruising on my bike and find all these crazy little towns, with these old churches, post offices and tumbledown buildings, and I'd get off the bike and go in and have a poke around. I found it all fascinating. To me, going on a run was all about riding, not riding to one spot then spending three days in a pub.

I'd be sitting back late at night by the campfire when I'd hear the bikes coming back in. Jock would be shirty with me. 'Where've you been all day, Caesar? You can't make Davo sergeant.'

'I can do whatever I want, Jock, when you're all pissed. Shadow don't drink, so he's going to be watching your back. I'm out here to ride. This is a motorcycle run, not a motorcycle drink.' It used to piss him and a lot of the blokes off, even my brothers.

*

ONE TIME I was riding with Sheepskin out at Liverpool when this cop car side-swiped us. He hit Sheepie and sent him into the gutter. We got off our bikes and the copper pulled up about 15 metres in front. Sheepskin charged. He was unbelievably strong and he hit the cop car's open door and just ripped the thing off. He knocked the cop out cold in his seat.

'You're going to have to get that door off the road,' I said.

He threw the door onto the footpath and we got back onto our bikes, hotfooting it off up the Hume Highway, then into the back streets and back suburbs all the way home, just hoping that the cop hadn't got our number-plates. But it all happened so quickly it appeared he'd had no time to do anything much, because nothing ever came of it.

Sheepie was one bloke you didn't want to mess with. He had a real hatred for the boys in blue. It wasn't the first time he'd attacked a cop in his car.

Once he tried dragging a cop out of the driver's window as the cop was trying to drive off down the street. I had to grab Sheepie and get him away. The whole clubhouse was soon surrounded. There must have been a hundred coppers there. I went out and had a talk with the head copper. I said, 'You can bring in the officer you allege has been assaulted. He can come through the clubhouse and check out all the members, but I think the bloke you're looking for was a hang-round called Hog. You should be able to find him.'

'A nickname?' the head copper said. 'That's not much good to us.'

'Yeah, well, that's all we know him by.'

'Are you willing to let us through the clubhouse with no trouble?'

'Yeah, come on in.' I escorted them through on the tour and they couldn't find Sheepie, so the senior officer went out and rounded up his blokes and off they went. We went out and yelled up to the roof, 'C'mon down, Sheepie. They've gone.'

My old mate Sheepie is now up there with Odin, my brothers, and all the other gods now. Rest in peace, buddy.

*

ONE NIGHT, we were sitting at the Como clubhouse on club night, Saturday. Jock was crook, so he hadn't turned up. We'd been out on our ride around Sydney, stopped at a couple of pubs on the way and the blokes were having a good time, drinking at the bar and around the bonfire. A few of them were up for doing something mad. So I told them about the boots and bandana run back in the early '70s.

Next thing you know, there's 35 Comancheros out on Parramatta Road riding down towards Auburn wearing only their boots, plus a few with bandanas. We got as far as Homebush before some cops saw us. We did a Uey and the cops put their sirens on, but we weren't pulling over for nothing. We hammered back to the clubhouse. Eight or nine cops joined the chase, but we beat them back to the club by a minute or so.

We got inside and were all getting our gear back on when the sirens wailed to a halt out the front. I went and fronted the sergeant, with all these headlights beaming on me, and the red and blue lights whirring about like we were at a disco.

'Youse blokes can't go riding up and down one of Sydney's busiest streets with no clothes on,' the head copper said.

'Did you get a complaint?' I asked.

'No, but you can't do it. It's against the law.'

'Show me it in your rule book.'

'I don't have a "rule book", I've got the law and I'm telling you that you can't do it.'

'Okay, sergeant, you won't see us do it again.'

'Okay, I'd better not. That's good enough.' And he left.

I didn't say we wouldn't do it again. Just that he wouldn't see us.

The nude run set us up for another great night and we stood there and laughed and drank in the warmth of the bonfire, with our shrivelled prides coming back to normal.

33

WHO SHOT JR'S SHOOTERS?

Chance dropped in to visit me for my birthday in July 2014. As usual, the conversation went back to the old days and it inevitably found its way heading towards 1983, which turned out to be one of the saddest and most momentous years of my life, up till that time.

It all started on 6 June, when I got a call from JR's missus, Cheryl.

'Johnny's dead,' she said, all distressed. 'Can you come over?'

I threw my colours on and jumped on the bike, booming out of the shed and racing the 10 kilometres or so over to his place, not knowing whether he'd had a heart attack or what. I rushed in. Chance was already there, but I hardly noticed him because JR was lying on the floor, not far from the door, blood pooling out, darkening, in a circle around his head.

'What happened?'

Cheryl told me that JR had invited Popeye Wilson and the three Sattler brothers over for a business meeting. She knew who they were, because they'd been over there before for a barbecue. But JR must have suspected something, because he put Cheryl into his little cubbyhouse behind the grandfather clock before they arrived.

From there, she saw it all go down through the peephole. He let them in, she said, then turned his back to lead them towards the lounge room. Popeye Wilson drew his gun and put one in the back of JR's head without JR knowing a thing. 'He hit the floor and the Sattler brothers took turns putting another one in each,' she said.

They were the type of blokes who'd want to be able to skite that they'd hit the mighty JR.

'He broke one of his own rules,' I said. 'He turned his back on someone he didn't trust.'

It didn't make a lot of sense to Chance and me. Popeye Wilson idolised JR. If JR said, 'Lie down in that puddle – I want to walk over the top of you', he'd do it. Popeye used to get about in a chequered sports coat, slacks and a little cloth cap like you'd see jockeys wearing at track-work. The Sattler brothers were big blokes, Kings Cross scum. Never saw them in a fight. They hung around Popeye Wilson because he had a bit of a name as a hitman. He'd knock off someone for two grand.

Cheryl was shattered. 'What do we do?' she said.

'Ring Abe,' I said. 'He knows how to sort these things out.'

So she did, and Abe said he was coming over.

As to what happened next . . . ? Well, let's just say that one of the people there that night blew his cool. He grabbed JR's twin Berettas, got on his bike, rode into the Cross and found Little Lenny Baker, who told him that the Sattlers and Popeye Wilson were at the Cockatoo Club,

Scrooge McDonald's gambling joint down the end of Victoria Street. He walked in and saw old Scrooge.

'They're in the back room, bragging about what they did to JR,' Scrooge said.

Whoever it was, he strode down the narrow hall to the back room and kicked the door in. Popeye Wilson got it first. One to the head, one to the chest. No formalities. He started putting them into the Sattler brothers; into the knees, the hips, the gut, the nuts, made them squeal, before he put them away. But this was a big hot-headed mistake. What he didn't do was find out who put the contract out on JR.

If I'd found out – if whoever had found out – that person would have been in a lot of strife, too. That, however, remained a mystery.

There was no investigation into JR's death. I'll say this for Mr Sin, when he was close to someone, he really took care of them. He thought of JR as a son. Abe had an interest in a funeral parlour and he must have known a tame doctor to sign the death certificate. The story that went out was that Johnny Regal was killed in a car crash. Abe would have ensured the cops ran dead on any information to the contrary.

JR's funeral service and cremation were held out at Waverley. I didn't go. I'd been to too many funerals. And I felt bad for Cheryl. She never believed in the life that Johnny lived and I didn't want to be there reminding her of that life. Not that I was going round killing people for him or anything, but we were best mates. So I let Donna go. She came back and said Cheryl was upset that I hadn't been there. Cheryl didn't blame me for anything, Donna said. As a matter fact, she told Donna she thanked me for what I did to help her. Not that I did much.

There was no investigation into the deaths of the Sattler brothers and Popeye Wilson. Abe took care of that, too. I assume the Cockatoo Club got cleaned up and the bodies were left to the fishes.

I'm only telling the story now because JR is gone and no one knows who Chance is. Mr Sin's gone, so nothing can come back on him. And I think 98 per cent of the people involved in that night are in tombstone territory. One or two who might be left wouldn't say a thing because, even at this stage, they live by a code and know that it doesn't matter how long things go by – whether it's 12 months or 40 years – if you do the wrong thing, you end up in the ground.

We'll just leave it at that. But me and Chance reminisced on my birthday in 2014 about how the three of us used to get down into JR's bomb shelter and churn through hundreds of rounds and have a great old laugh through all the smoke and the noise. 'The number one whacker in the country, with soft drink in his fridge.' He was a fun bloke to be around.

After JR's death, Cheryl moved to the Eastern Suburbs and opened a restaurant in Double Bay. It was very good and very successful. Donna and I used to go there for special occasions. I guess a lot of Cheryl's patrons would have lost their appetites if they'd known who her old man had been. But above all, he was a top bloke and a great mate.

34

CRACKS IN THE COMOS

As I had built the Comancheros, I knew that Jock's two main sidekicks, Snowy and Foghorn, were getting pissed off. Neither of them were big blokes and neither of them were bluers. They were more backroom political types and both of them saw their power base disappearing as the club got bigger and tougher. The Comos had a rule where if you were a life member you didn't have to ride your bike. You could attend meetings, vote, go on runs, do everything every other member could do, but you didn't have to ride a motorcycle. It was a bunch of shit. Snowy and Foghorn didn't ride. I used to always be going on at them about it. 'At least ride once a month. Snowy, I've never even seen you on a motorcycle.'

They got into Jock's ear and that's when things started to sour. When I first came to the club, they were big fish in a small pond, but the pond had got a whole lot larger.

Until things went bad, Jock and I were fairly tight. Like, the day after he and I were in the Wisemans Ferry fight, Donna and I went up to his place and sat around in the pool with him and his wife, Vanessa. Had a barbie and a great time. For a long time, I respected the man. To a point, I still do. I might get in the shit from my brothers and other people for saying that, but I think if it hadn't been for Foghorn, Snowy and Kraut – one of his new recruits who couldn't ride and who got about in all this Nazi regalia – I don't think things would have gone the way they did. I think I'd still have been the sergeant-at-arms of the Comos, serving under Jock as president.

I know everyone blames Jock for what happened and I blamed him at the time, too, but when I've talked to Sheepskin over the years since, he's been pretty adamant that it was Foghorn and Snowy in Jock's ear all the time bullshitting to him about the Campbells and other members and how we wanted to take over his club. That was the furthest thing from our minds. We didn't want his club. If he'd got rid of Foghorn and Snowy when Sheepskin told him, he would have had the biggest and toughest club in the country.

Just to recap on what I said in *Enforcer*, early on in my time at the Comancheros, Jock formed the Strike Force, who were like an elite inner circle of his. He asked me to join first up, but I refused because I didn't like the idea of having almost a club within a club. I thought all members should be equal and that having an exclusive group would cause resentments. And that's the way it proved to be. Foghorn, Snowy and Kraut became key members of the Strike Force and were always causing trouble, spreading rumours that this bloke didn't like that bloke.

It got to the point where Bushy and Sheepskin wanted to kill each other, Chop wanted to rip Kid Rotten's head off and Lard and Shadow wanted to get into it. I had to get over to Jock's place one day because Lard had made the mistake of calling up Shadow and offering him on, which would have meant Lard would have lost his colours and Shadow might have too – because he would have ripped him three ways from hell. Shadow had never been beaten in a fight and Lard had never been in the sort of fight that me and my brothers used to get into. So I got over to Jock's, got on the blower and stopped Shadow from coming out. The only reason I got on to him was that his bike wouldn't start. He was having trouble with the carby. It was the only thing that saved Lard from a stint in ICU.

It was only later that we realised that Lard had no beef with Shadow, it was all Foghorn and Snowy stirring the pot.

Sheepskin was a member of the Strike Force, but he was the voice of reason there and he used to keep me informed about what was happening. Sheepie and I realised that something was gunna happen; that this couldn't keep going. Foghorn then started stirring trouble between Davo and Jock, spreading stories that Davo was gathering support for a challenge to Jock's presidency. And they told Davo some shit about what Jock had said about him. It got to the point where Davo was gunna beat the shit out of Jock. You just can't have people wanting to beat the shit out of the president of your club.

So there was already a lot of tension in the air when, in August 1983, Jock gave Opey and me the job of finding a new clubhouse. Within a few weeks, we'd signed a lease on a beautiful but rundown old waterfront mansion at Birchgrove, in Sydney's inner west. The Comos were moving up in the world just as they were about to be torn apart.

While the club was still in the middle of moving the bar and all our memorabilia over to the new place,

Shadow and Chop caught Jock screwing another member's old lady. This was such a huge contravention of the code that it meant the loss of colours for anyone, including the guy who'd founded the club 15 years earlier. Shadow and Chop were going to bring it up at the next meeting, where it would have led to automatic expulsion. But they didn't get a chance to do that, because Jock didn't turn up to the next meeting, or the next.

When he eventually did show, he was with Sheepie, while the Strike Force sat outside with guns. He waited for silence, then announced, 'I'm splitting the club in two.' We all sat staring at him. 'I've started a chapter out west,' he went on. 'It's to be called the west chapter and I'm going to be president. This is going to be the city chapter and, Caesar, I want you to be president. Whoever wants to come with me can leave now, but there's one rule in the west chapter, and that is that I have the final vote on everything.'

Only one member, Bear, and one prospect, Bob, got up to join him.

Jock had outmanoeuvred us. He kept his club by breaking it in two.

The funny thing was that, if Jock had come to me instead of staying away from the meetings, I could've got him off that charge. It emerged that this old lady he had screwed had had it off with a few other club members as well, and I think we could have worked something out. I would have kicked her out of the club, for a start.

Anyway, Snoddy asked me if he could be president and I agreed. I loved being sergeant.

I go into this in a lot more detail in *Enforcer*, but the main thing to come out of it all was that all the best blokes – except Sheepskin – were with the city chapter. All the top bluers, the partyers, the blokes who loved to ride, were with us, while Jock was left with just the rump of a club – so he had to start recruiting frantically to build his numbers back up.

Right from the start, the tensions mounted. Jock invited only one member of the city chapter to his wedding. When we turned up at Molong for the national run the next month, he and Snoddy almost got into a fight within minutes of us arriving. Our city chapter blokes were gathering ready for a blue. But I would never fight a man wearing the same colours as me, so I got us all out of there.

It ended up that, in little more than two months after the split, the city chapter voted to leave the Comos. After a long debate about what to do next, Shadow remembered Snoddy talking about a trip he'd taken to the States and the stories about a top bunch of old-school bikers he'd met in New Mexico – the Bandidos. After a short discussion, we voted unanimously to ask them if we could start a chapter in Australia. Snoddy was given the job of getting on to the Bandidos' Albuquerque chapter president Ha Ha Chuck, who got on to Ronnie Hodge, the national president. We didn't get to speak to Ronnie Hodge direct, and so we had a nervous week waiting to hear if we'd get the go-ahead.

Snoddy rang Ha Ha from the clubhouse on a Sunday night. Ha Ha said it was a goer, and Snoddy said, 'Wait a sec. I just have to ask the big feller.' 'Who's the big feller?' Ha Ha asked. 'That's my sergeant-at-arms, Caesar Campbell.' I said, 'Yeah, let's give it a go', and so that's how the Bandits started in the land of Oz. All because of Shadow's idea and Snoddy's friendship with Ha Ha.

35

THE BEST CLUB IN THE WORLD

The Bandidos started in Australia on 22 November 1983. That's the day the first set of colours arrived back from the embroidery place as a test sample. I gave the embroiderers the go-ahead to make up the rest of the batch while I got Donna to sew that first set onto my cut. As soon as she'd finished, I put the colours on and went out for a ride. Anyone who's read *Enforcer* will know the first stops were Snoddy's and Shadow's places. It was a great feeling to be the first bloke in Australia to fly the colours of the best club in the world. For ten days, I rode around Sydney making sure everybody who was anybody knew the Bandidos had arrived. It was among the proudest times of my life. I also had the first Bandido tattoo, the first Bandido T-shirt, the first belt, the first belt buckle, the first Bandido boot buckles. People might think I'm gloating, but I'm not. To me it was a really special honour. Even though it's only a small bit of their history, I'm still super-proud to be part of the Bandido nation. And always will be. Every man who puts on that cut for the first time should be the proudest man in the world.

A couple of blokes have come out claiming they were wearing Bandit colours in August 1983, but they're getting confused by the fact the Comos split into two chapters in August. I've got dated photos showing us all on the October run to Molong where we're all still wearing Comanchero colours.

There were 29 members, five prospects and another two hang-rounds, Maverick and Sleazy, who became prospects in May 1984. (They've both gone around saying they were original members, but they weren't.)

So now we were Bandidos. Our colours were so new that the red and gold glowed off our leather vests. Me and my brothers were still the front line, the battering ram, the wrecking crew for the club, so nothing changed there.

Getting back to the good times . . .

In December and January, 1983–84, we went for a run up to Port Macquarie and we took along the McElwaines' dad, Big Bad Bob. He was only a little bloke but he had a big heart and was a top feller. We had a roarer of a time and when we got back he put on a big do for us at the pub he owned, the Terminus at Pyrmont, to show us his appreciation.

He employed topless barmaids at his hotel and he got them all doing a strip show for the members. There were a few hookers provided, too. It was a really good night. I had the prospects out watching the bikes. With no old ladies to look after, I didn't have to wander around the pub checking up on everybody, so I just sat with my back into the corner as usual and watched me brothers party and I had a good look at some really nice tits. I must admit it, I'm a tit man. It's one of the reasons I love my woman so much, she's got it all.

Anyway, I did go for a look around at one point. Out the back of Big Bobby's pub, he had a large aviary with Major Mitchell cockatoos and other interesting birds in it. I found Wack out there with one of the barmaids giving her a knee-trembler. The whole aviary was shaking. I went back to my corner and continued watching the brothers enjoy themselves. Sometimes the brothers used to wonder how I could be having a good time by just watching everyone else have a good time. I just did.

There'd often be one of the brothers trying to talk me into having a go at one of the strays or, like on this night, one of the topless barmaids doing a strip. With Donna, I never needed to do that. She was the only woman I ever wanted, the only woman I got excited over. I'm not just saying that because she's working on this book with me – it's a fact and she knows it. To this day, I still get a tingle in me balls when I see her getting changed.

She was the perfect outlaw's old lady. When I said I was going out on club business, she never questioned me, never asked where I'd been when I got home, and sometimes I could be gone for days. If I had to get up and go out at 2 am and not be back till 6 am, she never queried it. If I was out most nights of the week . . . never a question. She looked after me.

And there was no better example than this night at the Terminus with all the topless barmaids. I was in there till about 3 am, when I left the club in the capable hands of Shadow. Snoddy had had a bit too much to drink. Shadow and I had the deal where he'd arrive a bit late and I'd leave a bit early and he'd take over as head of security.

The old lady put on the tomato, cheese and ham sandwich when she heard my bike pulling in. She got me a can of Coke while I put the bike in the garage. I came in through the back door. Brought in three of the dogs with me and they were all running around the house at 100 miles an hour.

'Calm them dogs down, they'll wake Daniel up,' she said.

So I put the dogs out the back. Daniel and Lacey were both still sleeping, so I got into my toasted sandwich and I suppose being a tit man and seeing those tits all night and seeing my old woman walking around topless, we ended up on the couch before I'd finished half my sandwich and had a nooky. It was a great end to a good night.

*

IN MARCH 1984, there were about 30 of us at the Rock and Roll Hotel. We'd been there for a couple of hours when one of our prospects, Tramp, rushed in and said 60 or 70 blokes were coming down the street towards the pub. I went out the front and saw 'em all walking down together. I recognised a couple of them as wharfies. This was going to be good.

I had a word with the pub manager: 'If you let these blokes in, it's gunna be on. Your pub's gunna get wrecked.' He came out the front with me and, as the wharfies reached the first bike in our line of bikes, he told them the pub was off limits to them tonight.

'But we drink here all the time,' one of them said.

'Well, we're drinking here tonight,' I said.

They made a few remarks about bikers and I looked over my shoulder and the whole club was coming out through the door. *Well, this is it. It's gunna be on here,* I thought.

Bull walked up on one side of me and Snake on the other. Shadow was just next to him, with Wack, Chop, the McElwaines and Snoddy forming the rest of the front line.

Like I've said, I try to make peace in these situations. But there was one big bloke who had a bigger mouth. He was really giving the outlaw biker thing a run for its money, so I dropped him. Right hook under the ear.

It was on. Even though we were outnumbered more than two to one, the whole club just went forward as one and we drove them back and out onto the road. The McElwaines were getting into it. My brothers were dropping blokes all over the place. I saw Little Charlie whacking into a bloke with a pool cue. He brought him to his knees and gave it to him in the back of the head before moving on to another one. I have to give it to Little Charlie – he wasn't the biggest or the strongest and he'd never learnt to fight, but he always backed you up. Same as Roach. Roach couldn't fight, but he was always there beside you. Junior, too. They were the type of bloke that I always thought made up the core of a club.

I looked over and saw Kid Rotten doing a backwards swing kick, catching his bloke under the ear, dropping him cold. Then he did a sweep kick and took down another bloke. Kid surprised me. I knew he'd done martial arts and I'd seen him fight one-on-one. But when you're badly outnumbered, everything is different. He came to the front line and got stuck right into it.

It wasn't a bad blue that night. The wharfies stuck it out, too. They tried to look after their mates. I don't mind giving credit where it's due. But in the end, by the time we heard the familiar sirens coming down the hill towards us, they were all on the ground, except for a few who took to shanks's pony.

Everyone went to their bikes and I made sure that the old ladies were all out of the pub with us. I went through the pub twice, checked the toilets, which I always did to make sure we never left anyone behind, made sure every bike had a rider and every bloke who had brought his old lady had her with him. And when we headed off, we headed off strong.

Whether there'd been trouble or not, I was always last to take off, checking that there were no stalled bikes, then I swung out around the pack and gunned it to the front, sitting alongside Snoddy, with Shadow on his other side.

We went riproaring up past the cathedral into the city, gunning out over the new Western Distributor and the old Glebe Island Bridge all the way back to the clubhouse. We put the bikes away and sent the old ladies inside. Barring a few members who went in to make sure the clubhouse was all right, every member was outside for the next 90 minutes watching and waiting to see if the coppers turned up. And if they did, they weren't taking anyone from our club without a fight. On that night, I was very proud of all the brothers in the club. It was another reason to feel so honoured to be a Bandido. I knew we had a bunch of blokes we could count on.

And with tensions growing between us and the Comancheros, we were going to need every bit of guts we could muster to face off against our old clubmates, who we were hearing were out willy-nilly recruiting a huge number of blokes we didn't know.

CAESAR'S LAW

XVII

THE SECRET OF A HAPPY MARRIAGE

Find the right partner and treat them right. Have a good sex life. But a better-than-good sex life is better. I've always had that. I think most blokes find it a bit hard because they've got to be the one always putting the word on the old lady, whereas for me and Donna it's more like 65 per cent her way. I don't have to worry about asking because she's always over the top of me.

Most outlaw bikers don't belt their old ladies. That's a fallacy. Most outlaw bikers look after their old ladies. It's the strays that get the hard time because they come around knowing that they're going out with blokes who have already got old ladies. Before I met Donna, I always had a rule that if I was going out with another chick and a chick put it on me, I'd always tell them I had a girlfriend but they'd still want to come out and open their legs so you don't knock it back.

Since meeting Donna, I've never stopped looking, but I never crossed that line again. That's one thing that's kept us together. She's always trusted me.

36

STICKS AND STONES MAY BREAK HIS BONER

My weekly routine involved going to the clubhouse every Wednesday afternoon. Wednesday nights were meeting nights, so I used to check out the clubhouse to make sure everything was right. There was no way I was going to let another club get in under our guard the way my brothers and I had done with the Undertakers and a couple of other clubs. Aside from making sure we weren't going to get ambushed by the Comos, I'd check that the place had been cleaned in the morning by the prospects. This day I went in with Shadow and Chop. We opened the door and there was no sign of anyone about until we heard some moaning and groaning. We followed the noise into the bar area to find the prospect, Sticks, with his jeans round his ankles, 'flying commando' – no undies on. He had this mad-looking device attached to his cock that he was pulling at. The device, that is.

'Caesar, I can't get the fucking thing off,' Sticks said. 'I been stuck here for fucking hours. It's killing me.'

It turned out to be a vacuum-sealed pump that he'd bought at a sex shop in the Cross. It was supposed to increase the size of your cock. He was so keen to make it larger, he'd kept pumping it until something went wrong. Now it was sealed in place and he couldn't budge it. We naturally spent a long time laughing before we started thinking of ways to fix Sticks's cock-up.

Chop went over and grabbed the thing. It looked like it was made from a hard, clear plastic. Chop had his gloves on, because we'd ridden over. He grabbed hold of the thing and gave it a good yank, but it wasn't going anywhere. Sticks screamed with the pain.

I turned to Shadow. 'Go out into the back shed and grab a hammer.'

'What are ya gunna do?' Sticks said, scared shitless.

'Well, if Chop can't pull it off, you're either going to be stuck there with it till all the members turn up, or we give it a whack with the hammer and see what happens.'

'What about me cock?'

'Don't worry, there's not that much of it.'

Shadow came back with the hammer. 'Give it a hit,' I said to him and turned to Chop. 'Hold the end of it.'

So Shadow hit the cock pump in the middle and the plastic cracked but didn't break. He gave it a second whack and it shattered. Sticks was free but it had left him with a big dark-blue mark around his pubes. And his balls were hugely swollen. At least it had increased the size of something.

Later that night, part way through the meeting, Chop couldn't resist. He had to tell everyone what had happened. Blokes couldn't stop laughing. Charlie fell off his stool. Lout was bent over holding his guts. The meeting never quite got back on track after that. But it was good for club morale. It helped bring us all together at a time when we needed a distraction. We needed reminding of all the laughs you can have in a bike club.

*

BIG TONY and Rua knew. They had a more entertaining weekday routine. They'd catch the ferry from Long Nose Point jetty just metres away from the clubhouse over to Circular Quay. There, they'd pick up office girls and bring them back for lunch and a sunbake on our back lawn, which came right down to the water.

So there was one Wednesday afternoon when I rocked in and heard someone calling out, 'Who's that?'

'Caesar.'

'It's Big Tony. Come up and help me.'

I went upstairs and here was Big Tony tied to the bed, naked.

'Now, how did you end up in this predicament?' I asked.

'I brought back three chicks from Circular Quay. I was rooting two of 'em. They wanted to tie me up. So I let 'em. But their girlfriend was on at them about getting back to work, so once they finished rooting, they got dressed and took off, laughing their heads off.'

I undid Tony. 'Well, we better check out the clubhouse.' We had a good look around, but nothing was missing.

That night, I raised the matter at the meeting and said that, from now on, if any member brought a chick back to the clubhouse they were never under any circumstance to let themselves get tied up just for a root. Tony was lucky nothing was taken. He'd have been in the shit, big time.

*

ANOTHER TIME, probably in March '84, Snoddy, Shadow, Snake, Bull, Chop, Wack and I were riding down Parramatta Road when a cop car pulled us over. There were three cop sheilas in the car, so maybe one of them was a probationer. They did a licence check on all of us and while they were doing that, Shadow, Snake and Snoddy started chatting them up. Once you broke the ice, female coppers always seemed keen to know if us outlaw bikers really did all those things we were supposed to do to women.

'Well, why don't you come out with us and find out?' Snoddy said, a twinkle in his eye.

Shadow saw that it was working, so he chimed in, as did Snake. Both of them could turn on the charm when they wanted to and, before you knew it, they had these cop sheilas agreeing to meet them at the Royal Oak in Parramatta that night.

And they turned up, too.

Lout was the manager there, so when the sheilas started to look like they were gagging for it, he opened up the big lounge area out the back which they usually kept closed unless they had a band or a big do on. Snoddy, Shadow and Snake took the three of 'em in there and fucked the arses off them. After a couple of hours, the cop sheilas came out looking quite happy and went away knowing outlaw bikers are something else when it comes to the bed department, the bar department and the pool table department. I think it had to be a first – three blokes from one club rooting three cop sheilas on the same night, same place.

*

THE LAST weekend in April 1984, we were going on a run down to Bega on the New South Wales far South Coast. We stopped in at Wollongong. The guys wanted a drink. There happened to be a band on at this pub, so one drink turned into five. As the time ticked over, it didn't look like we were going to make Bega – 340 kilometres further south. There were sheilas everywhere, plus a local bike club who weren't too happy that the Bandidos were in there and that all the local chicks were heading towards us.

Anyway, I got the boys out of there with about 20 sheilas now riding on the back of various bikes. We went about 40 kilometres down the road to Kiama, where we found a paddock near the beach. There was nothing but drinking and rooting going on the rest of the night. So I spent the night making sure no one got into any real strife.

Come next morning, I was a bit on the tired side and I'm walking around the campsite having a look and there's sheilas lying everywhere, drunk as skunks, half of 'em half-naked. There were Bandits lying around with their jeans down and their cocks hanging out. It looked like a bomb site of sexual destruction. But the boys had had a good night, well and truly. I sent a prospect to a phone booth to call taxis to pick up these sheilas. The brothers had had such a good night they didn't want to continue on to Bega, so we had a vote and it was decided we'd head back to the clubhouse. About eight or nine chicks were still there and some of the brothers asked if they wanted to come to Sydney.

They were only too eager to come back with us, so we headed back up the Princes Highway, through Sylvania and over Tom Uglys Bridge. As usual, we took up most of the road. We finally got back to Birchgrove around lunchtime and all the fellers put their bikes in the garage. We had a huge garage that could fit about 45 bikes. We got 'em all inside, got the girls in and Opey pumped up the stereo. The drinking began again and after a couple of heart-starters, the sheilas were taken up to the bedrooms. Where there wasn't a spare bedroom, there was a lounge. Even the pool table got used. That caused a bit of drama, because a few of us wanted to play pool.

We had this little place underneath called 'the dungeon' where Lard used to sleep. I volunteered his bed. Two of the sheilas were taken down there. Lard wasn't that upset, because he was with one of the sheilas. So that freed up the pool table, giving some entertainment for those of us who weren't rooting or waiting for a root. The music pumped. Darkness fell. When it came to about 2 am and things were still raging – which is what happens when you're a Bandido, you party, you rage, you fight and you ride – I had a word to Shadow. 'You can watch 'em till about 9 am, then kick 'em out and send 'em on their way. That'll be the weekend over.'

'All right, Ceese. Done.'

I headed home. I came in the back door and Donna and I sat on the lounge and turned up the music. I was telling her about the weekend. It had been a bucks run, which she knew I didn't like. She knew I liked to have her on a run with me. There were others who felt the same way, but we were always outvoted. You've gotta go with the vote. I was telling The Woman about it when I apparently fell asleep.

She laid me down on the lounge and covered me with a blanket and I had a good five or six hours' sleep before I woke up and did what I always did after a run – got out the cleaning gear, rolled the bike into the yard and started polishing. The Woman used to come out and bring the kids. They'd sit out there with drinks and food. It was a three- or four-hour job.

*

253

In June 1984, me and all my brothers drove over to have a drink and a meal at Birkenhead Point. We walked into the tavern and there was a big bunch of footballers already there watching what appeared to be something like a Miss Birkenhead kind of contest going on. I gathered from the logos on the footballers' jackets that they were from a well-known rugby union club in the eastern suburbs. I recognised a couple of them as bouncers from the Cross. They must have been emboldened by having so many mates from about five grades there with them, because a couple of them brought up the Wrecking Crew and started mouthing off, trashing us. Next thing you know, Bull and Snake have belted a couple and we've suddenly got an entire rugby club barrelling towards us – all of them in good nick and most of them fairly big.

But we knew the pub inside out. We were near the entrance, where you went up to the first floor where they had bands. We backed ourselves into the hallway and up the wide stairs, fighting all the way, until we got to the top, then we just took them two at a time, punching these blokes out. *Whack! Whack! Whack! Thump!* Everyone except Wheels. He didn't go *Whack*. He used to just pick them up and throw them all over the place.

So, after about 15 minutes in this ruck, the usual sirens came wailing in the distance and these union players decided they didn't want to get locked up, so they scarpered. We got out the side entrance to the car park. Our cars were on the second level of the car park, so we just opened the doors from the second level of the pub and walked straight out, while the cops were running into the pub down below on the first level. We got into our cars and drove off.

I had Wheels in the car with me and, while I drove him home, we talked about the Wrecking Crew's reputation. 'It follows you everywhere, don't it, Caesar?'

'That it does, Wheels, but who gives a fuck! Ever since we got the name and before it, we've never been beaten. It'll be interesting the day that we do.'

To this day, though, we never have been beaten. Some of us aren't around anymore. They're up in the Ride Forever chapter having a good time and I'm looking forward to joining them. We will always be super-close.

CAESAR'S LAW XVIII

UN-MANLY GROOMING

What do I say to blokes who shave their chests and wear cosmetics?

I think they oughta put skirts on and wear high heels. You can't be a man and do all that shit.

37

WORKING WITH CHANCE

Sometime in early- to mid-1984, I got a phone call from the Widowmaker. He wanted to meet at Sweethearts. The reason Sweethearts was such a popular meeting spot for people doing things they didn't want the coppers to know about was that it used to be swept daily for police bugs. People around the Cross knew it was a safe place to do business. We met there this night at 8.30, standing out the front for a perv at the sheilas working the street, before we went in and ordered a milkshake each. We probably looked just as funny to the people who knew who we were as we did to Joe Public visiting the Cross. Here were these two big bikers, sergeants-at-arms, both sipping on their shakes which came in these great, heavy glasses.

'What's going on?' I said. 'I thought you were out of the business. Is it club business?'

'Nah mate, it's not club business,' he said. 'We got no problem with your club. The friendship between you and me keeps our clubs pretty steady.'

'Yep, so what's the problem?'

'Well, as you know, I've virtually given up doing what I was doing.' He probably wouldn't have said it exactly like that. We used to have a bit of a code, but getting on all these years I can't remember what it was.

Chance said he'd been offered one more really big job. The pay was too good to pass up. Mr Sin was in a bit of trouble and needed someone to disappear.

'The bloke's up in Queensland,' he said. 'He's got a pretty hot couple of bodyguards. I can't go popping 'em off all over the place. So I was wondering if you were interested in coming up to deal with them?' He must have seen me hesitating, because he added, 'The pay'll be good. It's gunna be worth your while.'

'Chance, it's not about the money,' I said. 'Me and the club are going through a bit of trouble at the moment.'

'Yeah, I've heard about the Comos. It'll only be up and back. You'd only be looking at ten to 12 hours.'

'Well, all right. I'll handle the muscle for you. What's the go?'

Chance told me he'd been watching this guy for about three weeks. He was an American mafia type who'd been trying to move in on Abe's turf. He'd announced that he was coming to Sydney and Abe was going to have to pay him a percentage from all his business dealings. This was a done deal, the Yank said, because he represented the big boys from Las Vegas. Abe didn't take very kindly to this.

So Chance had gone up to the Gold Coast where this bloke was staying to check him out. Chance had watched him regularly going from nightclub to nightclub with his two bodyguards. He knew what his patterns were. So that was where he wanted to hit him.

The muscle was American too. He'd seen them in some blues when people had got in their way. 'These blokes can really handle themselves and they're not shy about pulling a piece, either,' he said. 'One of 'em carries a knife.' He described it to me and I said, 'Oh yeah, that sounds like one of those navy Seals' Ka-Bar survival knives. Where's he carry that?'

'Down the back of his neck.'

'Down the back of his neck?' I thought that was a pretty funny place to carry it.

The more we talked about them, the more I could see that these two blokes had spooked Chance. We'd done the other job on the country estate where there were six. And a few of those blokes were pretty hot special-forces types too. But this pair had him rattled.

So we got on a plane to the Gold Coast. In *Enforcer*, I'd said that my first-ever flight was when I was extradited back from Perth in 1986, but that was actually my second time in a plane. I hadn't wanted to mention this flight at the time, for obvious reasons. I was nervous as all get out. Chance wanted the aisle seat, but I said, 'You're not getting me sitting near the friggin' window.' I didn't want to see how high we were. I sat in the aisle. As we took off, I was having a heart attack, feeling every shudder, hanging on tight, certain that the plane was falling to pieces. Chance just sat back, chilling out with the headphones on.

Anyway, much to my surprise, we arrived safely. We walked out into the airport car park and Chance went straight over to a silver/grey Mercedes and felt under the back left wheel arch. He pulled out a magnetised keyholder and we jumped in. 'It's a rental,' he said, but he didn't explain who got it for him.

We got to a pre-booked hotel and Chance pulled his kit out of the car boot and brought it in. He had the whole bag of goodies. It was just like the movies. He laid everything out on the king-sized bed and checked it all, pulling his piece apart and putting it back together, loading his magazines, checking the springs, fiddling with the silencer.

So we waited until well after dark before we went out on the town. Chance seemed to know where the target would be. We went up an elevator to a restaurant and bar high above the Gold Coast strip.

The place was raging, smoky. The music loud. Michael Jackson, Madonna, that type of thing. You could hardly move through all the people. I was wearing my black jeans, black shirt and bandana, with my hair plaited back tight. It wasn't hard to feel inconspicuous in the throng.

We moved slowly through the crowd until Chance nudged me and gave a tilt of the head towards a table with a view out over the glittering strip. The guy was easy to spot. He couldn't have looked more like a Mafioso if he'd come off the set of *The Godfather*. He had the dark Italian features, the white suit, black shirt and white tie. His black hair was slicked back and a big stogie dangled from his lips. The muscle was with him, looking every bit like two presidential bodyguards. Business suits. Neat hair.

'Fuck me roan,' I said, as we hung back near a thick column. 'I know one of them. I fought him in the round-ringing. His name's Randy.' He was an ex-army Ranger. I'd decked him in about one minute thirty. 'He's not going to be any problem. Just as long as you cover the gun side of things.' I was confident Randy wouldn't recognise me. My beard had been pretty wild in the fighting days, but it was a neatly trimmed goatee now.

The other bloke was a bit bigger and carried himself real well. I watched him walk and I could tell he had a bit of style about him.

We found a spot near the toilets. And we waited. (Just remember, this could well be the three per cent fiction part of the book.) The plan was to use Chance as a distraction, then I'd come in and take them out. We waited and waited until finally, about 1 am, our man needed to relieve himself. These two blokes positioned themselves outside the bathroom door and were blocking anyone else from entering, as Chance had told me they would. Chance got up, acting pissed, and went to push past them. 'Fucking let me in,' he slurred. 'I've gotta fuckin' piss, mate.'

I came up behind him with my eyes half closed, doing my best impersonation of a drunk. I might never have been blotto myself, but I'd sure observed a lot of smashed people. 'C'mon, let me mate in,' I said.

I gave Chance a big shove and pushed him through them to the door. They turned to grab him and, as they did that, I bundled them both up and shoved them through the door. I went smash with a right hook into Randy's face and he went down. I don't think he even saw me. The other bloke got a good one on me. Gave me a black eye. I closed in on him, snapped his arm, then just put a sleeper on him and put him out.

The target was there at the trough, freaking out. He got down on his knees. Begging. I think he knew what was coming.

'You've got ten minutes,' I said to Chance and stepped outside to keep watch while Chance did whatever he did in delivering Abe's Go Fuck Yourself.

When Chance came back out 30 or 40 seconds later, I went back in and grabbed the bigger bloke under the arms and pulled him up into a sitting position. I got the door partially open and held it there with my foot while I flopped him against the door so that, as I closed it, he'd fall against it to make it harder for anyone else to get in. Nearly broke my wrist as the door slammed shut under his weight while I had one hand round the corner trying to keep him in position.

The bouncers hadn't even noticed the kerfuffle. We walked calmly to the exit, got into an express elevator, and hit the down button. 'That was bloody good thinking with the bloke against the door,' Chance said as we zoomed to the bottom.

'Thanks. But you can count me out of your jobs in the future if they're going to be like this. Hundreds of people and we're stuck up the top of a gigantic building with only a couple of friggin' elevators to go down. Give me the six security guards on an estate any day. At least there were a dozen ways out of there.'

We walked out and hopped in the Mercedes. Chance turned south and we drove. He didn't tell me what the plan was and I just thought we must have been driving it all the way back to Sydney, but after about 200 kilometres he turned off into one of those tourist towns on the North Coast of New South Wales. He parked and opened the door.

'Now what are we doing?' I said.

'We're switching cars.' He walked over to an XC Falcon Cobra, threw his gear in the boot and jumped in. It turned out to be one of his own cars. We drove through the night and the morning all the way to Sydney.

Some time later, Chance showed me a newspaper article about the case, but that was the only thing I ever heard about it again.

*

THE JOB paid handsomely and I took the money out to my stash in the garage. My nest egg had been steadily growing from the round-ringing and collecting for more than a decade. Inflation had worked badly against me in the '70s, but it was still a tidy sum. Every time I got a nice big collect or had a win in the ring I'd stash most of it away in a big plastic suitcase. And then I'd needed to get a second big plastic suitcase. I kept both of them behind a false wall in my garage at Ashfield. By the middle of 1984, it had grown to $1.9 million. For easier access, I also had a little box under the floor in the back room of the house. It had $33,000 in it.

My plan was to buy a house for Donna for Christmas. In July 1984, not long after the Gold Coast job, I saw a real estate agent in Bowral in the Southern Highlands south-west of Sydney. The agent showed me a huge Federation-style house on over 10 hectares that had been meticulously looked after. It had five enormous bedrooms, including a wardrobe as big as the lounge room at the place we live in now. The land was divided into paddocks with the painted white post-and-rail fences like you see in the pictures of horse studs in Kentucky. I'd been into horses since I was a kid, so this would have been perfect.

I had enough to buy it with plenty of change. It wasn't that I was ever going to retire from the outlaw life to be a country gentleman, but I could see a future where we slowed down a little out there. The trouble was, I wanted it to be a surprise closer to Christmas, so I thought I'd back off for a few months and hope that it was still on the market in October/November.

HOW TO DO A SLEEPER HOLD

The choker hold is probably the easiest one to try. It's not the best but it's the simplest. Think back to when you've seen a bloke in a movie wrap one arm under a bloke's chin and other around the back of his head, then goes to snap his neck. Instead of snapping the neck, you just squeeze the larynx with your lower arm and that chokes 'em till they pass out. You've just got to learn how long to put it on for. You can feel the body weight drop as they go unconscious, so you don't want to go too far past that.

I always take them straight to the ground so they're easier to control. I know a lot of blokes do it standing up. But there's a risk there that if all his body weight is being supported through the throat, you can crush his larynx as he drops. He can choke on his own blood. So that's why I always take them straight to ground.

You can do it so you can knock a bloke out for 15 to 20 minutes, but you've got to be careful because if you go that little bit too long then you'll croak 'em.

The better sleeper hold is where you put your hand under the bloke's chin same as the other way, with your other hand over the top, but you get your fingers around their vagus nerve and the artery. As you squeeze them with the arm to choke them out, you also squeeze the nerve and the artery. You can knock them out for an hour if you do it that way and you also paralyse the left arm and left leg, so it puts them out of action for some time.

But this isn't something that anybody can just do. I practised it for years when I was doing the *kyite*. We'd do special exercises for the strength in our fingers. All the fellers in the *dojo* were super strong in their wrists, hands and fingers. So we could do it pretty easy whereas the average bloke wouldn't be able to do it. We used to have blokes that would come in and we'd practice on them. I don't know why they did it. They were all Korean and they'd just march up and pay their respects to the *sensei*. But they'd let us get in and find the vagus nerve and the carotid artery on the left of the neck. There was no way I'd let anyone knock me out. That's a sensation I've never felt.

38

THE WORST DAY
OF MY LIFE

We were just a new club. We had very little history
and suddenly we'd been plunged into a war with
the Comancheros, who were starting to do some crazy
things.

Up to that time, if two clubs had irreconcilable differences, one would attack the other at a pub, at their
clubhouse or at a prearranged site like a park. They'd slog
it out with just about every sort of weapon short of guns
and bombs. They kept it away from the public. The club
that won might take the colours of the losers, but they'd
leave the others to pick up their wounded.

Jock knew there was no way his club could ever beat
us in that sort of situation, no matter how many blokes
he recruited and no matter how much he drilled them
with his little formations and war games. If he wanted
to go to war with us, he had no choice but to resort to
guns and other crazy plans. The first volley was fired at

266

the clubhouse one night when a few blokes were inside. Chop and a few of the others who were there were really shocked. It was a shame. It was the dawning of a new era.

Someone shot at me and Donna while we were riding to the clubhouse. Left a hole in my petrol tank. They poured oil and diesel on the curve at the bottom of a hill near the clubhouse trying to bring us all down, not caring if there were old ladies on the back or what.

Through the winter of 1984, it escalated. There were more shots fired, a few small-scale blues, a few blokes run off the road. But because we were so confident in our ability to smash the shit out of the Comos, we never felt the need to arm up. I strapped an aluminium baseball bat to my handlebars, but that was it.

I'd been sergeant-at-arms of the Comos and the Bandits for near on five years and during that time not one member went to jail or got badly hurt – not until Junior got put in hospital by a bunch of Comos who attacked him while he was with his old lady. That's what kicked off the whole war.

John Boy was killed in a bike accident in 1982 and Knuckles was severely injured in another one a year later, but until 2 September 1984, Father's Day, I'd managed to keep everybody pretty safe.

And as the blokes who gathered at Lance's place on that day knew, I wanted to go to the Caringbah Inn because it was a longer ride and they had bands on there. But I had a whole heap of blokes talking over the top of me about going to the Viking Tavern at Milperra for a swap meet. If I'd done what I normally did and listened to my gut feeling, we'd have gone to Caringbah and there wouldn't have been any Father's Day massacre at the tavern.

We would have heard on the grapevine how the entire Comanchero club turned up at the Viking Tavern with guns and walkie-talkies waiting for us. We would have known that they'd taken the war to a whole new level and we would not have been taken by surprise again.

Far from preparing for war, the Bandidos began the day at my son Daniel's fourth birthday party. We left the old ladies and the kids there, in a corner-block backyard that was in full view of Frederick Street, Ashfield. We weren't bunkering down for a battle. We rode to Lance's and decided where we'd go next. Snoddy had spent the previous few days in Griffith, shooting and getting to know a bunch of blokes who wanted to open a Bandido chapter down there. So he drove straight up from Griffith that morning and met us at Lance's place, with a shotgun and a carbine in the back of his station wagon, buried deep under the rest of his camping gear. They were the only guns we entered that car park with.

*

THE MINI-SERIES *Bikie Wars* portrays us all riding in on bikes, many of us armed. Snoddy's got a gun attached to his back as do a bunch of the other Bandidos.

Then everybody just stares at everybody in slowmo for a full three minutes while the dramatic music plays. The whole show is filled with lots of blokes just staring somewhere. They had so little material to fill six episodes, I guess they had to pad it out with montages.

What really happened was that Snoddy's Falcon was first into the driveway of the sprawling ranch-style pub, followed by Bull's Holden, then me on my Harley followed by the rest of the club. We turned right into one of the car park rows shaded by skinny gum trees, but there were no spots to stop. The place was crowded with people and stalls. The smell of barbecuing meat filled the air. Snoddy and Bull drove slowly through the car park until a car pulled out in front of Snoddy, blocking his way. I looked back to check on the rest of the blokes and I saw that they were all in the car park. That's when I noticed the first sign of trouble.

Jock's sidekick, Foghorn, was driving a ute in behind us. He stopped, blocking our way back out. I watched him get out of the ute carrying an M1 carbine – the American World War II semi-automatic – and run down into the crowd towards the pub.

I looked down and saw a bunch of Comancheros standing about three car park rows below us. They all had shotguns on their hips. I saw Leroy, who had become their sergeant-at-arms, among them. I looked around for Jock, but couldn't see him. I figured that, as usual, he'd sent his blokes out while he stayed back at the clubhouse.

There was no time to think. We weren't ready for a gun battle. And we were trapped. I figured if we walked or ran out of the car park, we'd be shot in the back. I think they expected that when we saw all the guns we'd go to water, panic and throw our colours down, or whatever. They'd obviously forgotten who they were dealing with.

I got off my bike and started walking straight towards them without bothering to get the bat off my handlebars. I just strode down between the rows of parked cars, yelling: 'Put down your guns and fight like men.'

That was about the only detail that the *Bikie Wars* got right. They have that ugly, tubby little bloke who plays me walking down there and saying, 'Why don't you put the guns down. Fight like men.' Then they've got him staring at some bloke for a bit trying to look tough before he pushes the bloke's gun upwards, it fires into the air and then it's all on.

The television fight lasts for just two minutes before they give Snoddy some magical ability to call it off, before you have to sit through three more minutes of Snoddy staring into space while the spooky music plays.

In reality, when I was walking down towards the Comos, I was thinking that if I could just get to Leroy, he'd probably put down his gun and have a go at me, one on one. The other thing flashing through my head was that the closer I got to them, the better chance I had of grabbing a couple of them and snatching their guns. That way, if anyone started shooting, I had something to shoot back with.

I was about one car-length away from Leroy when I challenged him directly.

'You really want to go, one on one?' he said.

'Yeah, put down your gun and let's do it. If you win, we'll drop our colours. If I win, youse drop your colours and that's the end of the war.'

'You're on.'

Leroy was a big boy, and super-strong. A real hard bloke. He put his shotgun down against the car and shaped up.

I thought I was alone, but then I looked back over my right shoulder and there were my brothers Shadow, Chop, Bull, Snake and Wack, along with Davo, Gloves, Roach, Lance and Zorba all spread in line just behind me. Bear was running down towards us. They'd all come down to back me up and I felt this intense pride. None of us had a gun. This was what it was all about, punching on when the odds were against you.

Then I realised that they were the only ones. The rest of the club had either stayed back with the cars or run out into the street.

I looked back at Leroy. Standing just behind him was a Como by the name of Hennessey, shaking like a leaf, his gun still at his hip. I thought, *This bloke's gunna be a real worry.* He was staring at my brother Snake, and

Snake was calling him all the names under the sun. I knew this Hennessey didn't want to start shooting, but that he might just because he was so scared of Snake.

Snake said something like, 'Put the gun down if you're not gunna use it. If you're gunna use it, use it.'

There was a bang and Snake went down. He'd been hit in the gut. He sat there with his hands over the wound, blood spurting out of his stomach.

I went cold.

At that moment, I just wished Jock was there so I could've snapped his neck.

I heard Snoddy, still up at his station wagon, calling Chop and Shadow to come back up and join him. Snoddy had to get round the back of his car and throw all his camping gear out to get to his two pig-shooting guns and the ammunition.

Back down where I was, Leroy picked up his gun and ran behind a car. Straight in front of me in a tight little group were Sparra, Tonka and Snowy, all with shotguns hanging by their sides. They started to raise them, so I charged. I got my left arm wrapped around the barrels of their guns and had them pointed at the ground while I barged the three of them back onto the front of a car, pinning them down with my body. I was really giving it to Tonka while holding the other two down. Tonka hit the deck and I stomped on his chest and head with my Johnny Reb boots, crushing one side of his skull. I did everything I could to get him out of it until he went limp. Then, still holding Sparra down, I started belting in on Snowy with my elbow. He fell to the ground, soft as, unconscious.

That left just me and Sparra. With my left hand still pinning down the shotty in his right hand, he used his left to start throwing punches. I used my spare hand to grab him by the throat. I tried to go for the vagus nerve on the side of his neck. If you know the right spot, you can knock a man out or kill him by hitting the vagus nerve.

I looked over my shoulder and saw Snake sitting there still holding his guts in, blood pouring through his hands. Leroy was standing over the top of him, his shotgun down by his leg virtually pointed at Snake's head like he was about to finish him off.

I zoned out. The world went red. I gripped harder into Sparra's neck. I felt the shotty drop out of his hand and I squeezed harder. I felt my fingers ripping his skin. I saw blood coming out, and felt my fingers go deeper into his flesh. I felt the side of his neck rip away as he hit the ground screaming.

I looked up and saw sneaky little Glen Eaves, Jock's brother-in-law. He was a tiny bloke with a real big mouth when he had a lot of blokes around him. He'd been in the army and he was lying on the ground in a firing position, pointing the shotty at me. For some reason, I think to get a better shot at me, he tried to get up onto his knees. But as he tried getting off the ground, he stumbled and the shotgun discharged into the ground near Sparra. I saw Sparra jerk, so I figured something had hit him. When they later took him away and did the autopsies, they found the wadding from a shotgun cartridge in his neck and concluded he'd been killed by the shotgun.

But only after half his neck had been ripped out.

Once the shooting had started, it came from everywhere. All I could hear was gunshots, but with all the rows of parked cars it was impossible to see where they were coming from. I looked around: there were Como colours climbing the back fence out of the car park, a bunch of them jumping into a green XY Falcon and heading for the bottle shop entrance. They took the door off the bottle-o, they were trying to get out of the car park that quick.

Most of the Bandidos who'd come down with me had got back to Snoddy and Bull's station wagons by this stage.

Snake was still sitting there with the blood spurting out between his fingers. My only thought was to get to him, and anyone who got in my way was a dead man. I took a step towards him. I saw Bull had this really huge Como down at the front of his car, kicking the shit out of him, while the bloke was trying to crawl under his car to get away.

A Como came towards me and I grabbed him by the hair and started laying in. Davo was standing alongside me fighting another Como I'd never seen before. Davo was a real good bluer, and he'd just finished this bloke off when I saw another Como coming up behind him with a bowie knife. I had my hands full, so all I could do was yell out to Davo. He turned around just in time. Instead of getting it in the middle of the back, he got it up under his arm. Didn't that get him started! He turned around and beat the shit out of the bloke.

I finished with the bloke who'd just come at me and took another step towards Snake when, for some reason, I turned to my left. *Bang!* I felt it in the right shoulder. I staggered back a metre. I'd been hit hard by something. I didn't know what it was. I was stunned. It was a strange feeling. I always figured that if you got shot with a serious weapon, you'd get a burning, hot feeling. But it wasn't like that. It was just like getting hit with a baseball bat. I'd been hit with a .22 before, but that was more like a pinprick. I soon realised this was a shotgun blast when I saw blood spurting out of a lot of holes. My arm went numb.

Then I felt another thud – this time to my chest. It was like another baseball bat, but this time I knew straight-away what it was. Blood spurted out of my arm and my chest. Breathing became difficult. I coughed and blood came out.

I think I went down on one knee, because I was bent over when a Como by the name of Alan came at me with an iron bar and, *Whack!*, he hit me on the side of the head, which I didn't like.

I just went *whooshka*, swung my hand out and caught him right in the nuts. He hit the ground alongside me and I grabbed him by the throat. I tried to rip his throat out, and I don't know if it was from being shot or what, because my wounds were on my right side, but I just couldn't get enough power into my left hand to do it.

I got to my feet, took the iron bar off him and hit him with it, then put the heel of my boot into his mouth. His teeth went everywhere and I started stomping on his head.

I could hear Chop and Shadow, about 6 metres off to my right, yelling, 'Bandidos! Bandidos!' It's a sound I'll always remember. They just seemed to keep yelling out, and even though I'd been shot twice, hearing my brothers yelling gave me strength.

Lance and Zorba were over bashing some Comos, Glovesy was still giving it to someone. I looked up and I was hoping to see the rest of the club come screaming towards us, because I knew if the lot of us had gone these blokes we'd have run over the top of them. But it didn't happen.

I saw the Como JJ and his old lady down between two cars looking up at me pointing a handgun. I can't remember to tell the truth whether it was JJ or his old lady with the gun, because I had blood spurting into my eyes and I was feeling real dizzy, but knowing JJ it was probably his old lady. She had more balls than he did. I was looking down there through this haze and then all of a sudden I felt *Whack!*, in the forehead. I didn't think

I'd been shot, I just felt this thud and then a burning sensation and blood was in my eyes. I was staggering around blind, but I heard a voice. It was Bull. 'Get out of here, Ceese!' I wiped my eyes and saw Bull and Wack heading towards Snake.

I started finding it really hard to breathe. And then all I heard was Bull yelling, 'Get out of here or you're going to die.' He was right.

I looked up to Snoddy's Falcon about 10 metres away and saw him leaning out of it shooting towards the Comos who were about 10 metres behind me. There was Chop and Shadow standing out in the open, back where I'd been, just a couple of metres from the Comos, firing away with guns they must have snatched off the Comos, screaming to the other Bandits to get up to the street.

As I staggered up, I felt, *Whack, whack, whack*. Little stings in the back. I knew from experience that they were probably .22s but I didn't know what was going on. It was too hard to see through the blood.

'Fuck it.' I stopped to turn around and go back down there to kill as many of them as I could before dying. Then something inside said to me, 'No. Walk out.' So I turned around again and lurched back up to the left and out of the direct crossfire.

My right leg was dragging and I couldn't feel my right arm. It was hard to breathe, but I just kept going and made it to the road. I saw all these Bandits up there. 'Go down and help your brothers,' I yelled, but I'm not sure how loud it came out. They might not have heard a thing.

Knuckles came up and grabbed me under the left arm. Lout and Bernie came over. Both of them yelled to Hookie to come and help me. One of them waved down a car and it turned out to be this sheila who knocked around the club, Big Sue. Lout, Hookie and Bernie threw me into the back of her green HK or HT Holden and I remember the car moving and seeing red and I was playing the last few minutes over in my mind. The numbness turned to pain. I remember Lout saying, 'We've got to get him to the hospital,' and hearing sirens.

Suddenly, someone was helping me up a hospital driveway, leaving me there on the ground outside. Later, I found out that one of them had run over and rung the bell to Emergency and the nurses had come out to find me lying there.

I was supported through some glass doors and now there were nurses all around me. I was on a bed or a table.

I was the first person from the tavern to reach the hospital. I could hear on the radio that they'd interrupted the program to report a bikie shooting in Milperra. The Asian doctor who was working on me said, 'What's going on down there?'

I was thinking, *Fuckin' just fix me up*. The pain was getting worse.

The nurses tried to make me as comfortable as possible, but the doctor was trying to get my colours off me.

'You're not having me colours,' I said.

'You've got to take them off so I can examine you.'

There was no way anyone was getting my colours. I'd been shot every which way. I'd seen my brother shot. I'd smashed and probably killed one bloke by ripping half his throat out. All for these colours. There was no way they were coming off.

'I've got to examine you,' he said. There was a running argument for about five minutes and I took a swipe at him. 'My colours stay here.'

'You'll die if we can't get them off.'

I had my left hand over my chest holding the vest under my right arm so they couldn't take it. Some wardsmen came in and they had enough blokes to hold me down. I didn't have the strength to resist. They cut the vest up the right-hand side and along the top of the shoulder, so they could slip it off.

I heard the doctor say, 'We've got to stem the flow of blood from his head.' Something sharp got stuck into my head, then the doctor was pulling at something in my forehead. 'Does this look like a bullet to you?' I heard the doctor asking the nurse.

It turned out that JJ or his old lady had shot me in the head with a .38, which miraculously just lodged in my skull without penetrating.

Then the quack yelled out to a nurse that my lung had deflated. He grabbed a rod about 30 centimetres long with a thread on it like a self-tapping screw. He came up to me and thumped it in under my right arm, and started more or less screwing it in through the side of my chest.

I took a deep breath, and that's the last I remember.

CAESAR'S LAW
XX

IS THERE A GOD?

Yes.

I say a prayer to my old man, my grandfather and my ancestors every night. And I ask the big man upstairs to look after my woman, my children and grandchildren, and to make sure they have long, healthy and happy lives.

When God considers it's my time I'll come, no problems.

I went to church seven days a week from the age of four. My Dad's dad, Joey Campbell, used to drag me along to the six o'clock mass every day and he'd do the 10 o'clock on Sunday as well. When I was almost eight I became an altar boy and I did that till I was about ten.

Believing in God helps you through life. If you don't fear death, you fear nothing. Donna worries that once you die there's nothing more there. With me, I'm the opposite. I didn't know my brothers had been killed on Fathers' Day 1984, but when I flatlined and they put me out in the hallway I saw my father and my grandfather and some of my grandfather's brothers, and I saw Chop and Shadow with them. So I firmly believe that once you go, they're all there waiting.

My grandfather looked like photos I'd seen of him as a young bloke. I believe that when you go, you don't go up as a 70-year-old, you go as what you were in your prime.

But I also believe that when men who have lived violent lives die, the only way to get into heaven is to fight a battle angel. And when men like me (and there are only a few, like Achilles, Genghis Khan, Attila the Hun, and Angus the Red Campbell) die, we have to fight the king of the battle angels to get into heaven.

39

I DIED FOR THIS CLUB

I didn't find out until I woke up weeks later that Chop and Shadow had been killed doing what Campbells always did – going forward, protecting their brothers in the front line. No matter what the current Bandidos have been told, there's an undeniable fact that some of the original Bandidos you're riding with now would not be here today if it hadn't been for my brothers Bull, Snake, Chop, Wack and Shadow. They saved a lot of Bandido lives that day. If anyone who was out there on Father's Day at the tavern says different, they're a liar. They stood their ground, unarmed, with guns pointing at them from everywhere down in the middle of that car park and they defended their brother Bandidos. And Snoddy is included in that. If it hadn't been for Snoddy providing the covering fire, three-quarters of the club could have been killed and it really would have been a massacre, instead of four Comos dead, two Bandidos and one innocent bystander. Every Como had a gun and we rode in with fuck-all.

Of all the clubs that I've had anything to do with, the Bandidos are the club I respect the most and the one I hold in the highest regard. The members who wear the fat Mexican today should be the proudest men in Australia.

I died for this club, too. The doctors lost my pulse and gave up on me. With all the other casualties rushed into emergency, I got wheeled into a corridor with a sheet pulled over my head. If it hadn't been for a nurse noticing the sheet moving an hour and a half later, I might have died. Somehow, I came back. There were five or six Bandits who wished I hadn't.

I beat myself up something fierce over what happened on Father's Day. I didn't stick to my gut feeling. I let Snoddy overrule me when I suggested we send some blokes down there to check out the tavern before we went. My two brothers died that day. Snoddy committed suicide in prison seven months later, and my brother Wack, who was shot in the arm at Milperra, developed cardiomyopathy in jail and died in 1987. If it hadn't been for the shootout, he would have got proper treatment and survived. (Snake recovered well from his belly shot.) So the toll was heavy. I've got that to carry on my shoulders.

When I was lying in the coma after Milperra, the coppers raided our house. The warrant they handed to Donna said it was to search for me, but I was under police guard in ICU at Bankstown Hospital. They went through the place like a bad smell. They stole Donna's leather jackets, her leather jeans. They stole eighty or ninety grand worth of jewellery. There were female coppers there rummaging around like the Boxing Day sales. The cops took my martial arts trophies, even my *gi* – the black karate uniform. My leather pants, a leather jacket. They took my photo albums. That's why

I haven't had the best array of pictures for these books. I've had to rely on photos that my mum and sisters had. And they found the plastic suitcases with $1.9 million in them.

I know I said in *Enforcer* that they stole a smaller amount. I didn't feel ready when I wrote that to explain how I got it all, but since I've now told you what I did, I might as well tell you what I lost.

I walked out of hospital before I was charged and, when they eventually arrested me, in February 1986, I got offered so much money by the cops to dog on my club you wouldn't believe it: thousands of dollars a week for the rest of my life, plus a house, to turn Crown witness against my brothers. But I didn't. I never could and never would.

Needless to say, our lives would be a lot different had that money not been stolen. By the time I got out of prison in 1990, I was almost 44 years old. The peak earning years in my profession were behind me and life was never the same again.

*

I ALSO fudged over another story in *Wrecking Crew*. While I was in prison, Abe got convicted on tax matters, because Jim Anderson turned against him. Abe was in the Long Bay hospital wing. He got a message to me that there'd been a contract put out on his life and that a bloke with a heavy reputation had managed to get himself into the hospital wing to do the job.

I told the screws I had chest pains. I knew that with my family's history of heart problems they'd have to put me straight in the hospital. And they did, but then they went and gave me an angiogram. They put the probe up through my groin, checked out my arteries, the whole bit. I would have been sent straight back to the Metropolitan Training Centre with a clean bill of health, except when they took the probe out of the artery in my groin they didn't tie the artery off properly so I bled really badly into my leg. The whole thing swelled up and turned black and blue. So, even though my heart was good, they stuffed up my leg and I really did need to stay in hospital.

Abe's room was next to mine and, at the first opportunity, I went in to say hello. His room was decked out with cosmetics and skin lotions. He had about five little foam heads to put his toupees on. He pointed out to me who it was had the hit on him, so I waited for the shift change to come on. The staff used to go down the corridor to have a yak, so I hopped over to this bloke's bed. I grabbed him and got him in a choke hold with my thumb in his eye. 'If you ever go near Abe Saffron, you won't ever wake up again,' I said. 'You're going to go bye-byes now. In the morning when you wake up, I want you to think about how lucky you are and to realise that you might never have woken up.' I throttled him tighter. 'And you tell your bosses (Abe apparently knew who had put out the contract) that they can be got at too. I've got plenty of friends on the outside. And Abe's got more . . .' I choked him out into slumberland.

He was cured and gone the next morning.

CAESAR'S LAW
XXI

HOW TO SURVIVE BEING SHOT

There's no real art to it. I've been shot that many times I couldn't tell you the number. But I can tell you that I just don't like giving in to anything.

It's like when I go into hospital for these operations and they tell me I've got a ten per cent chance of coming back out. I just treat the disease or the problem as a Como. None of them are getting over the top of me. A positive outlook has a lot to do with it. Plus meditation.

I do a lot of meditation. I got taught it when I was doing the *kyite*. I can't tell you how we do it, but it's the sort of thing where once you learn to do it, it takes about 20 minutes to get in the zone, and once you're there, you can zone yourself out and stop pain. I could get my heart rate down to nine when I was practising it a lot. One of the doctors at Bankstown Hospital reckoned that that was probably what happened when they thought I flatlined after Milperra. He said, 'You probably went into your meditation to control the pain you were in and you instinctively took your heart rate down that low. So it's gone down to being almost non-existent and the machine didn't pick it up.'

I don't know if that's right or not, but everybody should do meditation. Especially if there's a chance someone might be coming after you.

40

CLUB BUSINESS

After prison, nothing was the same for my brothers and me, and the Bandidos. Just like happened at the Comancheros, we made a lot of our club brothers feel inferior because of the way we always took it upon ourselves to be up front in the fights. If anything, the feeling got stronger in the Bandidos. A lot of our club brothers resented the fact that when blokes from other clubs wanted to talk to our club, they'd seek out the Campbells. Mainly me, but if I wasn't around they'd want to talk to one of my brothers. The fact was, we knew a lot of blokes from over the years. This made a lot of other brothers unhappy or jealous.

A clique got together that didn't want us in the club anymore. Especially after Father's Day, when new blokes started joining. And prison can make a man lose his balls. Once they've been inside, a lot of blokes don't want to go back. The Campbells were portrayed as loose cannons who might start another war. Not that we would intentionally. Me and my brothers back down from no one. And we avenge those who wrong us. But I'd given my word to Kid Rotten and Mum and Donna that I wouldn't go after the Comos. Mum had already lost three sons to that war. One wasn't killed by the Comos. I consider that the cops and the DPP murdered Wack by opposing his bail when they knew he was dying.

Anyway, facing these internal pressures, gradually my brothers left the club. Wheels retired, Bull retired, Snake had some argument with the new national vice president, Mick K, and made an agreement with him. I don't know what that was about. My son Caspar had joined the club while I was inside and rose to become a sergeant-at-arms. We became the first Australian Bandido father and son to ride together and the first Bandido father and son sergeants, but he retired too. He'd wanted to be a Bandit since he was 14. He was born for it, but that just shows the pressures that were going on at that time in the mid-'90s.

One of the retired outlaws we've got down here in the Snowy Mountains is PJ. I've known him since 1970. He only retired in the early part of the 2000s. His club can be proud of him, but God he's a pest. He's forever asking questions about what happened between me and Mick K and I keep telling him, 'Donna put it in the second book, *Wrecking Crew*.' He says, 'I know, I've read 'em both, but I can't help thinking there's more to the story between you and Mick K. Every time he was around our club at a party or whatever, he couldn't help himself boasting about how he'd fooled ya.'

'Yeah, him and five others. But while they wear the same patch as me, there's nothing I can do about it.'

In short, Mick K knew I wasn't in on his way of doing things. He told me that the Americans were going to close down the Bandidos in Australia if I didn't leave the club. I was a fool to believe him. But I wasn't going to retire and I wasn't leaving the club. I said, 'Let 'em come and try and take me colours.'

'Nah, you've got to do it for the club,' Mick K said, hitting me on my soft spot. I'd do anything for the club. My brothers had died for it, and I almost had too. We went back and forth and I got him to agree that we'd pretend I'd retired for 18 months until things had cooled down, but it was really just 'special leave'. At the end of the 18 months, I'd come back and resume my membership as normal, with no time lost, so I'd get all my anniversary badges, all the T-shirts. I thought I was doing the right thing by my brothers and my club, but I was getting stabbed in the back.

He was meant to tell four other blokes about the deal, but he never did. He showed off a set of colours that he said was mine. (They were Lurch's old colours.) He said I'd handed them in. Then, about a year later, he went and got himself wasted, shot in the basement of the Black-market nightclub in November 1997, and our secret deal died with him.

I wasn't going to go rushing in there and jump up and down just after the guy, plus another member and a prospect, had been put in the ground. So I waited. I was waiting for someone to come and see me and hear my side of the story. And to this day I've been waiting for some of the young blokes who've read the books, especially *Wrecking Crew*, to come and ask my side of the story.

I think everyone who's lived long enough has had a time where they trusted someone because they believed them to be a brother or a really top mate and they got conned. That's what happened to me. I lost my club. Aside from family, I lived for being a Bandido. I still am a Bandido, so it's really hard when I see a pack of my brothers riding down the road and I can't put my colours on to join them. I only ever wear the colours now on Shadow's, Chop's and Wack's birthdays, and sometimes on Father's Day I ride up to their graves at Rookwood. On their birthdays, I ride up to a spot in the mountains. I spend a couple of hours sitting up there thinking about them and about the world. Then I ride home and take the colours off and put 'em away till the next time, and if that offends anyone, well that's too bad.

I never handed my colours in. I never retired. I never left the club. I don't mean any disrespect to the club or the new members, but the original members should know what me and my brothers did for the club. I know a few tried to tell them the truth about my situation, like Lance Wellington and Rua. But they got shot down in flames.

It's just too bad that things happen like this and people are just too scared to stand up and tell the brothers in the club what Mick K was really like. For him, money came first, money came second, money came third, girls came fourth – and the club was just a way of getting both.

And it would be remiss of me if I didn't mention Dukes McElwaine. Probably out of all the original members, he tried hardest to tell everyone that I'd been stabbed in the back and that he had come down and seen me and saw that I still had my colours. He said that trying to tell the club members was like talking to a brick wall. He said Mick K had his little crew spread that much money around that people just weren't interested in listening. Dukes was a real brother.

I said, 'Thanks, Dukes. It's nice to know that there's at least a few brothers out there where loyalty and honour count.'

'Don't worry, Caesar. It'll come good. People will realise what you and your brothers did for the club.'

Sadly, Dukes had some personal problems later on and ended up not being around the club much and I didn't hear a lot more from him. He had an accident and busted his arms up pretty bad and spent a bit of time in hospital. He just tended to keep to himself after that. I was really hurt that no one bothered telling me that he'd died when he did. I didn't find out till about two months after his funeral. If I'd known, I'd have been there no matter what. Top man, top member of the Bandidos. It's good to see that his son Luke has joined the club and followed in his dad's foot-steps. If he can be half as good as Dukes, he'll be a really good member. I know what it's like to lose your dad when you're still young. I wish him all the best with his club and personal life.

I'm just waiting for someone at the club to step up at a meeting and say we should do the right thing by Caesar and give him his badges and his anniversary T-shirts and show him the respect he deserves.

It's been claimed to me that I left the club when I handed over my colours. But everyone knew what my colours looked like. For a start, there were the bullet holes through the leather where I'd been shot at Milperra. Any Bandit is welcome to come down and have a chat and see them for himself. I'll be buried in them. I hope my club pays me that little bit of respect in the end and gives me a club funeral, but if they don't, well, they say karma's a bitch.

There does seem to be a bit of a change coming in the club. Snake has made friends with three or four of the new breed and, after they've got to know him, they've turned around and told him things were completely different from what they'd been told. It's good to see some of the newer members are starting to check out things and not listen so much to the stories they were told about the Campbells.

We're not the boogie men we've been portrayed as. What the young Bandidos don't realise is that there are a lot of Campbells who are proudly retired from the club, and I'd like to think that if the club was ever at war again, or if we were needed in any way, that we'd come and do what we can.

I don't hold any grudge against the club. I do hold grudges against four or five blokes who are in my club, and I will to the day I die. But I brought in the rule that one Bandido does not fight another Bandido and I'll stick to it till that day too. If I had actually left the club, there would be five blokes out there who would never have ridden again, because they wouldn't have any kneecaps. But that could only happen if I wasn't a Bandido ... and I am, so they've got no worries. I'll always back up the patch.

So when PJ brings it up, I do get a bit worked up and he'll end up going, 'Calm down, big feller. I didn't mean to get you upset. I just wanted to know for sure.'

'Yeah, but PJ, I get sick of these questions. It's not just you and blokes from other clubs. It's everyone here in the mountains. If I go to Sydney, it's me own relatives, my sons and my sisters. You wouldn't believe how much I get asked about it. And I can't go right into it because a lot of it is still club business and you know the rules about club business.'

CAESAR'S LAW
XXII

FAMILY BALANCE

A lot of outlaw bikers have this thing where they think that if you're going to be completely 100 per cent outlaw and devoted to your club, you can't have a real family life. That's a load of crap and the Bandits can prove that. I had a really good family life and a top club life. To prove it, my son Caspar came into the Bandidos when he was old enough and ended up being sergeant-at-arms of the Bandit chapter.

Kid Rotten has got two sons in the Bandits. I believe one's the president. So Kid's had a good family life. It goes to show if you work on balancing it out, you can get it right. If you think your life has got to be just like you read in *Easy Rider* or *Live to Ride* magazine, you'll probably get it wrong. A bloke has just gotta work it out himself. And the bloke who has a really good family life has a really good outlaw life, and they're the type of blokes I want in my club.

41

STRONG MEN, STRONGER WOMEN

When I first came up to the Snowy in the 2000s, I also met Bear, who was president of the Rebels' Snowy Mountains chapter. Me and him got on like a house on fire. I'm proud to call Bear brother. And I'm proud to call his son Cub brother as well. We've adopted them as Campbells and we're proud to have them.

They've since moved away, but when I was in Canberra Hospital, I had Bear and Cub come down from the North Coast and spend days with me. I didn't know they were there, along with Bull and Snake and my son, Daniel. When I came out of the coma, the first person I saw was Donna. She was holding my hand. In the background were all my brothers standing with Bear, Cub and Daniel. Bull grabbed my hand and started rubbing it. 'Come on, big feller, come out of it. Fight. You've been a fighter all your life. Don't let this take you.'

Gradually, as my vision cleared, I could see my daughter Chyanne's face. This might sound funny, but I've got a Superman doll I call Supernut and when my vision cleared up I saw Supernut sitting on my chest. My daughters had brought it for me.

I spent nine days in the coma and then another two and a half weeks there. I had Bear and Cub backwards and forwards from the North Coast. Same with my brothers and daughters. Daniel and Donna were there full time. It means a lot when you see how much your family thinks of you. And I had mates like Witch, Chance, Irish and PJ come to see me in the ward. It was good to see old outlaw bikers who didn't forget their brother. And I'd like to thank all the nurses at ICU and Ward 7 for the care they gave me.

Chance and I were having a conversation up in the ward just after Bear and Cub had gone home. I'd especially wanted Bear to meet Chance. Chance said, 'Isn't it funny that you and me – a couple of blokes that have done what we've done over the years – death has sort of been a mate to both of us. Death has sat on our shoulders. He's been on your shoulder more than once. You've been over the line a couple of times. I've been there once. We keep coming back. I suppose in the professions we were in, it was bound to happen that death would be a riding mate. When you think about it, he's a constant companion for any outlaw biker.'

'It's funny you say that. I said that to me brothers when they started outlawing, that being an outlaw biker was the most dangerous thing you could do, except for going to war for your country. I still stand by that.'

'Yep, I'll agree to that. How are they treating you?'

'The nurses have been great. Just as good as the ones up the mountain.'

Donna was in a big recliner chair they'd brought in for her. I had a chest infection, a kidney infection, a liver infection. Mum was crook at the time, too. She came down from Sydney and spent of bit time with me.

She was the best mum in the world. She died a few months later at the age of 88. She'd been a mother to a lot of Bandits. Snoddy, Dukes, Lout, they all used to go see her. She had 14 kids – plus we adopted Chop – and she raised them mostly by herself, with a bit of help from me after Dad died at age 46 in 1969. If there's ever been a sweeter, gentler woman put on this earth, I don't know of her.

In saying that, she was also one of the toughest. She put the extra into extraordinary. She was a great match up for my dad, who is the greatest man to come out of Newcastle. When she died, Mum had 89 grandchildren. Sixty-five per cent of them were male. That's a testament to any woman. Mum, if you're looking down, I love you. Always have and always will. You've always been the best mum. If Donna hadn't come along, you would have been easily the best woman, but I'll call it a tie between you and my woman.

It was a strange thing to see all these tough blokes from the Wrecking Crew – toughest blokes ever to put a leg over a Harley – all shattered because this sweet, gentle little woman had passed away. Everyone in the family was shattered. All the neighbours where she lived for the last 30 years – they were all shattered too. Everyone in Woolloomooloo went to Mum for advice and support whenever they had a problem. She was one of a kind.

*

PJ's THE big joker in our gang of retired bikers. We were down the pub probably in November 2014, not long before I got shot, and he was saying to all the fellers, 'Do you remember the old saying about strong men and weak men?' Irish pops up and says, 'Yeah, but you'd have to change it around if you were to say it today. Back in the old days it was, "Strong men go to outlaw clubs and weak men hide behind a blue uniform, a badge and a gun." The strong men still go to outlaw clubs but the weak men hide behind a blue uniform, a badge, a semi-automatic, a Taser, capsicum spray, a baton, body armour. And then they have the tactical response girlie squads to back 'em up.'

Irish turned to me. 'Caesar,' he said, 'you're the best known for getting into blues. Out of all these special squads, I take it you've offered plenty of 'em on, one on one. I know there have been a few coppers who have taken you up on that offer and stepped out from behind their badge and their gun.'

'Yeah,' I said. 'There have been a few.'

'But did any blokes from these special squads ever step out from behind their uniform?'

'Not one.'

I told them how the cops still harass us. They couldn't waste the taxpayer's money anymore if they tried. 'My young bloke walks out the front door and he's followed by one to two police cars everywhere he goes. They sit outside Woolworths if he goes shopping. They search him once a day. He's clean as a whistle. Not one of 'em has ever offered to step around the corner one on one with him. They've red-flagged him. There's always got to be four or five of them there to search him. Daniel's as tough as they come. He's a top amateur boxer. He's a qualified *muy thai* instructor and these blokes don't know what they're messing with. I've told him to keep his hands in his pockets. He's been off the road for about three years now, because every time he drives they harass the shit out of him.'

And PJ said, 'Wow, your young bloke's got it good. I remember back in the day if the coppers were to pull you over there had to be ten or twelve of them.'

'Yeah, but that was a long time ago, PJ,' I said. 'I can remember the same thing happening with you and with Chance and Guitar and Juno and Alex from the Rebels. It happened to a lot of us. You got pulled over and the coppers would stand 6 metres away waiting for reinforcements before going through your bike.'

Then we talked about the time the Galloping Gooses got this guy up at Mt Colah. He'd done something he shouldn't and they tied him to a tree and did a bit of barbecuing. Some bushwalker found him and called the cops and next thing you know it's in the paper that 'Hells Angels barbecue man'. That week, all the Hells Angels in Australia had been in Melbourne. Just shows that the media and the police don't worry too much about the truth. The headline 'Galloping Gooses BBQ man' doesn't sound nearly so good.

*

As us old-school outlaw bikers sat round a table in Cooma having a drink recently – me with my orange juice and everyone else with Wild Turkey – we were talking about the way things had declined between outlaw clubs and the police force and how it was the worst it had ever been. Scotty said, 'I think it's because 95 per cent of coppers these days think they've got to prove they're RoboCop. Plus, to try and break the clubs up, they're fitting everyone up more. In the old days they'd plant a bit of pot on you and you'd get a fine or you might go away for a few months, but these days they're planting guns on the blokes.'

I agreed.

They've got huge power. They can set you up or put it out there that you're an informer. It just takes one junkie or one bloke facing ten years for half a key of speed to get the offer of six months if he just tells such and such that he heard you giving him up in the cop shop while he was there. Or they just plant two keys of coke on you.

'They'd do anything these days to put an outlaw biker off the road,' I said. 'Right down to pushing bikes into traffic.' They do it subtly, just nudging you, waiting for the big truck to come past so it takes out your front end, but a member of the public passing by won't even notice. They'll just see an outlaw biker and if he retaliates all they'll see is the biker attacking an innocent police car. The life of an outlaw biker isn't easy. And it's not for everyone. You've got to be strong. If you can do ten years in an outlaw club, you're doing well, especially these days.

I watch a lot of the young blokes in outlaw clubs today and I know they would love to have lived the life that my brothers and I lived back in the early days and, if given the chance, they would have been just as well-known as Guitar, Nino Palazaro, Matchie, Sheepie, Metho Tom and my brothers. It's just a different culture today. I'm not saying it's bad, it's just different. I'll respect anyone who'll put on an outlaw patch. You've got to have guts and you've got to have honour.

✳

I OFTEN get asked who the toughest blokes on the scene were back in my day. Outside of my brothers, it would be Sheepskin, Les Markham from Corporation of Sin, Brian Mason from the Mobshitters, Nino Palazaro from the Gypsy Jokers and Gino Vella (even though I never had a run-in with him, my spies tell me he was pretty good).

If I had to rate the club presidents, that would be easy. That would be Alex Vella from the Rebels. He had a dream to make his club the biggest in the country and he saw that dream fulfilled. Unfortunately, I think it's starting to unravel a bit without him here. Even though he lived in Australia most of his life, he was not a citizen and when he went back to Malta in 2015, the government cancelled his visa, stranding him over there. If the government had any brains, they'd let him back in the country, because the Rebels are a better run club for them and Joe Citizen and the cops when Alex is there.

Best club? Well, that's a given. The Bandidos are the best club in the world. Always have been, always will.

CAESAR'S LAW
XXIII

MY MOTTO

One of the great sayings that went around back in the early days of outlaw clubs was held up as almost being a holy truth. And I think it still is. 'The two most important days in your life are the day you are born and the day you find out why.'

That might mean different things to different people. But if you're an outlaw biker you should know what it means. I know I do.

My personal motto is: 'Always be the one they fear, and fear no one.'

In recent times, Donna has become Facebook friends with Mark 'Hammer' Dixon who used to be Chopper Read's bodyguard. I like his motto: 'When in doubt, knock 'em out.'

42

PIE FIGHTS

Skipping back to the early Bandido days, it was about April 1984, and Snoddy, Shadow, Wack, Chop, Dukes, Bear and I had gone on a ride down to Fitzroy Falls, 140 kilometres south of Sydney. We had a look at the falls and they were spectacular. We got ourselves some lunch at a bakery and as we came out with our pies, another well-known outlaw club pulled in. They allowed Jap bikes and others, as well as Harleys. There was a bit of an argument. Snoddy had an apple turnover full of cream and he shoved it in this bloke's face. It was on. Shadow hit another bloke in the mush with a hot steak and mushroom pie. There were pies and cakes flying all over the place and once we ran out of ammo, the blue really got going. There were seven of us and about 15 of them.

We cleaned their clocks and left them lying on the footpath or hanging over their bikes. As usual, someone had rung the cops, but we weren't worried because this was another outlaw club and no matter how much you might not respect them, you knew they weren't going to dob you in. So we rode off. I knew a back way up behind Bowral and we got home and sat back at the clubhouse and all had a good laugh about the pies and especially the apple turnover.

Why I bring this up is because on 12 July 2015, when I was still recovering from the sickness that came from having been shot eight months earlier, The Woman and I had gone for a drive to Nimmitabel, a quaint little town 37 kilometres south of Cooma. We pulled up at the bakery with our nose in to the gutter. That's the way they park up here in the mountains. When we came out with our pies, there was a bunch of bikes, 12 or 13, parked next to us. It was some social club with a tiny patch on their backs. As we got in the car, the bloke closest to me, a big boy about 30, decided to give me some lip. 'Good look for a biker to be wearing ugg boots,' he said. 'But then you're fairly old, aren't you?'

'It's a better look than that fucking postage stamp you've got on your back.'

'You can't talk to me like that, old man, I'm the sergeant-at-arms of this club.'

'Yeah, well it can't be much of a club if they let pussies like you in it.'

'Fuck you. You're gone.'

I was expecting him to get off his bike on the side away from me to keep his bike between us, but he didn't. And then he started taking his jacket and vest off. He got the vest off and – as social riders often do – left his colours on the back of his bike. He had no neck, no clue. He had huge arms. He was a muscle head, into the 'roids. In those key seconds as he took his jacket off, I sized him up, visualising how the fight would go like I'd always done.

These days, I try to thump 'em in the throat if I think it's going to be tough. Get it over quick.

My right hand is pretty fucked. I've got peripheral neuropathy, where you get severe hot electrical shocks in different parts of your body. The fingers that the bloke from Satans Riders broke outside the Venus Room still give me grief and I got shotgun pellets in that same hand at Milperra. The second knuckle got shot out of my right pinkie and I had another slug go through other knuckles on my right. So I struggle to even make a fist with that hand. The left gets the peripheral neuropathy pretty bad. I'll be out on the bike and I'll find it hard to get my fingers flexible enough to move the clutch.

So, I've got to be tactical. And it's amazing how you can lift when the need arises.

When this bloke had his jacket half off, because he was on my side of his bike, I was able to get at him and I just pounded him in the larynx, my hands like a knife. Didn't matter how big his arms were if they were all locked up in his jacket. He went back and hit his head on the gutter. Spat blood. I bet he was suddenly pretty happy that I was wearing ugg boots, as I jumped on his head.

'You didn't fight fair,' I heard one of his mates say, coming towards me.

I got him right up under the corner of the jaw, just under the ear. I heard a bone crack as he went down like a ton of bricks. A third bloke came at me and I got him in a stranglehold.

'If you're looking for a fair fight, join the girl fucking guides. If you blokes think riding Harleys and having a little postage-stamp patch on your back makes you tough, you've got another think coming. There's no such thing as a fair fight in the outlaw world. There's just fights.'

I heard a bloke yelling, 'I think that's Caesar Campbell', while I strangled the bloke, making up my mind as to whether I'd knock him out or snap his neck. I wasn't in a real good mood. I felt *thump, thump, thump* on the side of my head. So I let the bloke fall to the ground and turned around and looked at this other guy. I must have looked pretty mean, because he took off like a scared rabbit down to the end of a row of bikes where all the rest of them were. Another one, a tall bloke, about six foot six, was going, 'We don't want no trouble, Caesar. Pig's a bit of a hothead. He's only 28. He hasn't had the experience that you've had.'

'I don't give a fuck if he's 28, 18, or 88. Who's the prick who's just run down there?'

'That's Bear.'

'Well from now on, right from this very second, his name's Rat.' They looked at me, confused. So I continued. 'I've got a brother called Bear and I'm not going to have some big girl like him running around using the same name. If I hear you're still calling him Bear, or if I hear of anyone in your club still using the name Bear, I'll close your club down. If my brother Bear was with me right now, the whole 13 of you cocksucking wimps would be lying on the footpath waiting for the ambos.'

'Come on, look, you've smashed up three of me blokes, can't we forget it?'

'Yeah, I can forget it . . . For now. But if I ever hear of you calling anyone in your club Bear, I'll get me brother Bear and we'll come and destroy ya. You'll find out what real pain is, sport. You'll get the thrashing of your life.'

43

CATCHING UP WITH CHANCE

Chance and I kept in contact and our lives ran fairly parallel. In 1984, he got shot doing a job that turned out to be half a dozen more bodyguards to deal with than he'd anticipated. He was pretty badly hurt, but he had the brains to handle it. He drove a couple of suburbs away, got out of the car and dripped his blood all over the footpath just down from a takeaway food joint. He ended up in hospital and, when he got well enough for the coppers to interview him, he told them he was getting out of his car and was going over to get something to eat at the takeaway joint when a car went by and opened up on him. He dragged himself to his car and drove to hospital. He had the bloodstains on the footpath to back it up.

Later in 1984, nothing to do with his paid work, he ended up in a fight for his club against the perennial foe of outlaw bikers, fucking footballers. He got stabbed with a broken pool cue, so he ripped it off the bloke who'd been jabbing it into him and used it on him, but instead of the footy player getting charged with assault occasioning grievous bodily harm, Chance copped it. The footy player got off with self-defence, even though he stabbed Chance first. That's the life of an outlaw biker.

Chance took it on the chin. He went to jail, did his time, and got out not long before me.

After we got out, Chance and I met up at Sweethearts. We were having a yak and he asked, 'Are you still doing what you were doing before?'

'Nah. I've given it up,' I said. 'I still do anything for the club or my family, but these blokes up here can find themselves another collector and enforcer.'

'Yeah, I think the Widowmaker's shelf life has run out, too,' he said. 'I think I'll put that to bed.'

His old lady had got in his ear, telling him it was time to give it up, but I think he knew it too. Abe's power was on the wane. Mr Sin had also come out of jail around the same time as us. While he still owned half the politicians, judges and coppers in the state, the other half wanted to make a name for themselves by bringing him down. It looked like his empire – and all the protections it offered – was crumbling.

'There's only two blokes beside me who know who the Widowmaker is,' he said. 'You and Mr Sin. From what I hear, he won't be around for too much longer, so there'll be just me and you. Caesar, I say this with the greatest respect: I hope we both grow to be old men to enjoy our families and our clubs.'

'I'm with you on that, Chance. Amen.'

Well, it's worked out partly that way. I got to enjoy my family and friends but not my club. Chance got all three.

To this day, he's never been busted – never even been investigated – for his professional occupation. He might have come out of retirement once or twice there in the early '90s, but since then he's led a life similar to mine except he was active with his club a lot longer. He's always been a top bloke and a great friend and I'm proud to call him brother.

It was funny that he moved down to the Snowy Mountains too. There are a lot of retired bikers here from outlaw clubs. There's the eight of us, sometimes nine, who get together on a semi-regular basis to have a yak and go for a ride, but Chance and I are always on the phone. He's always dropping into my place or I'm dropping into his.

We talk about the old times and JR comes up a lot. So there we were recently on the lounge at my place, the outlaw and the hitman, when I thought I'd get something cleared up that I'd been wondering about for a while. I knew roughly how many people JR had put into the ground. It was 35 or 33 – JR wasn't too sure himself. 'I don't want to be nosy,' I said to Chance, 'but how many did you do?'

'We've known each other for that long and you coulda made a lot of money by giving me up, not just from the cops but from the blokes up the Cross. So I don't mind telling you. It was between 60 and 80.'

'Geez, that's a bit vague,' I said. 'Was it 65 or 70 or what?'

'Let's just leave it there between 60 and 80.'

'Even 60's a hell of a lot of blokes. You might as well just tell me.'

'All right, it was between 70 and 80,' Chance said.

'You're not going to tell me the exact number?'

'No, I'm not.'

'Fuck, that's a lot of blokes to have put in the ground.'

'Caesar, back in the day and even now, you wouldn't believe the blokes that molest kids, the rockspiders. I hate 'em and I would have put 'em away for nothing, but I was getting paid to do it. They came from all walks of life: politicians, the entertainment industry, the cop force, everywhere. Every time I got a job to hit a rockspider, my night was made. Of course I hit other people for other reasons, but even then I didn't do it just for the money. There always had to be a reason. Mr Sin knew that. Everyone I put in the ground needed putting in the ground.'

'If people only knew that you existed.'

'Well, by the sound of it, they're going to know soon. You've asked me if Donna can mention me in this new book, so they're going to know about the Widowmaker now.'

'Yeah, they're going to know there was a hitman nicknamed the Widowmaker,' I said. 'But they're not going to know who he was. I'm not going to do that to you. But that's not what I'm talking about.'

'You know that every second bloke who was a regular up the Cross had heard the rumour of the Widowmaker,' he said. 'Crims in Melbourne had heard about him and if they heard the Widowmaker was coming for them they'd fucking take off for Brazil.'

'That's true,' I said. 'A lot of people did know about the Widowmaker, but no one ever guessed it was an outlaw biker. Who would have ever thought that an outlaw biker could be the biggest hitman in the country?'

Chance smiled. 'That used to peeve JR, didn't it?'

'Yeah, but you gotta admit, he was good at what he did,' I said.

'Caesar, he was the tops. There was only one better, and that was probably just because I got more jobs. If you count the bodies it was me, but JR was a real craftsman. He knew what he was doing and he worked hard at being the best.'

'Yeah, that's good of you to say that, Chance.'

'Look, I know you and JR were the best of mates back in the day and I hope you and me are still the best of mates.'

'Always,' I said. 'I've done things for you and you've done things for me. There's a bond when two blokes have done for each other what we've done.'

'That's right. It's been a privilege shaking your hand. The first time I did it, I'd heard about ya and it was a privilege back then, and it's a privilege now.'

'Same here.'

'Give me 15 minutes and I'll get the old bike out and we'll go for a run.'

'Righto. How about Dalgety?'

'Sounds fine. We'll have a meal at the pub and look at the Snowy River.'

'Sounds good.'

So that's what the Widowmaker does these days. He rides with his mates up into the Snowy Mountains and we go to places like Dalgety, sit out the front and watch the Snowy River roll on by. We cruise to places like Jindabyne and ride up to the top of the mountain and into Victoria and go to places like Mansfield. Just because we're retired from our clubs doesn't mean we don't ride. We have a good time. I wouldn't like to be the person who got on the wrong side of Chance even now, because I reckon you'd still end up in the ground if you pissed him off.

All you paedophiles, you better stay away from the Snowy Mountains.

I talked to Chance not long back when the idea for this book came up and I asked him if he minded if I mentioned him. 'I'll leave that up to the old lady,' he said.

So I asked his old lady. 'You can tell the story of the Widowmaker,' she said. 'But just don't mention his real name or his club.'

44

NOT THE END

They say life's a journey and you go from one place to another till you reach the place you consider home – and for me that journey took me from the Gladiators to the Comos to the Bandits. That was home.

The outlaw life is a hard life, but it's a good life and it's one I'd never give up. I was born to outlaw. And I'll be an outlaw till the day I die. And that's the way Chance feels and PJ and all me old mates from back in the 1960s and '70s.

In this book, I've decided to tell a lot more than I was prepared to tell in the first two books, but remember, 97 per cent of it is fact, and three per cent is fiction. By now, you've figured out why.

I've got hundreds of hours of tapes detailing more about the blokes up the Cross and things I've done. They're 100 per cent fact, so they can't be published until after I'm gone. It'll take about four books to fit it all in.

I remember everything. Everything Abe did, and George and Paddles, the coppers. Everything. Where bodies are buried. Where people think bodies are buried, but they're not. All that stuff.

These tapes are, of course, well hidden, and I've got it so that there's a couple of tapes that will be left in reserve so that if anything happened to my family, they would be published. And all shit would break loose.

I've often been asked if I feel regrets or guilt for what I've done.

I don't.

I've never, ever started a fight. I'll give my oath to that on my old man's grave. Every fight I've been in, someone's started it with me or someone else and I've gone in to help them. So I don't feel sorry for anyone I've hurt, because they started it. The jobs I've done – I'd only do them if the person in my opinion deserved to be put in the ground.

Chance is good with it, too.

He's pissed off for my sake about what happened between me and my club. Even though he retired from his profession a long time ago, he still comes up to me and says, 'Just give me a few names, Caesar, I'll make sure they disappear. We've been too close for too long. I hate seeing you disrespected.'

I tell him not to worry about it. It's between me and other people.

'If you ever change your mind, just give me a list,' he says.

'Well, that won't be happening.'